John Jamieson

A Historical Account of the Ancient Culdees of Iona,

and of their settlements in Scotland, England, and Ireland

John Jamieson

A Historical Account of the Ancient Culdees of Iona,
and of their settlements in Scotland, England, and Ireland

ISBN/EAN: 9783337323202

Printed in Europe, USA, Canada, Australia, Japan

Cover: Foto ©ninafisch / pixelio.de

More available books at **www.hansebooks.com**

A HISTORICAL ACCOUNT

OF THE

ANCIENT CULDEES

OF IONA

*And of their Settlements in Scotland
England, and Ireland*

BY

JOHN JAMIESON, D.D., F.R.S., F.A.S.E.

AUTHOR OF "AN ETYMOLOGICAL DICTIONARY OF THE
SCOTTISH LANGUAGE," &c., &c.

POPULAR EDITION

GLASGOW: THOMAS D. MORISON
LONDON: SIMPKIN, MARSHALL, HAMILTON & CO
1890

EDITORIAL NOTE TO POPULAR EDITION.

IN issuing a popular edition of this important and standard work, it may be well to recapitulate a few particulars regarding its distinguished author, who may be termed the national philologist of Scotland. The son of a Glasgow minister, he was born in 1759, and, in due course, educated at the university of that city, where he especially distinguished himself in linguistic and philological studies. At the age of twenty-two, he was licensed to the ministry, and became pastor of a church at Forfar, where he gained the thorough esteem and confidence of a full congregation through the faithful and able discharge of his clerical labours and duties. For sixteen years he continued his pastoral duties at Forfar, during which period he married the daughter of a neighbouring proprietor, who gladdened the course of his long life, and died only a year before his own decease.

During the period of his pastorate at Forfar, Mr. Jamieson became the author of no fewer than six publications, some of which excited much interest at the time. But none of them have lived in the same sense that some of his later works have done. Neither are any of his earlier productions of such a kind as one would expect to come from an enthusiastic, word-sifting antiquary. Among others of this period we find *The Sorrows of Slavery: A Poem containing a Faithful Statement of Facts regarding the Slave Trade;* as also *Eternity: A Poem addressed to Free Thinkers and Philosophical Christians;* there is also *A Vindication of the Doctrine of Scripture, and of the Primitive Faith concerning the Divinity of Christ,* in reply to Dr. Priestley; a work of a different nature, and which attained to great popularity, and ran through many editions, was the one entitled *Sermons on the Heart.* By these and similar labours, Jamieson won for himself an honourable name in the field of literature.

In 1796, Jamieson became pastor of Nicolson Street Church, Edinburgh. The literary capital of Scotland was no doubt the proper place of residence for such a man; and the facilities for philological and historical research to be had in Edinburgh, would still further increase his zest and natural bent for such studies. Before the publication of his great work, Jamieson, still issued other two books of considerable consequence. In 1802 there appeared, in two volumes, *The Use of Sacred History;* and in 1806, *The Important Trial in the Court of Conscience*, both works of considerable note. But in 1808-1809, there came from his pen, his greatest and by far the most important of his works, namely, *An Etymological Dictionary of the Scottish Language*, first issued in two volumes quarto, then, in 1825, increased by a *Supplement* of other two volumes, making in all four quarto volumes. The enormous importance of this herculean literary attempt, to the Scottish people at large, and to the interests of philology, can scarcely be over-rated. Jamieson's aim and scope in undertaking and carrying out this great work were as follows :—1. To illustrate the words in their different significations, by examples from ancient and modern writers. 2. To show their affinity to those of other languages, and especially to the northern. 3. To explain many terms, which, though now obselete in England, were formerly common in both countries. 4. To elucidate national rites, customs, and institutions, in their analogy to those of other nations.

In 1811 he published the present work in large quarto size And in 1814 appeared his *Hermes Scythicus; or, The Radical Affinities of the Greek and Latin Languages to the Gothic;* and four years afterwards, there came from his pen *A Grammar of Rhetoric and Polite Literature.* He also edited two very important national products, which, on account of their obselete language, were fast being forgotten, but through his judicious editing again, were restored to use to a great extent, namely, Blind Harry's *Wallace*, and Barbour's *Bruce*. Pre-deceased by his fourteen children, and also by his wife, Dr. Jamieson died in Edinburgh in 1838, in the eightieth year of his age.

In issuing a popular edition of this important and significant work, and thus bringing it within the reach of all, the publishers think they have done right. Though on a most important subject, and such as should be of interest to all intelligent and patriotic Scotchmen; the book hitherto has been within the reach of the wealthy only. For many years back, the book could not be purchased for less than several pounds sterling. In order to permit of this being a popular edition, the foot-notes almost entirely in Latin, and the appendix likewise almost entirely in Latin, have been omitted. From the nature of the two items referred to, the general reader would be quite unable to make any material use of them. In other respects, the book in its entirety, is as it came from the author.

AUTHOR'S PREFACE.

WHEN the author engaged in this disquisition, it was not with the remotest idea of writing a book on the subject. His sole design was to collect a few materials, to be afterwards thrown together, so as to form an article in a literary work, to which he had promised to contribute. But, from the contradictory assertions of learned and able writers, concerning the Culdees; from the variety of topics regarding their history or character, which demanded particular attention; and from the indispensable necessity, in an inquiry of this kind, of producing original authorities; he soon found, that it was in vain to think of giving any tolerable account of this celebrated society within the usual limits of an essay. Various difficulties have occurred, indeed, in the progress of this investigation. But, in consequence of persevering in it, he has had the satisfaction of meeting with facts, which seem to have been formerly overlooked ; and he flatters himself that he has been able to set some others in a new light.

Although far from thinking that the work can be free from mistakes, he is conscious that he has done all in his power fairly to exhibit the testimony of antiquity on this subject. If it shall appear to the candid reader, that the author has in any measure elucidated this obscure, but important, branch of our ancient history, he will not regret his labour.

CONTENTS.

CHAPTER XII.

CHAPTER XIII.

CHAPTER XIV.

CHAPTER XV.

AN
HISTORICAL ACCOUNT
OF THE
ANCIENT CULDEES OF IONA.

INTRODUCTION.

THERE is no portion of the Scottish history, which has a higher claim to attention, than that which respects the Culdees. Nor are the natives of Scotland alone interested in it. Whatever be the peculiar influence of national attachment, or of local connection, this is a subject which merits the regard of all who bear the name of Protestants. By various writers, indeed, it has either been industriously consigned to oblivion, or, if brought into view, grossly misrepresented. But, happily, amidst all the obscurity and fable, in which the more early part of our history is involved, such gleams of light now and then break forth, as not only to demonstrate the existence, but to elucidate the character, of a succession of men, who, while they were an honour to their country, were at the same time an ornament to the Christian name. Nor is their claim to attention enfeebled, from the circumstance of their appearing in a remote corner of the earth, as champions for the simplicity of our faith, and for the independence of the Church, at the very time that error and tyranny had extended their baleful empire over the continent of Europe. They, in this respect, resemble the Waldenses, who, hid amidst the almost inaccessible retreats

2

of Piedmont, and environed by the natural bulwarks of the Alpine regions, during the same dark period, preserved the truth in its purity, till the time appointed for its more general dissemination arrived.

CHAPTER I.

Of the Name, CULDEES.—*Conjectures as to its Origin.—Of the first preaching of the Gospel in North Britain.—Of the Mission of Palladius.—Iona the principal seat of the Culdees.—Said to have been the immediate Successors of the Druids.*

THE name of CULDEES, or KELDEES, was given to a body of religious men, who chiefly resided in Scotland, Ireland, and some of the adjacent isles. The etymon of the name has exercised the ingenuity of the learned.

According to Boece and Buchanan, they were called *Culdei,* q. *Cultores Dei,* or worshippers of God, from Lat. *colo* and *Deus.* Spotswood thinks that they were named from the cells in which they lived.

Lloyd, bishop of St Asaph, after saying that he had not met with the word, in this form, "in any author before the time of Giraldus Cambrensis," justly observes: "Then it was a very usual thing to find out Latin derivations for those words of which men did not know the original. And thus the *Kyldees,* or *Kylledei,* came to be called *Culdei,* or *Colidei;* that is, the worshippers of God; being such as spent their whole time, or a great part of it, in devotion."

Others have embraced still more far-fetched etymons. Bishop Nicolson says, that Culdee signifies "a black monk," as being meant to denote the colour of the cowl, in the Irish language, *culla.* Some have supposed that the word has been borrowed from the Greeks; in the same way as the names bishop, presbyter, deacon, and monk, have come to us from them: for their monks, confined to cells, were called Κελλεωται.

The origin assigned by Obrien is certainly very plausible. In Irish, he says, it is *Ceile De,* from *ceile* a servant, and *De,*

God. Goodall adopts this etymon, observing that, " in more ancient MSS. the word is not written *Culdei*, but *Keledei*; and that the more learned in our old language affirm, that it is compounded of *keile*, a servant, and *Dia*, God."

Dr Smith gives the same etymon. For he views the word *Keledei* as merely the Latinized Gaelic phrase *Gille De*, which signifies *Famuli Dei*, or, servants of God. This derivation has also the sanction of Dr Shaw, in his History of Moray.

Toland, however, contends that *Keledei* " is from the original Irish, or Scottish, word *Ceile-de*, signifying, separated or espoused to God."

It has also been said, that " Gaelic *cuil*, and *ceal*, signifying a sequestered corner, cave, &c., those who retired to such a place were called *Cuildeach*, in plural, *Cuildich;* which they who spoke or wrote Latin, turned into *Culdeus* and *Culdei*, altering only the termination." Nearly the same account is given by another writer. " *Culdee*," he says, " is a Gaelic word, signifying a monk, or hermit, or any sequestered person. *Cuildeach* is common to this day, and given to persons not fond of society. The word is derived from *Cuil*, a retired corner."

" Their name," according to another learned writer, " was probably derived from the notion of their retreat, and seclusion. In the Welsh, *Cêl*, which means shelter, a hiding, would form the name in the plural thus: *Celydi*, *Celydiaud*, *Celydion*, *Celydwys*."

Although both the etymons last mentioned have peculiar claims to attention, yet I am disposed to prefer the latter, from *cuil*, *ceal*, or *cêl*, a retreat; not merely because it requires no change of the initial syllable, but because it is most consonant to the established sense of *Kil*, retained in the names of so many places, which, in an early age, have been consecrated to religion. But of this more fully afterwards.

When this name was first imposed, it is impossible to

ascertain. Without paying any regard to what our historians have said of the establishment of Christianity, by a prince designed Donald I., we may safely assume, that there must have been a considerable number of Christians in the northern part of our island about the time assigned to his reign, that is, towards the close of the second century. For Tertullian, who flourished in this age, asserts, that the gospel had not only been propagated in Britain, but had reached those parts of the island into which the Roman arms had never penetrated. This perfectly agrees with the defence, made by the Culdees, of their peculiar modes of worship. For they still affirmed, that they had received these from the disciples of John the Apostle.

Scotland and Ireland have contended for the honour of the origin of the Culdees. Some of our writers pretend to trace them to the beginning of the fourth century. The Irish say, that this order of monks was first instituted in their island, by Columba, A. 546: and afterwards, by the same apostolic presbyter, in Scotland. Till his time, indeed, we have no evidence of the existence of any societies observing a particular institute; though there seems to be no good reason to doubt that the doctrines by which the religious of the Columban order were distinguished, were held in North Britain long before.

It is said by Prosper of Aquitaine, that " Palladius, being ordained by Pope Celestine, was sent to the Scots believing in Christ, as their first bishop." The same thing is asserted by Bede, in the very language of Prosper. This testimony has occasioned a great deal of controversy. The generality of our Scottish writers have contended that his mission was to the country now denominated Scotland : and many things plausible have been advanced on this side of the question, especially by Goodall. It has, particularly, been urged, that ancient writers were so little acquainted with the northern part of our country, or that lying beyond the

Forth, that they viewed it as an island distinct from Britain; that they sometimes called it *Hibernia*, and its inhabitants *Hiberni;* and that the position given to the country is applicable to Scotland only. But there can be no doubt that Bede was well acquainted with both countries; and, though he sometimes calls the inhabitants of Ireland, and at other times those of North Britain, Scots, yet, when he gives an account of the mission of Palladius, as he immediately proceeds to speak of the Scots and Picts, who took possession of Britain all the way to the wall, it appears that he here uses the term as denominating those who had come from Ireland, as allies of the Picts, and soon after returned to their own country. For the very same people, whom in his Chronicle he calls *Scotti*, he in his History designs *Hiberni*. Now, it cannot be conceived that Bede would call those *Hiberni*, whom he knew to be inhabitants of Britain.

It must be admitted, however, that it forms a considerable difficulty, that Marianus Scotus, who wrote about the year 1060, and who was himself an Irishman, should use such language as seems necessarily to imply, that he considered the mission of Palladius as meant for the benefit of the inhabitants of North Britain. For, having expressed himself in the very terms used by Prosper, he adds: "After him was St Patrick, by birth a Briton, consecrated by St Celestine the Pope, and sent to be archbishop of Ireland. There, preaching for forty years, with signs and miracles, he converted the whole island of Ireland to the faith."

But while it may be supposed that Palladius went first to Ireland, there is reason to believe that he thought himself bound to visit those Christians also who resided in the country, now called Scotland: for it has been asserted, that he died in the northern part of this island.

A learned writer considers it as "likely that he passed over to Britain from the north of Ireland, and died in Galloway, held by the Piks after 427." But he seems to go too far when he says: "Not a church was ever dedicated to Palladius in Scotland, nor is there a trace of him in our history or tradition."

Fordun, confining the mission of Palladius to the Scots of Britain, says that King Eugenius gave him and his companions a place of residence where he asked it. In the MS. of Coupar, there is this addition; Apud Fordun, in *lie Mearns*; i. e. "at Fordun, in the Mearns." This perfectly coincides with the modern account. "This parish [Fordun] is remarkable for having been for some time the residence, and probably the burial-place, of St Palladius, who was sent by Pope Celestine into Scotland, sometime in the fifth century, to oppose the Pelagian heresy. That Palladius resided, and was probably buried here, appears from several circumstances. There is a house which still remains in the churchyard, called St Palladius's Chapel, where, it is said, the image of the saint was kept, and to which pilgrimages were performed from the most distant parts of Scotland. There is a well at the corner of the minister's garden, which goes by the name of Paldy's Well."

To this it may be added, that the annual market, held at Fordun, is still universally, in that part of the country, called Paldy, or, as vulgarly pronounced, Paddy Fair. This is a strong presumption that a church had been dedicated to him there; as it is a well-known fact, that at the Reformation, when the saints' days were abolished, the fairs, which used to succeed the festivals, and were denominated from them, were retained. Hence their very name, from Lat. *Feriae*, holidays. Camerarius asserts, on the authority of Polydore, Vergil, that "the precious reliques of this saint were formerly worshipped at Fordun; and that the shrines, containing these, adorned with silver, gold, and jewels, had been repaired by William Scheves, archbishop of St Andrews."

It is said in the Breviary of Aberdeen, that Palladius died at Longforgund in Mernis. Although Longforgan, formerly written Forgund, seems to be a place of very considerable antiquity, the description here given cannot apply to it, as it is situated in the extremity of Perthshire, on the borders of Angus. This place may have been substituted, by mistake, for " Fordun in Mernis." According to Sigebert, Palladius was sent to the Scots, A. 432. It would appear, that, finding his labours unsuccessful in Ireland, he had attempted the conversion of the Picts : for Fordun was in their territory. Bede informs us that Ninian converted the Southern Picts. These, it has been generally supposed, were in Galloway; as Ninian is said to have been bishop of *Candida Casa.* But, if Mr. Pinkerton be right in asserting that, A. 412, the date of the conversion referred to, there were no Picts in Galloway, and that those meant must be such as dwelt to the south of the Grampian mountains; Palladius most probably went thither for the purpose of reclaiming them from any errors into which they might have fallen, and especially with the view of bringing them into subjection to the authority of the bishop of Rome.

It may easily be accounted for, that there should be fewer traces of Palladius in our history, or local memorials of him, than of almost any other saint who resided in this country. To a people of so independent a spirit as that which characterized our forefathers, the ministry of any one must have been extremely unacceptable, whose chief object was to subject them to a foreign yoke.

CHAPTER II.

Of the coming of Columba into Britain.—Cursory view of his Life and Character.—To be distinguished from Abbot Columban.—Of the Island of Iona.—Of the Druids.—The Doctrine of the Culdees, and their Mode of Living.

FROM the preceding observation it must appear, that, even on the supposition that the primary mission of Palladius was not to Scots inhabiting Britain, Christianity had been received in the northern part of it long before the age of Columba. The southern Picts being already converted, this good man "came into Britain," as Bede informs us, "to preach the word of God to the provinces of the northern Picts."— " He came, at the time that Bridius [otherwise Brudi], a most powerful king, reigned over the Picts, and in the ninth year of his reign; and converted that nation to the faith of Christ, by his preaching and example; on which he received from them the forsaid island [Hii] in possession, for the purpose of erecting a monastery."

Columba was a native of Ireland, and a man of distinguished rank. He was indeed of the blood royal, being the son of Felim, the son of Fergus, who was grandson to the celebrated Niall of the nine Hostages, king of Ireland. His mother was Aithne, the daughter of Macnave. His paternal grandfather was Connal. from whom, according to Irish antiquarians, the district of Tirconnel took its name.

He was born A. 521, and educated under Finian, bishop of Clonard, Fenbar, Gemman of Leinster, and the far-famed St Ciaran. When he was about twenty-eight years of age, we are told, he founded the monastery of Dairmeagh, in Ireland, that, is, the Field of Oaks. Some have understood this of Armagh. Usher explains the term as denoting Durrough, in the King's county.   Others, again, view it as pointing out the modern Derry.

Zeal for the propagation of the gospel, among the heathen, has been assigned by some writers as the reason of his leaving his native country, while others have imputed his conduct to very different motives.   He has been accused, not only of intermeddling in political concerns, to which the clergy have unhappily been too prone in almost every age, but of abusing his influence so far as to excite great disturbances in Ireland.   It has been said that in consequence of some real or supposed indignity done to him, his own kindred entered keenly into his quarrel, so as to deluge the country with blood; and that his conduct gave so great offence to the ecclesiastics of that kingdom that they threatened him with excommunication.

It may be supposed that, in the earlier part of his life, he might in some instances be carried away by pride or ambition; especially as goaded on by a consciousness of rank, and partially under the influence of the restless spirit of the age in which he lived.   But we must conclude, either that his conduct has been misrepresented, or that he learned wisdom from the affecting proofs which he had of his own weakness. For it is acknowledged by all the writers of his life, that, after he left Ireland, he conducted himself with exemplary humility and self-denial.   The influence which he afterwards retained in that country goes a great way to vindicate him. Not only is it asserted by Jocelin and other writers that he founded a hundred monasteries, while some increase the number, including churches, to three hundred: but it is certain that the greatest respect was paid to him at the national council, or parliament, of Drumceat in Ireland, where he appeared as representative of the clergy of North Britain.

The accounts given of his miracles and predictions should be read with that allowance which we must necessarily make for the credulity of the times. In the memoirs of this saint nothing is related more ridiculous or incredible than what we find in the page of the venerable Bede.

The names of the companions of Columba who attended him to Iona have been recorded by various writers. Usher gives the following list, as extracted from an MS. in the Cotton Library. "These are the names of the men who passed over with Columba from Scotland [i. e. Ireland], when he first went to Britain. The two sons of Brendin, Baithen and Comin, who were both successors of St Columba; Cobthach, his brother; Ernan, the uncle of St Columba; Dermit, his servant; Rui and Fethuo, the two sons of Rodan; Scandal, the son of Bresail, the son of Endei, the son of Niell Luguid; Mocutheimne, Echoid, Thorannu, Moculir, Cetea Cairnaan, the son of Branduib, the son of Meilgi Grillaan."

Here, it would seem, there is some error in the enumeration, or in the punctuation; as, instead of twelve, we have thirteen persons mentioned.

To prevent mistakes, it is necessary to observe, that there were two eminent men, nearly contemporaries, who were both natives of Ireland, both founders of monasteries, both abbots, and both canonized; to whom the same name is frequently given, and who, from the inattention of ancient writers, have frequently been confounded with each other. These were Columba, and Columban or Columbanus. Our Columba landed in Hii A. 563, and died there in 597. Columban was educated in the monastery of Bangor in Ireland, under St Congall. He left Ireland and travelled into Burgundy, A. 589. Like Columba, he took twelve companions with him. Among these, according to Marianus Scotus, was the celebrated St Gall. In Burgundy, he founded the Abbey of Luxeville, which he governed for about twenty years; being then ejected by the persecution of Queen Brunechilde. Cave says that he was exiled from Luxeville by Theodoric,

king of Austrasia, because he too boldly reproved his libidin-
ous life. Hofmann calls this Theodoric, *Rev Galliae*. After
this he travelled through the greatest part of France; and
at length retired into Italy. Here, being kindly received by
Aigilulph, king of the Lombards, he erected the abbey of
Bobio, near Naples; where he died a year after, A. 615.

His life was written by Jonas, one of his disciples, a monk
of the abbey of Bobio; and published by Messingham in his
Florilegium.

Bede properly designs the apostle of the Picts Columba,
according to the best MSS.; although, in some editions,
Columbanus occurs. He marks the difference of the names,
when, in transcribing the letter from Laurence, Archbishop
of Canterbury, to the Irish bishops, he designs the other
Columbanum Abbatem in Gallis venientem. Smith is mistaken, however, when he says in the index of his edition of
Bede, that the letter of Pope John was addressed to this
Columbanus among other Irish bishops. For, as it was
written A. 640, this was fifty-one years after he left Ireland,
and twenty-five after his death.

In the Saxon Chronicle, the Abbot of Iona is denominated
Columba, and also *Columban.* By Sigebert he is designed
Columbanus. In the Chronicon Hermanni Contracti, he
receives both names; although the latter is also given to
Columban, Abbot of Luxeville. But in the index to Pistorius
they are both referred to as one person. Both Goldast and
Dempster are chargeable with the same carelessness.

Dr Smith of Campbelton has fallen into an error in ascribing to Columba the three poems which he has inserted,
with translations, in his Appendix. They were written by
the Abbot of Luxeville, and were published by Usher under
his name. The Archbishop of Armagh has given another,
also by Columban, beginning with these words:

Mundus ille transit, et quotidie decrescit, &c.

Besides the hymn in praise of St Kiaran, and another in

honour of St Brigid, three poems have been ascribed to Columba of Icolmkill; but all different from those published by Dr Smith. The first begins :

Altus Prosator, Vetustus dierum et Ingenitus.

The second : In te, Christe, Credentium : and the third ; Noli, Pater, indulgere.

It is the more surprising that Dr Smith should commit so gross a mistake, when he had in his hand Colgan's *Trias*, in which these three hymns of Columba are published.

Perhaps it deserves notice, that Colman, one of the disciples of Columba, the Bishop of Lindisfarne, who, rather than submit to the Roman rites, renounced his bishopric, and who afterwards settled, with his adherents, at Inisboufinde, was sometimes denominated *Columbanus*. As he left Lindisfarne A. 667, Usher very reasonably interprets the language of the annals of Ulster, under this year, as applicable to him. A. 667. Navigatio Columbani Episcopi cum reliquiis Sanctorum ad Insulam Vaccae Albae, in qua fundavit ecclesiam. Also, A. 675. Ejusdem Columbani Episcopi Insulae Vaccae Albae pausa ; that is, his decease. The reliques especially meant are supposed to be those of Bishop Aidan, which, according to Bede, Colman carried with him from Lindisfarne.

The memory of Columba is by no means lost, even in the Highlands of Scotland. A Highlandman, about to set out on a journey, thus expresses his wish for divine protection ; *Gilli Chalumchilli ghar pilli, agus ghar tiaunda ;* i. e. "May the servant of Columba of the cell protect and bring me safe home !" This invocation is especially used by Roman Catholics.

Claich Ichalmkilli is the name given to a small pebble brought from the shore of Iona ; that is, "the stone of Icolmkill." Stones of this description are still worn, by Catholics, as amulets. They are sometimes set in silver, and suspended over the heart.

A Gaelic proverb is still in use, which has a reference to Columba: *Uir! uir! air beal Orain ma'n labhair e tuile comh'radh;* "Earth! earth! on the mouth of Oran, that he may blab no more." Legendary tradition gives the following account of the origin of this proverb. When Columba first attempted to build on Iona, the walls, it is said, by the operation of some evil spirit, fell down as fast as they were erected. Columba received supernatural intimation, that they would never stand, unless a human victim was buried alive. According to one account, the lot fell on Oran, the companion of the saint, as the victim that was demanded for the success of the undertaking. Others pretend that Oran voluntarily devoted himself, and was interred accordingly. At the end of three days, Columba had the curiosity to take a farewell look at his old friend, and caused the earth to be removed. Oran raised his swimming eyes and said, "There is no wonder in death, and hell is not as it is reported." The saint was so shocked at this impiety, that he instantly ordered the earth to be flung in again, uttering the words of the proverb mentioned above. The place is still called *The Chapel of St Oran.*

It is not improbable, that this story was invented by some of the druidical enemies of Columba, in order to expose him and the Christian doctrine to ridicule; especially as the savage rite, attributed to him, was practised only by the heathen.

According to the annals of Ulster and of Tighernac, which Archbishop Usher seems disposed to follow, the island of Iona was given to Columba by Conal, or Conval, son of Comgal, king of the Dalriad Scots. But there ought to be some very powerful reason for rejecting the express testimony of Bede, who was so well versed in the history of this monastery; especially as Adamnan, the successor of Columba, who wrote his life, nowhere asserts that this island was the gift of the Dalriadic prince. As, however, it lay on the confines of both kingdoms, it might possibly be claimed by both; and what the one sovereign had given, the other might pretend to confirm. Adamnan, indeed, speaking of a plague which had been very fatal A. 702, says, that it visited all the world save "the Picts and Scots of Britain, who were divided from each other by Drum-Albin," or the Grampian mountains. But this determines nothing as to the extent of the Scottish territories a hundred and fifty years before, when Columba received the island of Iona in possession; or only about half a century after the Scots, under Fergus the son of Erc, landed in Argyleshire.

Iona was entitled to no pre-eminence from external circumstances. It is a small island in the Atlantic ocean, separated from the west point of the island of Mull by a narrow channel called "the Sound of I." It is about three miles in length, and from half a mile to a mile in breadth. "The view of Iona," says a pleasant writer, when describing his approach to it, "was very picturesque: the east side, or that which bounds the sound, exhibited a beautiful variety; an extent of plain, a little elevated above the water, and almost covered with the ruins of the sacred buildings, and with the remains of the old town, still inhabited. Beyond these the island rises into little rocky hills, with narrow verdant hollows between (for they merit not the name of vallies,) and numerous enough for every recluse to take his solitary walk, undisturbed by society."

This celebrated island has been variously denominated. "Its ancient name," we are told, "was *I, Hi*, or *Aoi* (as written in the annals of Ulster,) which were Latinized into *Hy-ona*, or *Iona*. The common name of it now is *I-colum-kill* (the Isle of Colum of the Cells), included in one of the parishes of the island of Mull." According to Toland, *I* signifies in Irish an island, and is often written *Hii, Ii, Hu,* to avoid making a word of one letter." But *Hu*, I suspect, must, in the first instance, have been merely an inaccuracy, in consequence of the double *i* being mistaken by some transcriber for *u*. Pennant gravely tells us, that "*Iona* derives its name from a Hebrew word, signifying a dove, in allusion to the name of the great saint, *Columba*, the founder of its fame." But this is scarcely more plausible than the traditionary account of the etymon of the name *Hii*, as related by Martin. "The natives have a tradition among them," he says, "that one of the clergymen who accompanied Columbus," as he erroneously designs him, "in his voyage thither, having at a good distance espied the isle, cried joyfully to Columbus, in the Irish language, *Chi mi*, i. e. I see her; meaning thereby the country of which they had been in quest: that Columbus then answered, it shall be from henceforth called *I*." What is said by Toland is far more natural. It seems to have been thus denominated from peculiar respect. "Bede," says an intelligent writer, resident in that district, "calls it *Hii*, but the proper name is *I*, sounded like *ee* in English, which in the Gaelic signifies an island, and [it] is called so by way of eminence to this day. Bede's mistake proceeded from his ignorance of the Gaelic. In [By] monkish writers it is called *Iona*, which signifies the Island of Waves. *Iona* is, in Gaelic, spelled *I-thona*; but, as the *th* is not sounded, Latin writers spell it *Iona*. The name is very characteristic of it in times of storm." But although *I* in Irish signifies an island, it affords no proof that Iona originally belonged to a Celtic people. For it is evidently the same word which occurs in the very same sense, although in a variety of forms, in almost all the Gothic dialects: Icelandic *ey*, Suio-Gothic and Danish *oe*, Anglo-Saxon *ig*, *eage*, Frisic *oge*, German *ey*.

There is, I am informed, a pretty general tradition in the highlands of Scotland, that the Culdees immediately succeeded the Druids, as the ministers of religion; and it is said, that they received the name of *Cuildeach*, mentioned above, as delighting, like the priests of heathenism, in retired situations. The reader may lay what stress he pleases on this tradition. But it perhaps deserves to be mentioned that, according to a writer formerly quoted, "the Druids undoubtedly possessed I before the introduction of Christianity. A green eminence," he says, "close to the sound of I is to this day called the Druid's burial place; Gael. *cloadh nan Druineach*. A cottager some years ago planting potatoes in this spot, and digging earth to cover them, brought up some bones, which the people of the island immediately concluded to be the bones of the Druids. The tradition is, that the first Christians banished the Druids, and took possession of their seats."

The tradition that the Culdees succeeded the Druids at no great distance of time might seem to be supported by a circumstance of an interesting nature, which has been mentioned by several writers in our statistic accounts; that *Clachan*, the name still given in the Highlands to the place where a church stands, originally belonged to a Druidical temple. Hence it is still said, "Will ye go to the stones?" or "Have you been at the stones?" that is, "Will you go to," or "Have you been at church?" But it is unnecessary to enlarge on this singular circumstance, as I have illustrated it pretty fully in another work.

It is probable that Druidism was not extinct even in the age of Columba. The history of Bede has been appealed to in proof of this: but many will hesitate as to the propriety of the appeal, as we have it on good authority that the Druidical rites were not practised by the Germans. A writer, however, of great ingenuity and of considerable learning, thinks that the Saxons, after the abolition of Druidism by the Roman Emperors, restored the same worship when they had conquered South Britain. The passage merits attention. For, although the author be viewed as proceeding on a false theory, he has brought forth a singular fact with respect to the meaning in the Gaelic language of a designation used by

3

by the venerable historian, which, if there be no mistake in his assertion, points out an analogy that could not have been supposed.

"I have already observed," he says, "that those victorious infidels [the Pagan Saxons], brought the word *Dry* from Germany [as being the name by which every German priest was called]. Together with the name they certainly introduced the office, being superstitiously devoted to Tuisto, Woden, and Thor. The history of King Edwin's conversion in Bede, and the great revolution brought about in the kingdom of Northumberland at that time in spiritual matters, is a sufficient demonstration of this position. One circumstance is sufficient for my purpose to mention concerning the conversion of Edwin. After Paulinus had exhorted Edwin to embrace the Christian faith, agreeably to the instructions he had formerly received from a person sent from the invisible world, the king summoned his friends and great council to have their advice and approbation. One of the councillors or princes was the pagan high priest, or *primus pontificum*. The name, or rather title, of this high priest, or *pontifex maximus*, was *Coifi*, or *Coefi*. I know not whether any one has attempted to explain the meaning of this word. It was, in my opinion, the common title of every druidical superintendent of spiritual affairs. The Highland talemakers talk frequently concerning *Caiffi*, or *Coiffie Dry;* and by these two words they mean a person of extraordinary sense, skill, and cunning. *Dry* undoubtedly signifies a Druid, a wise man, a prophet, a philosopher, and sometimes a magician in the Gaelic : *Coiffie Dry*, Bede's *Coiffi*, or *primus pontificum*, stands for the principal Druid, or what such a person ought to be, a man supremely wise and learned."

To do justice to this ingenious writer it should be observed that he has previously endeavoured to shew that "the *Tuisco* or *Tuisto* of Germany was the same with the *Teutates* of Gaul;" and that "the *Thor* of the Celto-Scythians of Germany," as he calls them, " was the *Taranis* of their neighbours to the south," that is, the god of thunder.

There might be Druids in Iona even after the arrival of Columba. He was opposed by Broichan, who is called a magician. Dr. Smith remarks, with respect to the sense of the synonymous term in Gaelic, that this signifies a Druid. But it is to be observed that Columba met with Broichan in the Pictish territories, at the court of Brudi, near the river Ness. But, although the Picts had undoubtedly priests of their own false religion, it remains to be proved that this was Druidical.

" Broichan had the merit, however," says Dr. Smith, " of dealing in a more open and avowed manner than some of his brethren. Odonellus (ii. 11) relates, that when Columba first landed in Iona, on Pentecost eve, some Druids who had been there disguised themselves in the habit of monks, and pretended they had come to that place to preach the Gospel, with a request that he and his followers might betake themselves to some other place; but that Columba immediately discovered the imposture, and that they resigned the field to him."

Before returning from this digression, I trust that the inquisitive reader will forgive me for inserting a singular proof of the strong hold which ancient superstition takes of the mind. Mr. Ferguson, minister of Moulin, who died about twenty years ago, assured a friend, of whom I had my information, that there was in his parish an old man, who, although very regular in his devotions, never addressed the Supreme Being by any other title than that of Arch-Druid; accounting every other derogatory to the divine majesty. Notwithstanding the great difference between the Celtic and Gothic modes of worship, it is singular that in Icelandic *Drutten*, a term so nearly allied to *Druid*, should be the name given to God as denoting his dominion. Shall we suppose that this designation was transmitted to them from the

Gauls, who left the name of the Cimbric Chersonese to that country which in later ages has been called Jutland, that is, the land of the Jutes or Goths? I need not say that this country is divided from Scandinavia only by the Baltic; and that it has itself been inhabited by Goths for more than two thousand years.

The doctrine of the Culdees, as far as we may judge from that of Columba, was at least comparatively pure. As he was himself much given to the study of the holy scriptures, he taught his disciples to confirm their doctrines by testimonies brought from this unpolluted fountain; and declared that only to be the divine counsel which he found there. His followers, as we learn from Bede, would receive those things only which are contained in the writings of the prophets, evangelists, and apostles; diligently observing the works of piety and purity. Hence it has been said that "for several generations,—with the errors which at that time prevailed in the Church of Rome they seem not to have been in the least tainted."

They observed a certain rule in their monasteries, composed, as it is said, by Columba himself, and sometimes denominated the Rule of Iona. For a considerable time before this era, many truly pious men, knowing their obligation to separate from the world, had from human weakness interpreted the divine precept in a sense which it was never meant to bear; and, if they did not retire singly to solitudes and caves, yet viewed it as most subservient to the interests of religion to form regular monastic societies. But their mode of life was very different from that of the generality of those who have been called monks in later ages. According to Bede, "after the example of the venerable fathers,—they lived by the labour of their hands." When giving an account of Aidan, who was one of them, he says: "He neither sought nor regarded any of the things of this world. All the gifts which were conferred on him by kings, or by the rich of this world, he immediately distributed with the greatest cheerfulness to the poor who came in his way. So far was his mode of living removed from the indolence of our time, that he required of all his associates, whether clergy or laity, that they should give themselves to meditation, either by reading the Scriptures, or by being at pains to learn the psalmody."

We know, that, although their successors, in later ages, lived together, and had some things in common, their wives and children, or their nearest relations, after the death of any of them, divided their property, and even claimed the offerings which had been made at the altar. This is mentioned with regret by a Romish writer. But it shews that they had not, like the monastic bodies of subsequent ages, formed any ideas of aggrandizing their order, or of enriching the particular monasteries belonging to it.

So far were they from reckoning the connubial relation inconsistent with their character, that it seems to have been held in honour. For, even in the later period of their existence as a society, they, in some places at least, like the priests under the law, succeeded by inheritance. From the work last quoted, we learn that, in the church of St Andrews, the Culdees came into office hereditarily. In Ireland, also, where this body had great influence, there was a hereditary succession in the bishopric of Armagh, for fifteen generations. The Culdees at St Andrews, however, were not permitted, after they had entered into this monastic establishment, to keep their wives in their houses. But, perhaps, this ordinance was not framed, till, through the increasing influence of that system of superstition which "forbids to marry," they were in so far forced to yield to the tide of popular prejudice in favour of celibacy. This is the more probable, as Alexander Myln, prebendary and official of Dunkeld, says that the Culdees who, "after the usage of the eastern church, had wives, abstained from them when it came to their turn to minister."

Although it appears that they observed a certain institute, yet, in the accounts given of them we cannot overlook this remarkable distinction between them and those societies which are properly called monastic, that they were not associated expressly for the purpose of observing this rule. They might deem certain regulations necessary for the preservation of order: but their great design was, by communicating instruction, to train up others for the work of the ministry. Hence it has been justly observed, that they may more properly be viewed as colleges, in which the various branches of useful learning were taught, than as monasteries. These societies, therefore, were in fact the seminaries of the Church, both in North Britain and in Ireland. As the presbyters ministered in holy things to those in their vicinity, they were still training up others, and sending forth missionaries, wherever they had a call, or any prospect of success.

CHAPTER III.

In each college of the Culdees there were twelve brethren, and one who was their Provost or Abbot. It has been supposed that, as twelve priests accompanied Columba from Ireland, and settled with him in Iona, they afterwards retained this number in imitation of the conduct of their founder; while it is by no means improbable that in this circumstance he might allude to the apostolic college. The meaning of a passage relating to this part of the subject, which occurs in the extracts from the Register of St Andrews, has undoubtedly been misapprehended. It is there said of the Culdees that there had been in that church, *tredecim per successionem carnalem,* "thirteen by carnal succession." This has been understood as if it signified that, before the time that this account was written, there had been thirteen successions of Culdees at St Andrews, in hereditary descent. But the meaning obviously is that, as the established number in the College, according to the original institution by Columba, was twelve, with their Abbot or Prior, the individuals succeeded their fathers, in the way of inheritance. There is every reason to believe that this plan of hereditary succession had been unknown, till the Culdees, like other ecclesiastics, began to decline.

They chose their Abbot or President from among themselves. Bede informs us that "most of the preachers who, during the reign of Oswald [A. 635, and downwards] came from Scotland, were monks; and that the monastery of Hii," or Iona, "had for a long time authority over almost all the monasteries of the Northern Scots, and over all those of the Picts, and had pre-eminence in the government of their people."

By some it has been urged, and certainly not without great appearance of reason, that the government of these societies of Culdees bore a very near resemblance to the Presbyterian form. That there were some, who, in early times, were called "Bishops of the Scots" cannot be denied. But it would be the height of prejudice to object to the name, if rightly interpreted. It is as scriptural as any other. It is most evident, however, that these bishops, whatever they were, cannot be viewed as diocesan bishops.

So far were they from possessing the exclusive right of ordination, that it does not appear that they were themselves ordained by bishops. As far as our historical evidence extends, they were not only chosen and sent forth, but ordained by the College of Culdees at Iona. These monks seem to have been mostly presbyters. It may well be supposed that they are the persons whom Bede designs *Majores natu Scottorum*, when he says that King Oswald " sent to the Elders of the Scots, amongst whom, during his banishment, he had been baptised, that they might send him a bishop, by whose doctrine and ministry the nation of Angles, which he governed, might be instructed in the Christian faith." It is natural to think that the application had been made to them, by whom the bishop was sent. Now, the historian says that Aidan was appointed, *destinatus*, from the island which is called Hii. He afterwards relates that Finan, who succeeded Aidan, was appointed, *destinatus*, from the island and monastery of Hii. Colman, who succeeded Finan, was also sent from this monastery.

It cannot be supposed that the power referred to exclusively belonged to the abbot, or that these bishops had their authority from him singly. Colman expressly declares that he received his episcopal honours, of what kind soever they were, from the College of Elders. Defending his mode of celebrating Easter, in the synod held at Straneschalch, he says : "The Easter which I keep I received from my Elders, who sent me hither as Bishop; which all our ancestors, men beloved of God, are known to have celebrated in the same manner." Here he ascribes his mission to Presbyters, undoubtedly as including all the solemnities connected with it. Had he been ordained by persons of a superior order he would unquestionably have at least made some allusion to them; if not with the view of adding to his own respectability, at least as giving greater authority to the ritual for which he contended.

It must be admitted that, according to Bede's narrative, there is something in the conduct of Finan which does not seem entirely consonant to the view given of the ordination at Iona. Peada, prince of the Midland Angles, upon his conversion to Christianity, having received four presbyters from Finan, for the instruction of his people; one of these, Diuma, was afterwards ordained by Finan to be bishop of that nation. Whether this should be ascribed to some greater attachment on the part of the Saxons to the model of the Roman church, I shall not presently inquire. But unless we suppose that Finan renounced the tenets of his mother church we cannot hence conclude that he viewed the office of a bishop as essentially distinct from that of a presbyter.

Whatever was the distinguishing character of the Bishops of the Scots, or those sent from Iona under this name, it is evident from Bede that their authority was very different from that of those called diocesan. "That island," he says, "is always wont to have for its governor a Presbyter-Abbot, to whose authority both the whole province, and even the bishops themselves, by an unusual constitution, ought to be subject; after the example of their first teacher, who was not a bishop, but a presbyter and monk."

Why does the venerable writer use the phrase, *ordine in-usitato*, but because this plan of government was so different from that of the Church of Rome, to which he adhered? From what is here said it might seem that these bishops had been subject to the Presbyter-Abbot only. But if we compare this with the language which he puts in the mouth of Colman, it appears at least highly probable that the subjection spoken of was due to the whole college, with the abbot as their president. For it may reasonably be supposed that this subjection would continue to be given to all those by whom, as Colman expresses himself, the bishops were sent. They must, at any rate, still have been subject to one, who, according to the modern ideas of episcopacy, was inferior in office.

Lloyd, Bishop of St Asaph, has strained every nerve to set aside the force of the testimony from Bede. It may be proper to examine his reasoning on this subject particularly; as it has been said by a learned writer of our own age, that the bishop "has completely prostrated the adversaries of his order, and demonstrated episcopacy to be coeval with Christianity in these isles."

Because Bede sometimes speaks of "the provinces of the Northern Picts," and "because it is familiar with him to call a bishop's diocess by the name of a province," the writer concludes that, therefore, "as far as one can judge by his words, he meant nothing else, but that all the province or diocess, which was under the Bishop of Hy, did then belong to that monastery." But, in the first place, this is evidently to beg the question. For he has produced no proper evidence that there was a Bishop of Iii. The plural term, *episcopi*, clearly implies that, whatever was the extent of the province, it, according to the conviction of Bede, had more than one bishop. To avoid the force of this obvious reply, on the ground of his previous assumption that "there could be but one bishop at a time," in "one province or diocess," he says,

"It might have been successively, and so I understand the place." But, if the language of Bede has any meaning, it must refer to a plurality of bishops living at one time. Otherwise the climax is lost. Nay, the assertion is good for nothing: for, if the whole province was subject to this Presbyter-Abbot, it needed no ghost to tell that the clergy in it were also subject to him.

In the second place, this assertion contains one of the most glaring fallacies that can well be imagined.—"He meant,— that all the province or diocess, which was under the Bishop of Hy, did then belong to that monastery." Could the Bishop of St Asaph really believe that Bede meant this? Could he believe that Bede could not express his meaning more clearly? nay, that he said the very reverse of what he meant? Here there is such a gross change of terms as can scarcely be paralleled. Bede speaks of a province; therefore he meant a diocese, several centuries before a diocese was known in our country. He speaks of bishops in the plural; and he could refer only to one bishop at a time. He asserts, that "all the province, and also the bishops themselves, ought to be subject." But, according to Lloyd, he could only mean that the province was under the bishop, that is, was subject to him. He directly inverts the idea of the original writer, and substitutes a new one of his own, as to territorial property;—it "did belong to."—But to whom did it, even in this sense, belong? To the Presbyter-Abbot? No; even this would be yielding too much. It belonged to "that monastery."

The fact undoubtedly is, that Bede uses the term province, not in an ecclesiastical, but in a civil sense; in the same sense in which, in the preceding part of the chapter, he speaks of "the provinces of the Northern Picts," and of "the province of the Bernicians:" and it appears most probable, that he here uses the term, in the singular, with the same latitude as when he uses it in the plural, as denoting the whole territory of these Picts.

The argument might, indeed, be carried farther. Did I contend, that the phrase, *omnis provincia*, ought to be rendered, every province; as the passage, according to this view, would be completely disencumbered of the mighty "province or diocess of Hy," this version might be urged with considerable appearance of reason. It might be said, that it has been thus translated by a writer who cannot be suspected of any partiality in the cause; that this use of the Latin term is not only supported by the best authorities, but is perhaps the most common; that, in the present instance, it is the most obvious signification; that this gives a satisfactory reason for the mention which is made of bishops, more than one province being referred to by the ancient writer; and that *omnis*, in this sentence, should naturally be viewed as having a retrospect to what he had said a little before, in the same chapter, that "Columba came into Britain, to preach the word of God in the provinces of the Northern Picts."

There is, indeed, every reason to think that the expression ought to be understood with still greater latitude, as referring to what occurs in the preceding chapter. There, when speaking of the observation of Easter, he had said, that "after this manner the northern province of the Scots, and the whole nation of the Picts, continued to observe Easter-Sunday." Now, if we shall suppose, that by "the northern province of the Scots," he means Argyleshire, we have at least three provinces in North Britian referred to, including the two under the Pictish dominion. In this sense, undoubtedly, he uses the phrase, *provincia Scottorum*, in the fifth chapter of the same book, when giving an account of Oswald's desire to have a bishop from this province But, even according to the concession of Gillan, the term is to be viewed as still more comprehensive. For, when Bede, in the third chapter, speaks of the *septentrionalis Scottorum provincia*, or northern province of the Scots, Gillan says, that by this "he not only means the North of Ireland, but the western

Scottish islands, and those parts of Britain that were inhabited by the Scots." He agrees with Sir James Dalrymple, in viewing these northern Scots of Ireland as under the jurisdiction of Iona.

But if it shall be urged, that the north of Ireland is meant in the preceding extract from chapter third, because, a little downward, he speaks of "the nations of the Scots, which inhabited the southern parts of the island of Ireland," as having learned to observe Easter canonically; I shall not be contentious. Although this should be viewed as a province in Ireland, it cannot be denied that it was subject to the monastery of Hii.

As the learned prelate, however, had laid it down as a fixed principle that there must have been a bishop of Hii, he points out the very place of his residence. "The Bishop of Hii," he says, "had his seat at Sodora, in that island; and yet might have all the North-Piets in his diocess, at first, as the Bishop of Lindisfarn had all the Northumbrians. And yet afterwards, when the North-Piets had more bishops, he that dwelt there at Hii might have only the isles to his diocess." As he has erected a diocess, and created a bishop, where neither can be found in history, it was perfectly consistent, that he should also fix an episcopal seat for him. The good bishop seems here as fast asleep as that "dreaming monk," Hector Boece, whom he accuses of following Jeffrey of Monmouth, in "turning a cloak into a man." He has, indeed, had less ground to go upon, than had Boece in making a man of the word *Amphibalus*. Because, in later times, some have been called "Bishops of Sodor," or "of Sodor and Man," it has been imagined, that the title must have had its origin from the name of a place. Some have said, that this name was giving to a holm, or small island, in the neighbourhood of Man, where they pretend that the cathedral stood. Others, among whom is Bishop Lloyd, have transferred it to Iona. But there is no more evidence, that there ever was a place of this name, than that the place was thus denominated from the Greek word *Soter*, as signifying the Saviour; which vain idea was necessary to complete the fable.

It is now well known, that the name Sodor, or the title *Sodorensis*, originated from the designation given, by the Norwegians, to one division of the islands in the neighbourhood of Scotland, while they were under their dominion. They called all those to the north of the point of Ardnamurchan, in Argyleshire, Nordereys, that is, the Northern Islands, and those to the south of this point, Sudereys, that is, Southern Islands; the latter division including Arran, Bute, Cumra, &c., and, among others, Man and Iona. The bishop of this province takes his title from the Southern Islands, because these were reckoned the most important.

The good bishop is indeed much puzzled with Bede's *more inusitato*. He first admits it in language abundantly strong: " But whatever diocess they had, it is certain that the bishops that sat there successively, till Bede's time, were all subject to the abbot of that monastery." Then he tries to account for it in this way, that in other places bishoprics preceded the monasteries, but here the monastery preceded the bishopric; adding, that the Pictish king and his people " gave him the island in possession for the building of a monastery; and withal, for the maintenance of it,—the royalty of the neighbouring isles; six of which are mentioned by Buchanan, as belonging to the monastery." "And therefore," he says, "though Columba found it necessary to have a bishop, and was pleased to give him a seat in his island [that is, Sodor,] and perhaps to put the other islands under his jurisdiction, yet it is not strange that he thought fit to keep the royalty still to himself and his successors."

But what is all this to the purpose? Here we have another sophism, an evident change of the terms, or rather, of the subject. Bede's language evidently respects spiritual subjection on the part of "the bishops themselves;" and Lloyd can devise no better plan for getting rid of the difficulty, than to understand the language as if it had been meant of temporal subjection.   I have already observed, that the ecclesiastial writer evidently uses the term province in a civil sense; and as including not only the north of Ireland, but most probably also the whole territory of the Northern Picts. But did this jurisdiction, which Lloyd denominates "the royalty of the Abbots of Hii," include not only the north of Ireland, but a great part of the Pictish dominion?   Has not Dr. Lloyd himself circumscribed it within the compass of a few adjacent islands?

He finds himself, indeed, in a strange dilemma here: and seems at a loss to determine which side he ought to prefer. He has previously affirmed, that, according to Bede, "all the province or diocess, which was under the Bishop of Hii, did then belong to that monastery."   Now, either the royalty of the abbot was confined to a few naked islands, almost uninhabited: and, according to this idea, the diocese of the bishop was scarcely as large as a modern Hebridean parish; or the bishop "might have all the North-Picts in his diocess:" and what must have followed?   Nothing less than a complete ecclesiastical dominion.   For we must believe, that the royalty of the abbot, and the spiritual jurisdiction of the bishop, were co-extensive.   Thus, in order to deprive the abbot of any ecclesiastical power, the learned writer confers on him at least half a kingdom in a temporal respect. He seems willing to convert an abbot into a prince, rather than that he should, in the slightest degree, infringe on the rights of a bishop.   He will leave royalty to shift for itself, if he can only guard the episcopate.

But although, in this place, the Bishop of St Asaph seems resolved to understand all the subjection, meant by Bede, in a temporal sense, or in relation to the royalty ascribed to the abbot; as if conscious that he trode on very insecure ground, he had previously endeavoured to provide himself with a different footing. "If," says he, "those that were ordained bishops of any diocess should afterwards come to retire in their monasteries, as Colman did at Hy for some time after his leaving York;—in that case, there is reason to believe that they lived under the ordinary government in the monastery, as they did before they were made bishops."

Here the good bishop takes up very different ground. The subjection to the royalty, or temporal jurisdiction of the abbot, or monastery, is transformed into subjection to the monastic rule. For he is so much nonplussed by the subjection to which Bede refers, that he is at a loss whether to call it temporal or spiritual: or, in other words, whether to view the supremacy of the abbot as territorial or conventual. He, however, takes both in: wisely judging, perhaps, that if he was wrong as to the one, he must be right as to the other. But even this supposition cannot avail him. For, whatever was the nature of the subjection which the bishops gave, it was given by the whole province. That it was not, therefore, subjection to the monastic institute, must necessarily be admitted; unless it be said, that all the inhabitants of "the province of the Northern Picts" subjected themselves to the rule of Columba, or, in other words, became monks.

But, in order to prove that Columba "acknowledged the episcopal order superior to his own order of Presbyter," Lloyd further asserts, that "Columba did acknowledge that bishops were necessary for the ordaining of others into the ministry." The first proof is: "It appears—there was always one in his monastery, as Bishop Usher tells us out of the Ulster Annals, Prim. p. 701." Usher's own words, in the passage referred to, are: "The Ulster Annals teach us, that even that small island had not only an abbot, but also a bishop." This is somewhat different from there being "always one in his [Columba's] monastery." Usher, however, does not quote the words of the Annals, but immediately subjoins, in the same sentence;—"From which [Annals] it may perhaps be worth while to learn the first series of Abbots." He then adds a list of ten in succession, giving various notices concerning some of them. Would it not have been fully as natural to have given a list of the pretended bishops, if he could have done it? But, although "superior to Abbot-Presbyters," it is not a little singular that antiquity has thrown a veil over their names.

The occasion on which Archbishop Usher refers to the Annals of Ulster, as proving that "this small island had not only an Abbot, but a Bishop," particularly deserves our attention. It is when he wishes to correct what he considers as a mistake in Notker, who had said that "the Abbot of the monastery of Iona was viewed as the Primate of all the Hibernian Bishops." The good Primate of Ireland, with all his candour, could not easily digest this doctrine.

It must forcibly strike the mind of his reader, as very unaccountable, that, though he gives the names of ten abbots, or what he calls "the first series," he does not mention one bishop. It naturally occurs, that there must undoubtedly be some reason for this silence; either, that the archbishop found no names there, or that he had ground to doubt whether he could view the persons as properly bishops. Under this impression, I cast my eye on the "Extracts from the Annals of Ulster," which Mr. Pinkerton has appended to his "Enquiry," and met with the only passage, to which, it would seem, the learned Primate could possibly have referred. The whole proof is contained in these words: A. "711. Coide, Bishop of Hii, deceases."

Besides the ten Abbots of Hii mentioned by Usher, there were, according to these extracts, during the lapse of about three centuries, other nine, who are expressly designed Abbots, ten called *Coarbs*, and one denominated "Heir of Columb-cille." Johnstone, in his Extracts from the same Annals, gives the names of two abbots not appearing in Mr.

Pinkerton's.   But not another, besides Coide, is mentioned
as bishop.

In Colgan's list, as given from Innes's MS. Collections, we
find twenty-six successors of Columba, in the course of two
hundred and sixty-three years; and besides Ceudei, who is
evidently the same with Coide, only one of these Abbots has
the title of Bishop.   This is Fergnan, surnamed the Briton, the
third in this list; the same person with Fergnaus, who also
holds the third place in Usher's.   But Usher takes no notice
of his being a bishop; and Smith, who, in his Chronicle, calls
him Fergna, gives him no other designation than that of
Abbot.   His name does not appear in the extracts from the
Annals of Ulster.   Smith also mentions Coide under the
name of " St Caide or Caidan," but merely as Abbot of Hij.

To the article respecting Coide, Johnstone affixes the following note: " The Abbots of Iona, Derry, and Dunkeld,
are frequently stiled Bishops."   This remark seems to be
well-founded, from what follows in the Annals : A. " 723.
Faolan M'Dorbene, Abbot of Iona, was succeeded in the primacy by Killin-fada."   Conchubran, an Irishman, who wrote
the life of the female saint Monenna, about the middle of
the twelfth century, calls Columcille, or Columba, " Archbishop of Scotland;" though he must have known that, as
Bede says, he was merely " Presbyter and Abbot."   We are
at no loss to conceive, why, in later times, the title of Bishop
was sometimes given to the Abbots of such celebrated monasteries.   In an earlier period, this title could not be supposed to add anything to the dignity of one to whom " bishops
themselves were subject."   But afterwards, when episcopacy
extended its powers, and made far higher pretensions, it may
easily be imagined, that those, who adhered to the Columban
institute, paid this compliment to the prejudices of the times,
from the idea that it would add to the respectability of their
monastic presidents; especially as they considered them
fully entitled to it, from the primacy which they held.

It ought also to be observed, that not one of the bishops mentioned, in the lists referred to, can be viewed as supplying the friends of the order with an instance in point. For each of them was "Abbot of Hij," as well as bishop. Whether the title had been conferred on account of any mission, from which they had returned, as did the predecessor of Aidan, and Colman, I shall not pretend to determine: but not one of them is designed "Bishop of Hii;" all their relation to this island being marked by the term Abbot. It cannot reasonably be supposed, that, because one had been previously sent on a mission in an episcopal character, that this, in the event of his returning to Hii, should preclude him from being eligible to the office of Abbot. He certainly must have had an equal claim with any of his brethren. But the thing to be proved is, that "there was always" a bishop "in this monastery," besides the abbot, for discharging those ecclesiastical duties that did not belong to the latter. It must, indeed, also be proved, that he was "Bishop of Hy;" for otherwise this diocese must be deemed, if not "a monkish," at least a modern "dream."

The only thing besides, which has a shadow of proof on this subject, is mentioned by Goodal. But it scarcely merits a moment's consideration. "A bishop, called *Adulphus Myiensis ecclesiae episcopus*, subscribes the canons of the Council of Calcuith, A. D. DCCLXXXV., where the learned are of opinion, that, instead of *Myiensis*, it ought to be read *Hyiensis ecclesiae*." But if there be no better proof, that there was always a Bishop of Hii, than a supposed misnomer in a single list of members of a synod which met more than a thousand years ago, it is surely time to give up the argument. It would be fully as natural to suppose, that this was the subscription of the Bishop of Mayo, in Ireland. For it appears that Mayo was accounted a bishopric before this time. Bede observes, that, "in the language of the Scots," *i.e.* Irish, it was "named *Mageo;*" and that in his time it was "usually called *Muigeo*." Usher says, "we commonly name it *Maio*." He at the same time observes, that, in the Roman Provinciale it is designed *Mageo ;* and that the last bishop of this see, A. 1559, is called *Magonensis Episcopus*. *Mayensis*, however, is also used as the designation of the county.

Goodal seems to reckon it a sufficient reply to all the reasoning from the language of Bede, with respect to the authority of this abbot, that "Adamnanus, who himself was Abbot of Hii, tells us of Columba, the first abbot, that, having once called up a bishop, whom he at first took to be only a priest, to assist him at the consecration of the Eucharist, upon discovering his character, he desired him to make use of the privilege of his order in breaking the bread alone. 'We now know,' says Columba, 'that you are a bishop; why then have you hitherto endeavoured to conceal yourself, and hindered us from treating you with due respect and veneration ?'"

But this is undoubtedly of little weight, when opposed to the strong testimony of Bede: especially as it rests on the solitary assertion of a very credulous writer, whose work almost entirely consists of miracles said to have been wrought by the saint, of revelations made to him, or visions seen by him. From the manner in which Adamnan relates this part of the history, it appears that Columba discovered the bishop's character miraculously, or by some supernatural impulse. Over this Goodal prudently draws a veil; lest, perhaps, he should raise a laugh, at the expense of his countryman, for laying claim, even in so early an age, to the wonderful faculty of the second-sight. For, indeed, what is here ascribed to Columba looks very like this. "The holy man," says his biographer, "therefore approaching to the altar, and suddenly casting a prying look on his [the bishop's] face, thus addresses him ; 'Christ bless thee, brother. Do thou alone, as being a bishop, break this bread after the episcopal mode. Now we know that thou art a bishop," &c.

There must, indeed, be something very extraordinary in the episcopal office, that a miracle was wrought in order to make it known; not to say that this presbyter, amidst all his veneration, addresses the bishop with sufficient familiarity.

Adamnan, we know, strained every nerve to reduce the monks of Hii to catholic obedience; and might therefore deem it necessary to make their founder, Columba, speak that language which was most grateful to the Church of Rome. Such pious frauds have been. It is not improbable, however, that this story may have been interpolated by some monk in a later age. At any rate, all that can be inferred from this solitary proof, is, not that Columba did not claim an ecclesiastical jurisdiction over "bishops themselves," but that he paid this respect to a stranger, who had come from a distance, and did not belong to the province over which he presided. That he was a stranger is undeniable; for Adamnan calls him, de *Numinensium* provincia proselytus. This, as it is noted in the margin, is certainly an error for *Momoniensium*. The same word is also written *Muminensium*, and refers to the province of Munster, in Ireland, whence, it is most probable, this stranger came.

There is great reason, indeed, for viewing this whole story as a mere legend; as it rests on the ground of its being supposed that two presbyters were necessary for consecrating the Eucharist. For this idea, however, there does not seem to be the slightest foundation, from ecclesiastical history. This privilege was denied to deacons. "St Hilary assures us there could be no sacrifice, [such was the language of the times], or consecration of the Eucharist, without a presbyter. And St Jerome says the same, That presbyters were the only persons whose prayers consecrated bread and wine into the body and blood of Christ."

It may be added, that, if we could suppose this account to be true, it would clearly shew that, notwithstanding all the strong assertions which have been made on this head, no bishop, during the age of Columba, usually resided at Iona. Thus it proves rather more than the friends of diocesan episcopacy wish, as it destroys their own argument.

CHAPTER IV.

*Account of the Ecclesiastical Government of the Culdees conti-
nued.—Of the Mission of Bishop Aidan to the Northumbrians.—Mistranslations in the modern English Version of
Bede.—Of the Seniores at Iona.—Whether the Term denoted
Bishops, or Presbyters?—Whether the Culdean Government
resembled that of a modern University?—Of Gillan's reasoning.—If the Episcopal Missionaries to Northumbria were
amenable to the College of Iona?*

LLOYD proceeds, in his attempt to prove that the Culdees
admitted a difference as to office between bishops and
presbyters, by referring to Bede's account of the mission of
Aidan to the Northumbrians. One, whose name is said to
have been Corman, had been sent to them some time before.
But, from the austerity of his manners, not being acceptable
to them, he returned to his monastery at Hii. Here, "having
in a council of the seniors given an account of his ill
reception," says Llyod, "Aidan being then present and
discoursing well of the matter, all the seniors pitched upon
him, and judging him worthy to be a bishop, they decreed
that he ought to be sent; it follows that so they ordained
him, and sent him." But the conclusion which he deduces
from this account is truly curious. "Then at least there
were present two bishops for Aidan's ordination; and if the
see of Dunkeld was then founded, as old writers tell us, the
bishop of that place might make a third: or there might be
some other, of whom Bede had no occasion to tell us; for he
could little think that ever it would come to be a question,
whether Aidan were ordained by bishops or by presbyters."
This is certainly as commodious a method of securing a
quorum of bishops for **canonical** ordination as ever was

devised.   An appeal is made on one side of a question to a
passage in ancient history, in order to prove that there was
ordination merely by presbyters.   On the other side, it is
inferred from the passage, although it makes not the least
mention of the presence of bishops, that there must have
been at least two, if not three, present;—because, forsooth,
Aidan could not be regularly ordained without them.   But
how does Bede overlook these superior, and indispensably
necessary, members of the council?   For a very sufficient
reason.   The good man never once dreamed that in future
ages any one would be so foolish as to suppose that a person
would be ordained to the episcopal office, or to any clerical
office, without the imposition of the hands of bishops.   That
very historian who has told us, in as express terms as human
language could supply, that "the whole province, and even
the very bishops," were subject to this Presbyter-Abbot,
could not imagine such an absurdity, as that it would be
inferred from his words that the power could possibly
originate where the subjection was due.   Although he asserts
that it was "after an unusual manner," or "quite out of the
common order," that bishops should be subject to a presbyter;   how could it occur to him that any one would imagine
that their ordination might possibly be somewhat of the same
description?

In the English version of Bede's history, printed A. 1723,
this passage is, in two instances, rendered in such a way as
must tend to mislead the mere English reader.   It is said
that, on the return of the former missionary, they "in a
great council seriously debated what was to be done."   From
the language used, one would naturally suppose that this had
been a national council, called for the purpose;   or perhaps
something more than a mere national council, as including
delegates from the British, Irish, and Saxon churches;   a
council in which bishops could hardly be wanting.   But this
is a gross mistranslation, whether from design or not, I do

not pretend to determine. It is surprising, however, that any one who had ever read a sentence of Latin should find a great council here. Bede merely says : "They begun, tractatum *magnum* in *Consilio*—habere, to treat fully," or "to have much deliberation in the Council as to what should be done." And what was this *Consilium* ? It appears to have been merely the ordinary *conventus* of the presbyters or seniors. King Alfred accordingly renders it, in his Anglo-Saxon version, *gemote*, i.e. meeting.

Stapleton, the old translator of Bede, although warmly attached to the Church of Rome, has rendered the passage in a very different manner :—"He returned into his countre, and in the assemble of the elders he made relation, how that in teaching he could do the people no good to the which he was sent, for as much as they were folkes that might not be reclaymed, of a hard capacite, and fierce nature. Then the elders (as they say) began in counsaile to treate at long what were best to be done," &c.

There is another oversight in the modern version. " He [Aidan] being found to be endued with singular discretion, which is the mother of other virtues, and accordingly being ordained, they sent him to their friend King Oswald to preach." But the passage literally is : "Having heard this, the faces and eyes of all who sat there were turned to him ; they diligently weighed what he had said, and determined that he was worthy of the episcopal office, and that he should be sent to instruct the unbelieving and the illiterate, it being proved that he was super-eminently endowed with the gift of discretion, which is the mother of virtues : and thus ordaining him, they sent him to preach." Nothing can be more clear than that, according to Bede, the very same persons who found him worthy of the episcopate, both ordained and sent him. And who are these ? Undoubtedly, if there be any coherence in the language of the venerable historian, they were the all who sat there, or who constituted that conventual meeting which has been magnified into a "great council." For there is not the slightest indication of any change of persons. Nay, they were the very same who had sent his predecessor Corman, and to whom he at this time returned, and reported his want of success in the ministry. Having received his mission from them, he, although clothed with episcopal honours, considers himself as still subject to their authority. He, therefore, like a faithful messenger returning to those who had sent him, gives an account, both of his ill reception and of the causes of it. As far as appears from the narrative this council was held, not with any immediate design of appointing a successor, but merely for receiving that report from their former missionary, which it was his duty to give, and which it belonged to them, as his judges, to receive.

The old version gives no other view of the sense. "Al that were at the assemble, looking vpon Aidan, debated diligently his saying, and concluded that he above the rest was worthy of that charge and bishopricke, and that he shoulde be sent to instruct these vnlearned paynims. For he was tried to be chiefely garnished with the grace of discretion, the mother of all vertues. Thus making him bishop, they sent him forthe to preach."

Thus, it undeniably appears, from the connection of the history, that those who sat there were the *Majores natu*, or *Seniores*, to whom King Oswald had made application; the very same persons who had sent Corman, who received the report of his mission, who passed a judgment on his conduct in approving of what was said by Aidan concerning it, who determined or decreed that Aidan was worthy of the episcopate, who ordained and who sent him. And who were these persons? Let the Bishop of St Asaph answer the question. They were the "Senior Monks," as he designs them in one place, or "a council of the Seniors," as he calls them in another; carefully distinguishing them from bishops, two of whom, he thinks, must have been "present for Aidan's ordination;" although he is so very reasonable, that he will be satisfied if we give him but one, for he says, "If more could not be had, one might do it in case of necessity." But, as we have no vestige of proof from the record, that so much as one bishop was present, if all this was done by "a council of Seniors," or Presbyters, how can the inference be avoided that Aidan received presbyterial ordination?

Gillan seems fully aware of the consequence. He, therefore, takes different ground. He will not, with Lloyd, hazard the determination of the question on the bare possibility of the presence of three, of two, or of a single bishop. He invests all the Seniors with the episcopal dignity. "Oswald," he says, "earnestly desiring the conversion of his subjects, wrote to the Scottish bishops (designed here by Bede *Majores natu*, and in the 5th Ch. *Seniores*, the very word by which Tertullian designs bishops, *Apolog.* c. 39) entreating that a bishop, *Antistes*, might be sent to instruct his subjects." Concerning the predecessor of Aidan, he adds that he "made a report of his mission in a synod of the bishops and clergy, by whom Aidanus was appointed his successor."

Thus the friends of episcopacy contradict each other, as to the very meaning of the terms used by the ancient historian. The writer last quoted can scarcely agree with himself. For, in the course of two sentences, he gives two significations to the same word. In the first he says that it is the bishops who "are designed here—*Seniores;*" in the second, he enlarges the sense so as to include "the bishops and clergy." That the place referred to was the island of Hii there can be no doubt. Lloyd observes that here there could be but "one bishop at a time," as having charge of the province. But Gillan, in the first instance at least, finds as many bishops as there were seniors. This sense of the word he attempts to confirm by the authority of Tertullian, who, he says, designs bishops in this manner. But he has chosen one of the most unfavourable passages for the cause of episcopacy that he could have found in the book. Speaking of the ministry of the gospel, and of the exercise of discipline, Tertullian says: "Certain approved seniors preside, being admitted to this honour, not from the influence of money, but from character." His commentator Pamelius, although a bigoted papist, never thought of driving matters so far as our modern writer. For he thus explains the passage: "But least this should be believed to be a tumultuous assemby, these, he says, preside, who by all the Greeks are called Presbyters, but by us Seniors, not all, but those who are approved by the testimony of all."

The term was used in the same sense in the Cyprianic age. Hence Firmilian, an African bishop, in an epistle addressed to Cyprian, speaking of the necessity of preserving unity in doctrine, especially where there was a multitude of prophets, or public teachers, says: "Wherefore it is found necessary among us, that we, the seniors, and the presidents or bishops, should annually meet together, for putting those things in order which are committed to our care; that, if any matters are more important, they should be regulated by common counsel," &c. The same Pamelius, as he supposes that this epistle had been translated by Cyprian from Greek into Latin, says: "It appears to me that what is in Greek Presbyters, has been here rendered Seniors, in the same manner as the name President is substituted for Bishop; which, as it is still used by Cyprian, frequently occurs in this epistle."

It is singular, that, in this very epistle, Firmilian also applies the other designation used by Bede, to the rulers of the church. As used by him, it undoubtedly includes both the *seniores* and the *praepositi;* and shews that the church, in his time, had not entertained an idea of excluding Presbyters from the right of ordaining, any more than from that of dispensing baptism. Speaking of heretics, he says: "They can possess neither power nor grace, since all power and grace are placed in the church, where the *Majores natu*, the seniors, preside, who possess the power both of baptizing, and of the imposition of hands and of ordination."

Gillan clearly perceived that the same persons are said to judge Aidan to be worthy of being made a bishop, to appoint him, to ordain him, and to send him to preach the gospel in Northumbria. He therefore found it necessary to give a new signification to *Majores natu* and *Seniores*. But, conscious, perhaps, that this would not stand the test of examination, he endeavours to secure a retreat in the use of the term ordained, as if it must necessarily denote the gift of an office superior to that of a presbyter. "Now," says he, " what can be the meaning of his being thought worthy of the office of a bishop, and his being ordained? Certainly he was a presbyter before he was a monk of Hii, and a member of the synod, and spoke and reasoned, and made a great figure in it." But what assurance have we of this? Bishop Lloyd shews that many monks were laymen. Bede himself admits that of the many who daily came from the country of the Scots, into the provinces of the Angles over which Oswald reigned, and entered the monasteries, only some were presbyters. He seems to say, that they all preached or acted as catechists; but that those only baptized who had received the sacerdotal office. Having observed, that they instructed the Angles in regular discipline, he adds: "For they were for the most part monks who came to preach. Bishop Aidan himself was a monk," &c.

As he had already distinguished those who had the sacerdotal office from such as were merely monks, there is great reason to suppose that he means here to say, that Aidan had been a mere monk before his ordination as bishop.

His speaking and reasoning, in what is called the Synod, will not prove that he was a teaching Presbyter. He had this right, as being a member of the college. His "making a great figure" on this occasion proves nothing. For it appears to have been the first time that he made any figure; and that, before their meeting, they had never viewed his gifts as transcending those of his fellows, or once thought of sending him on a mission.

Having considered every material exception to the important testimony of Bede, with respect to the unusual mode of government observed at Iona, I shall only further observe, that it must appear to every one, who will be at the trouble carefully and candidly to examine his testimony, that it is not to be viewed as an incidental remark, in reference to the territorial rights of the abbot or monastery; but that, as he introduces it when speaking of the mission of Aidan, he evidently keeps it in his eye in the whole account which he gives of this mission. It is unquestionably meant as the key by which we are to interpret all his singular modes of expression on this subject.

We have seen, that his modern English translator has used considerable liberties with the text. But he had so much candour as to acknowledge his dissatisfaction with the attempts which had been made to invalidate the testimony with respect to the "unusual order." "This," he says, "the learned Primate Usher contradicts, and urges from the Ulster Annals his keeping a bishop always in his monastery; and his successor Adamnanus tells us, that he paid submission to a certain prelate upon breaking bread at the altar. *Adamnan. in vit. Columbi apud Canisii Antiqu. Tom. 5.* Yet this proves nothing against what Bede says."

Pennant gives a similar opinion. "In answer to this," he says, "Archbishop Usher advances, that the power of the abbot of Iona was only local; and extended only to the bishop who resided there.—But notwithstanding this, the venerable Bede seems to be a stronger authority, than the Ulster Annals quoted by the archbishop, which pretend no more than that a bishop had always resided at Iona [i.e. according to Usher's inference from them], without even an attempt to refute the positive assertion of the most respectable author we have (relating to church matters) in those primitive times."

But this is not all. I have said, that Bede still keeps this point, of the peculiarity of the ecclesiastical government at Iona, in his eye, when giving an account of the mission to the Angles. What he says, in the fifth chapter of his third book, concerning the choice, mission, and ordination of Aidan, in the meeting of the Seniors, has been particularly considered; and also his testimony, in the chapter immediately preceding, concerning the *more inusitato*. We must allow the ancient writer to be the best interpreter of his own language. Having asserted, that the "bishops themselves" were subject to the monastery of Hij, he immediately proceeds more fully to shew the reason of this ;—that they derived all their authority from this monastery. It is in the third chapter, that he enters on the subject of Aidan's mission. Here, after relating that, in consequence of his settlement at Lindisfarne, many of the Scots entered this province, preached the word with great zeal, and administered baptism, those, to wit, who were admitted to the rank of priests ; he subjoins, that churches were erected, and lands appropriated for establishing monasteries. "For they were chiefly monks," he says, "who came to preach. Bishop Aidan himself was a monk, forasmuch as he was sent from the island which is called Hii ; the monastery of which for a long time held the supremacy among almost all the monasteries of the Northern Scots, and those of all the Picts, and presided in the government of their people." In Alfred's Anglo-Saxon version, it is *Ealdordom and heanesse onfeng*. We see in what light this excellent prince understood the language of the historian. "It received the principality and exaltation."

This sentence supplies us with an incontestable proof of the sense in which we are to understand the unusual subjection mentioned in the following chapter. It is to be understood, as given, not to the Presbyter-Abbot exclusively, but to the Abbot in conjunction with the Seniors. For the supremacy is, in the third chapter, ascribed to the Monastery. The last clause of the sentence fully determines the nature of the subjection. It could not be temporal, or referring to territorial right. For the monastery of Hii not only held the supremacy amongst the monasteries, but " presided in the government of their people," i.e. not the inhabitants of these monasteries, but the subjects of the Scottish and Pictish thrones. Their jurisdiction, of course, must have been solely ecclesiastical.

Stapleton could have no other view of the passage. For he thus translates it : " The house of his religion was no small time the head house of all the monasteries of the northern Scottes and of abbyes of all the Redshankes, [the term by which he translates *pictorum*,] and had the soueraintie in ruling of their people."

It has been urged, that we can conclude nothing, from this unusual authority, against the establishment of episcopacy in Scotland, because the government of Oxford is vested in the university, exclusively of the bishop who resides there. But the cases are by no means parallel. For, 1. The government of the whole province was vested in the abbot or college of monks. It has been said indeed, that the kings of England " might have extended the power of the university " of Oxford " through the whole diocess, had they pleased, and that it would not have been a suppressing of the order of bishops." But, not to say that such a co-ordinate power would have been extremely galling to the episcopate, it has been proved that the power of the monastery extended far beyond the limits which Bishop Lloyd has assigned to the pretended diocese of Hii. 2. The power itself is totally different. Although the Bishop of Oxford be subject to the university in civil matters, as well as the other inhabitants of that city; what estimate would he form of the pretensions of that learned body, were they to claim a right of precedence, *regendis populis*, in governing all the people of his diocese; and, as a proof of the nature of the government, the same which Bede gives, of sending forth missionaries to teach, to baptize, and to plant churches? The bishop, I apprehend, would rather be disposed to view this as a virtual "suppressing of the order."

The supposition has been otherwise stated with respect to an university. It has been said: "When a bishop is head of a college, in any of the universities, (which has frequently happened) he must be subject to the jurisdiction of the Vice-chancellor, though only a priest, and perhaps one of his own clergy." In reply, it has been properly enquired: "Were the bishops of Lindisfairn no otherwise subject to the monastery of Ieolmkill, than the head of a college in any of the universities, becoming afterwards a bishop, must be subject to the jurisdiction of the Vice-chancellor, who may be a priest in his own diocess? Were they not ordained and sent by the monastery to be bishops of that kingdom, and even then subject to the monastery? The cases must, indeed, be viewed as totally dissimilar; unless it can be shewn, that the head of a college may be "sent, ordained, and consecrated to be a bishop of any diocese in England," and yet "continue subject to the university" from which he was sent.

It had been observed, in the vindication of Sir James Dalrymple's Collections, that the bishops sent to Lindisfarne could not "expect the ordinary concurrence of the abbot and college, because of the distance;" that they brought ecclesiastics with them from Hii, and that others came afterwards, to assist them in the conversion of the Saxons; and that those who left their bishoprics among the Saxons returned to Hii. Gillan attempts to turn aside the force of these observations by saying that "the Abbot's commands might have been transmitted more easily and safely from Hii to Holy Island, than from thence to the north of Ireland, if we

5

consider the boisterous sea, and the uncertainty of wind and waves;" and by asking, with respect to the teachers, "Whence could they have got them but from Hii?" and as to their retreat, "Whither should they go rather than to their own monastery?" But he seems in this instance to pay little regard to the history of the times; and entirely to overlook the intrepid spirit of the early inhabitants of the western islands and maritime coast, who were accustomed to venture to sea in such vessels as would now be deemed scarcely sufficient for crossing a river. We may well suppose that the intercourse by land from Hii to Northumbria was frequently interrupted by the wars between the Picts and Scots, or between the latter and the Cumbrian Britons. We know that, in the year 642, which falls within the thirty years allotted to the mission to Lindisfarne, Donald Brec, King of Dalriada, or of the Scots, was slain in battle by Hoan, or Owen, King of Cumbria. Now the missionaries from Hii could not go by land without passing through the Cumbrian territory, unless they had taken a very circuitous course.

From the poverty of our materials relating to this dark and distant period, it cannot reasonably be supposed that every difficulty which an ingenious mind may suggest can be fully obviated. But there seems to be sufficient ground for concluding that the missionaries sent to Lindisfarne were, even in the character of public teachers, amenable to the college at Iona. If they were not, they were completely independent: for they did not acknowledge subjection to the successors of Augustine, bishop, or archbishop, of Canterbury. Is it natural to imagine that the abbot and monks of Iona, who were so jealous of their superiority in other respects, would consent to send so many of their clergy into Northumbria, if they were from that moment released from all subjection, unless they chose again to submit to the mere monastic rule? It appears that Oswald, partly from early prejudice, as being himself educated at Hii, and partly perhaps from political motives, did not wish that the clergy in his kingdom should have any connection with a see that depended on a foreign authority.

In another point of view, it is hardly credible that the college at Hii would renounce all authority over these missionaries. When King Oswald applied to them for a bishop, it was not to preside over a church already organized, but to plant a church among a people, who, as the learned writer acknowledges, were " in a state of paganism." Now, has it been usual in any church, whether of the episcopalian or presbyterian form, that those who received a mission to preach the gospel to the heathen should be henceforth viewed as quite independent of the authority of those who sent them ? Besides, their being supplied with co-adjutors in the ministry from Iona must, by all candid enquirers, be considered as a proof of their continued dependence on that monastery. In a word, although we should plead nothing from the return of several of the bishops, the report which they gave of their conduct on their return to that very *conventus Seniorum* by which they had been sent must certainly be viewed as an incontestable evidence of their continued subjection, not as monks, but as missionaries. For the elders in their meeting did not merely receive such a report, but proceeded to judge of the conduct of the person, evidently claiming a right to inflict censure, if they judged it necessary.

We have one instance, at any rate, of the censure of reprehension, not only expressed by one member of this *conventus*, but evidently approved by all the rest. It is worthy of observation, indeed, that when the first bishop who had been sent to Lindisfarne returned on account of his want of success, and related this to the college of Hii, they acted precisely in such a manner as we would suppose persons to do who viewed themselves as having an inspection of Lindisfarne. We have no evidence from Bede that there was either any complaint made by Oswald against the missionary, whose name, it is said, was Corman, or any application from Oswald for a successor. The Seniors seem to have held a council immediately on Corman's return, and had much deliberation, or reasoning, as to what should be done, the result of which was, that they sent Aidan to Lindisfarne. Nothing can be more evident than that they acted as persons who were authorized to supply this vacancy.

The same writer asserts that "the Scots and Britons at the coming of Augustine into Britain, and for a long time thereafter, differed in nothing from the Church of Rome, but only in the observation of Easter, and a few rites and ceremonies." He afterwards admits that, according to Bede, Augustine demanded that they should "preach the word of God together with him, i.e. own him as their archbishop, and consequently the Bishop of Rome as the Patriarch of the western church : for the Pope had not as yet claimed the supremacy over the whole Catholic Church. He knew they embraced the same faith as himself."

Here we discern the true spirit of those old episcopalians, with whom the writer was connected. The attachment of many of them to Rome was far stronger than to any class of Protestants who did not acknowledge the divine right of episcopacy. But was it nothing for the "Scots and Britons" to receive a foreigner imposed on them in a character which they had never recognised, by an Italian priest whose claims they had never learned to acknowledge ? Be it so, that the Bishop of Rome had not yet assumed the title of Universal ; was it a matter in which faith was nowise concerned, to withstand the workings of "the mystery of iniquity," to oppose "the Man of sin" in every step that he took towards his exaltation ? This writer's idea of "the faith of the saints," whatever he might think of their "patience," is certainly very different from that of John the Divine.

Augustine held the synod referred to in the year 603. Before this time, towards the close of the preceding century, there had been a violent contest between the Bishop of Constantinople and the Bishop of Rome, with respect to the claim to this imposing title: and it was only three years after the meeting of this synod, or in the year 606, that the tyrant Phocas, by an imperial edict, gave it to the Bishop of Rome, settling the supremacy on him and his successors. If it was not unpardonable presumption in such obscure men as the clergy of "the Britons and Scots" to pretend to judge of a question of this nature; if they ever meant to oppose the encroachments of the great usurper, surely there was no time to be lost.

But whatever the warm adherents of an exiled and popish family, in this country, might think of the conduct of our ancestors; or what inference soever they might deduce from the language of Bede; we have a very different testimony from the pen of a celebrated Lutheran of another country, who may be viewed as an impartial judge on this subject, unless we suppose that he, as well as Sir James Dalrymple, was blinded by his sincere attachment to the Protestant cause. "The ancient Britons and Scots," he says, "persisted long in the maintenance of their religious liberty; and neither the threats nor promises of the legates of Rome could engage them to submit to the decrees and authority of the ambitious pontif, as appears manifestly from the testimony of Bede."

Gillan seems to view it as no inconsiderable concession which he makes to the ancient "Britons and Scots," when he admits that the adherents of Rome did not "think them hereticks." But the Britons and Scots treated them as such, and therefore refused to have any fellowship with them; as may be afterwards demonstrated.

It may be added, that, what judgment soever the Romanists formed of the Britons, the latter had no reason to think fa-

vourably of them.   Let us hear the evidence of one, who was
himself an archbishop and a warm friend of episcopacy,
concerning Augustine.   "Whilest he strove to conform the
British churches to the Romane in rites ecclesiastic, and to
have himself acknowledged for the only Archbishop of Britain,
he did cast the church into a sea of troubles.   After divers
conferences, and much pains taken by him to perswade the
Britons into conformity, when he could not prevail, he made
offer, that, if they would yield to minister baptisme, and observe Easter according to the Romane manner, and be assisting to him in reforming the Saxons, for all other things they
should be left to their ancient customs.   But they refusing
to make any alteration, he fell a threatening, and said, That
they who would not have peace with their brethren, should
finde warre with their enemies.   This falling out, as he fore-
told (for Edelfrid, King of Northumberland, invading them
with a strong army, slew at one time 1200 monks that were
assembled to pray for the safety of their countrymen) made
Augustine to be suspected of the murder, and did purchace
him a great deal of hatred : whether he foreknew the practice
or not, is uncertain, but shortly after the murder of these
monks, he himself died."

The monks referred to were chiefly those of Bangor, in
Wales.   Their abbot Dinoth was sacrificed with them.   Bede
represents this calamity as the effect of the prophecy delivered by the pious Augustine.   But there is every reason to
believe that the prediction was founded on a predetermined
plan.   As there had been a previous conference with these
monks, Archbishop Parker, speaking of what Bede relates
concerning Augustine's prediction, as if the war had been a
divine judgment in completion of it, says: "It is more
probable that he, having taken counsel with King Ethelbert,
not only knew of the war, but was himself the cause of it.
For he lived in the greatest familiarity with that king, at
whose persuasion and instigation Edelfrid brought this de-

struction on the Britons. It is affirmed, indeed, that in the first conference concerning these rites, Augustine, when he saw that the monks would not be persuaded, uttered his threatening: hence it is not improbable, that war was prepared against the Britons, if they should not comply in the second meeting. Some also assert, that Augustine met the kings at Caer-leon, when prepared for that battle."

Later popish writers, in order to exculpate Augustine, have attempted to shew that he was dead before this battle was fought: and, as we now have the Latin of Bede's history, it would seem that this worthy writer had said so. But the proof is evidently an interpolation. For there is not a word on this subject in the Saxon version; whence there is reason to conclude, that, in the time of Alfred the Great, by whom this version was made, this apology for the Roman missionary had not been devised. The language of Bede, indeed, shews how far he was blinded by his zeal for conformity to Rome. "And thus," he says, " was the prediction of the holy pontif Augustine fulfilled, though he had himself been long before removed to the heavenly kingdom, that these perfidious men might feel the vengeance of temporal destruction, because they had despised the counsels of eternal salvation offered to them." It is said by Amandus Xierixiensis, a friar Minorite, apparently of Xeres in Spain, that "this war was raised against the Britons on account of their disobedience to St Augustine; because the Saxons, who had been converted to Christianity, were resolved to subject the Britons to his authority."

CHAPTER V

Continuation of the Account of the Ecclesiastical Government of the Culdees.—Bishop Lloyd's View of the Ordination of Finan.—Of that of Colman.—Bede's Account of the Ordination of Aidan.—Of the Episcopate of Cedd.—Of the Conversion of the Saxons by Scots.—Testimony of the Saxon Chronicle.

I HAVE attentively considered all the principal exceptions which have been made, not only to the argument from Bede's assertion with respect to the government of Hii, but to that from the account which he has given of the designation, ordination, and mission of Aidan. His successor Finan had no higher authority. But it is not surprising, that the friends of episcopacy, after using so much liberty with the testimony of the ancient historian, should exibit a similar claim with respect to the appointment of Finan. This has been done by Bishop Lloyd in the following language: "After Aidan's death, Finan 'succeeded him in his bishopric, and in his stead received the degree of episcopacy,' saith Bede, again using the same expression, meaning (I suppose) that he received a degree higher than what he had before when he was priest."

Supposition is often of signal use, when there is a deficiency of evidence. There is obviously no foundation for the supposition which is here made. In neither of the passages referred to, does Bede insinuate that he meant any such thing. His language is: "But Finan succeeded him in the episcopate; and to this he was appointed from Hii, an island and monastery of the Scots." "Bishop Aidan being dead, Finan in his stead received the degree of bishopric, being ordained and sent by the Scots." When Bede says, that Finan "was appointed to this from Hii—a monastery of the Scots," he undoubtedly means that he received all that was included in his destination, or connected with it, from the college there, from the very persons whom he elsewhere denominates Seniors.   He received no other "degree of episcopacy," as far as we can learn from Bede, than what consisted in an ordination and mission by these presbyters.   It appears, indeed, that he had no other ordination, or consecration, than Aidan had before him.

I need scarcely add, that Lloyd makes the same attempt as to Colman, who succeeded Finan, saying, from Bede, that he "was a bishop of Scotland;" and that "the Scots sent him bishop to Lindisfarne."   But all that can be proved, is, that Colman received a mission from the monks of Iona.

The mode in which the venerable writer expresses himself concerning the mission of Aidan, who was a great favourite with him, may, I think, fairly be viewed as a key to all that he elsewhere says on the subject of these missions.   His words, from their very place, claim peculiar attention.   For they constitute the link between the account he has previously given of the appointment of Aidan, nay, of the peculiar model of ecclesiastical government at Hii, and the more particular narrative that he proceeds to give, both of the circumstances which led to the nomination of Aidan, and of those which attended it.   Having described the unusual government at Hii, he says: "From this island, therefore, from the college of these monks, was Aidan sent to the province of the Angles, who were to be initiated into the Christain faith, having received the degree of the episcopate.   At which time Segenius presided over this monastery, as Abbot and Presbyter."

If ever a writer, friendly to episcopacy, as Bede certainly was, had occasion to guard his language, as far as he could do it consistently with truth, this was the place.   Having, a few sentences before, described the peculiarity of the government, having said that the head of this college was not a bishop, but a presbyter: if Bede knew that, notwithstanding all the ordinations mentioned were by bishops, it was scarcely possible for him to avoid giving this caveat to his reader. But his whole language is so laid, as to appear a designed and formal confirmation of what he had said with respect to their singular administration. "Therefore," says he, on the ground of this very peculiarity, Aidan, whatever authority he had, received it not from bishops, but from "the college of these monks." Can his language be reasonably subjected to any other interpretation? But, does not Bede say, that Aidan "received the degree of episcopacy?" Yes; but, if there be any sense or connection in his language, he must have meant, that it was such episcopacy as presbyters could confer; an episcopacy, in conferring which none had any hand, who enjoyed a higher order than Segenius. Else why does he add, "At which time, Segenius, abbot and presbyter, presided over this monastery?" It would, certainly, have been far more natural to have told what bishops joined in conferring this degree.

Bishop Lloyd has been at considerable pains to prove, that all those, who were called bishops among the Saxons, received episcopal ordination. I do not see how it can fairly be denied, that, in one instance, the language of Bede can admit of no other interpretation. Having mentioned, that Cedd the presbyter had been sent to preach the word to the East-Saxons, he says, that "Bishop Finan, seeing his success in the work of the gospel, and having called to him two other bishops for the ministry of ordination, made him bishop over the nation of the East-Saxons:" adding, that he, *accepto gradu episcopatus*, "having received the degree of episcopacy, returned to the province; and, *majore, auctoritate*, with greater authority, fulfilled the work which he had begun, erected churches in different places, ordained presbyters and deacons, who might assist him in the word of faith, and in the ministry of baptism."

But, though the accuracy of this statement be admitted, it will by no means prove, that the episcopal mode of ordination was received in the northern part of Britain. This cannot be believed, in direct opposition to that evidence from facts which has been already exhibited. How then, may it be said, can we account for the difference as to the mode of ordination in the two countries? The difficulty may, at least partly, be solved, by supposing that the Church of Rome had greater influence among the Saxons than in North-Britain. About half-a-century before the ordination of Cedd, Augustine had been sent to Britain by Pope Gregory, for the purpose of subjecting it more effectually to his usurped domination. He had expressly ordained Mellitus to preach the gospel to the East-Saxons.

It is evident, that Augustine was extremely zealous for the episcopal dignity; for, before his death, he ordained Laurence as his successor, "lest upon his death," we are told, "the state of the church, as yet so unsettled, might begin to falter if it should be destitute of a pastor, though but for one hour: in which he followed the example of the first pastor of the Church, the most blessed prince of the apostles, Peter, who, having founded the Church of Christ at Rome, is said to have consecrated Clement his assistant in preaching the gospel, and at the same time his successor." According to Bede, indeed, Augustine had the dignity of an archbishop, and conferred the same on Laurence: although this is disputed by some writers of the episcopal persuasion, who assert that there was no such title in the western church at that time.

We also learn from Bede that "King Ethelbert built the church of St Paul, in the city of London, where Mellitus and his successors were to have their episcopal see." Thus every thing was cast, as far as possible, into the Roman mould.

Although the East-Saxons made a profession of the faith for some time, they apostatised, and expelled Mellitus. It was to the very same people that Finan afterwards sent

Cedd: and it seems highly probable that these Saxons, having been formerly accustomed to the greater pomp of that episcopacy which had been introduced by Augustine, might, upon their return to the profession of Christianity, refuse that submission to Cedd which they had formerly given to Mellitus; and might urge the necessity of his receiving that ordination which alone they had been taught to consider as canonical. Now, though we have seen that Finan himself had only that more humble ordination which was usually conferred in the island of Iona, he might judge it expedient, in the appointment of a successor to Mellitus, so far to comply with the prejudices of the people to whom he was sent as to ordain him by the imposition of the hands of the bishops. But, though he might deem such a compliance expedient, there is no satisfactory evidence that he viewed the office of bishop as essentially different from that of a presbyter. For, had he done so, he would have denied the validity of his own orders; and he could never pretend to take any share in conferring on another a power which he did not himself possess. Besides, it is admitted by Lloyd that when Bede says that Cedd was ordained by the Scots, we must understand the passage as intimating that the bishops whom Finan called in to assist him in ordination were also Scots. If so, they must have had the same ordination with Finan, that is, ordination by the presbyterial college of Iona. Here, surely, there could be no canonical transmission of the episcopal dignity. It would appear, therefore, that Finan viewed the difference as lying more in name than in anything else; as this designation, from the influence of prejudice, was reckoned more honorable than that of Presbyter.

It is true, indeed, that Bede speaks of Cedd as deriving greater authority from his episcopal ordination, and as ordaining presbyters and deacons in consequence of it. But it may naturally enough be supposed that the ecclesiastical historian expresses himself according to his own prejudices, and the general sentiments of the age in which he wrote.

Lloyd represents the great distinction between bishops and presbyters, even in the period referred to, as lying in the right of ordination; as if this had constituted the chief part of their work. But the humble monks of Hii had a very different view of matters. They considered preaching as the principal work of a bishop. Hence, according to Bede, Colman "was appointed to the preaching of the Word to the nation of the Angles."

It is admitted by Lloyd, that "if the Scots were governed only by presbyters, then Cedd was made a bishop by presbyters: which is all," he subjoins, "that our adversaries would have. But what if Cedd was ordained by no other than bishops: Then Bede's saying, any one was ordained by the Scots, will not argue that he was ordained by Scottish presbyters; nay, it will argue the contrary, unless our adversaries can bring at least one instance of a Scottish ordination by presbyters." Because Bede says that Cedd was "ordained by the Scots," referring to his ordination, mentioned above, by bishops of that nation, he deduces this general conclusion, that always when we read of one being ordained by the Scots, we are bound to believe that the persons who conferred ordination were diocesan bishops. This is, indeed, in the boldest manner, to infer a universal conclusion from particular premises. I do not say that it can be justly denied that this is Bede's meaning in the passage referred to: but I must reject the inference. For, although a historian in one instance uses a phrase in a different sense from that in which it is commonly used by him, we are not bound to understand it everywhere else in direct contrariety to the connection. Although Bede says that "the venerable bishop Cedd was, *ordinatus a Scottis*, ordained by the Scots," this is something very different from what, as we have already seen, he asserts concerning Aidan, Finan, Colman, and others, who are not only said to have been "ordained by the Scots," but to have received all the ordination they ever had before they left Hii; nay, to have been ordained and sent by Presbyters.

It ought also to be observed that Bede, when speaking of the episcopate, describes it only by the term *gradus*, and not by any one expression of difference of office or order. Now, it is well known that many learned men, who have opposed diocesan episcopacy, have admitted that the term bishop was very early used in the church, as denoting a distinction with respect to degree, while the office was held to be essentially the same. In what sense this distinction has been made may be afterwards explained.

It deserves also to be mentioned that, how little soever some now think of Scottish orders, it is evident, from the testimony of the most ancient and most respectable historian of South-Britain, that by means of Scottish missionaries, or those whom they had instructed or ordained, not only the Northumbrians, but the Middle-Angles, the Mercians, and East-Saxons, all the way to the river Thames, that is, the inhabitants of by far the greatest part of the country now called England, were converted to Christianity. It is equally evident that for some time they acknowledged subjection to the ecclesiastical government of the Scots: and that the only reason why the latter lost their influence was that their missionaries chose rather to give up their charges than to submit to the prevailing influence of the Church of Rome, to which the Saxons of the West and of Kent had subjected themselves.

The Saxon Chronicle, under the year 560, supplies us with an additional proof of the nature of the ecclesiastical government of Iona, in perfect consonancy to the account given of it by Bede, a proof which, notwithstanding the attempts that have been made to invalidate it, appears absolutely irrefragable. I shall give the sense of the passage as literally as possible. "Columba, Presbyter, came to the Picts, and converted them to the faith of Christ, those, I say, who live near the northern moors; and their king gave them that island which is commonly called Ii. In it, as it is reported, there are five hides [of land], on which Columba erected a monastery; and he himself resided there as abbot thirty-two years, where he also died when seventy years of age. This place is still held by his successors. The Southern Picts, long before this time, had been baptised by Bishop Ninian, who was trained up at Rome. His church and monastery are at Whiterne, consecrated in honour of St Martin, where he rests with many other holy men. Thenceforth there ought to be always in Ii an Abbot, but no Bishop; and to him ought all the Scottish Bishops to be subject; for this reason, that Columba was an Abbot, not a Bishop."

This proof is so strong and distinct, as scarcely to need illustration. Bishop Lloyd discovers great anxiety to over-throw it: but, to every candid reader, his attempts must appear extremly feeble. He supposes, that from the "words of Bede," (which we have formerly considered) "not rightly understood," this note has been "inserted into the later copies of the Saxon Chronicle." This, however, forcibly reminds one of the Socinian mode of reasoning. It is well known, that, when writers of this class are much puzzled with any passage of scripture, which opposes their system, they raise the cry of interpolation.

It might justly be asserted, that, here there is so great a difference, both in the mode of expression, and as to some circumstances mentioned, that no room is left for supposing that the annalist copied from Bede. But, although the bishop's conjecture were well founded, it would not at all invalidate the evidence, Let us even suppose for a moment that this passage has been inserted some time after the year 850, as he imagines; was this too late to know the model of government at Iona? Had not many of her delegates officiated in England, in the two preceding centuries. If Bede had expressed himself inaccurately, had not abundance of time elapsed, for enabling later writers to guard against a similar mistake ? Whether was a writer, let us say, a century after the death of Bede, or Lloyd, a thousand years after him, best qualified to understand Bede's meaning ? If this insertion was made so late, as by this time episcopacy had gained far more strength, is it not natural to think that a writer, immediately attached to the Church of Rome, would be so much the more on his guard as to the language which he used ?

But what the Bishop of St Asaph at first only supposes, he a little downwards roundly asserts. "These words of the Saxon Chronicle," he says, "A. 560, were all put in by a later hand. For the old Saxon Chronicle has nothing of Columba in that year." What he means by "the old Saxon Chronicle," I cannot easily conjecture. He could not refer to Wheeloc's edition, A. 1644. The learned Bishop Gibson, indeed, who published his in the year 1692, informs us in his preface, that Wheeloc had given his copy from two very imperfect MSS., both evidently written by the same hand, which contained merely fragments of the genuine Chronicle. Gibson's edition, from which I have quoted, was given to the public, only as the result of the most accurate investigation of the best MSS. In this work he had the assistance of the very learned Hickes, the first Saxon scholar that this country has produced. But even Wheeloc gives the controverted passage. Lloyd must therefore refer to some imperfect MS., containing merely an abstract.

He pretends that this passage must be an insertion, made " some time after the year 850," from what is said "concerning the Picts, that they dwelt at that time in the North Moores ;" as " it was about that year that the Picts were conquered by the Scots, and till then they continued in their old habitation." I need scarcely say, that the idea of the Picts being expelled by the Scots is now almost universally viewed in the same light in which the history of the government of the Culdees appears to the bishop, as "a monkish dream." This is, indeed, the proper distinction of the Northern Picts in the earliest period of their history. The language might, perhaps, be more properly translated, "near the northern mountains." The term occurs frequently in this sense in Alfred's translation of Bede; as, *In heagum morum;* in excelsis montibus: lib. iv. c. 27. Gibson has improperly rendered it by *paludes,* as if it signified marshes: in which sense it is also used. They are said to live "near the high mountains," because they are separated from the Southern Picts by the Grampians: and this is the very description of those Picts who were more immediately subject to the college of Iona.

It is evident that the writer, unless he meant to act as a base interpolator, must have lived before the date assigned. For he speaks of the monastery of Hii as still retaining its dignity and power. Nor can it be reasonably supposed that any subsequent writer would have made such an attempt: as he could have no end to serve by it, and the forgery must soon have been discovered.

I shall only add that Lloyd takes no notice of the different account which the Chronicler gives of the ecclesiastical government of the Southern Picts. For the contrast would have enfeebled, if it had not overthrown, his objection. The ancient annalist evidently knew well what he was writing. But observe the opposition stated. "In Hii there must be always an Abbot, not a Bishop." He seems to give the very ground of the difference in what he says of Ninian. He "had his education at Rome."

Henry of Huntingdon, a writer of high respectability who flourished about the year 1140, has given a similar testimony. His language so nearly resembles that of Bede that it may perhaps be said that he has transcribed from him. But it can hardly be supposed that a writer of his description would implicitly receive anything merely on the testimony of another. It would appear that he had informed himself concerning the truth of the statement given by Bede; as, after speaking of Columba, he says: "Whose successors, imitating his example, have made a conspicuous figure." Nor did he live too late to receive accurate information on this subject. For in his time the disputes between the Bishop of St Andrews and the Culdees must have made so much noise that we can scarcely suppose they could be unknown to him. There were still Abbots of Hii in his time; and he speaks as if they had still maintained their claim, however much their power had declined.

John of Fordun, one of our most ancient historians, says, that, before the coming of Palladius, "the Scots had, as teachers of the faith, and administrators of the sacraments, only presbyters and monks, following the custom of the primitive church." Lloyd is very angry with Fordun for this assertion. He roundly calls him "a dreaming monk:" and sarcastically says, that he "was pleased to discover this for the honour of his order no doubt." Sir George Mackenzie, however, has taken notice of the bishop's mistake in this instance; observing, that Fordun was "a Presbyter, not a Monk, as St Asaph calls him." Lloyd is disposed to disregard the whole of what is here asserted, on the ground, as would seem, that the writer was in an error in supposing that Palladius visited the Scots of Britain, because, he says, there were no Scots at that time. But it has been seen that there is a high degree of probable evidence, that Palladius resided for some time in the northern part of our island, and that he died there.

It is a singular circumstance, that, however much later writers have affected to despise the testimony of Fordun with respect to the Culdees, the Canons of St Andrews did not hesitate to avail themselves of it, when it was subservient to their credit in the meantime, though at the expense of giving a severe blow to episcopacy in an early age. As there had been a dispute, at a meeting of parliament in the reign of James I., with respect to precedency between the priors of St Andrews and Kelso: the king having heard the arguments on both sides, determined it in favour of the former on this principle, that he was entitled to priority in rank, whose monastery was prior as to foundation. "We have a proof of this," adds Fordun, "from St Columba, who is represented as arch-abbot of all Ireland, and who was held in such pre-eminence among the inhabitants, that he is said to have confirmed and consecrated all the Irish Bishops of his time." The whole of this chapter, not excepting the passage last mentioned, has been emboded in the Register of St Andrews.

Lloyd pays as little regard to the assertion of Major, and treats with still greater contempt that of Boece, who has said, that the Culdees "chose, by common vote among themselves, a chief priest, who had power in things belonging to God: and that, for many years after, he was called Bishop of the Scots, as it is delivered in our annals." Elsewhere he says, that before the time of Palladius "the people, by their suffrages, chose bishops from the monks and Culdees." Lloyd endeavours to set aside the testimony of Boece, by recurring to what is commonly admitted, that he is a writer entitled to very little credit. But how slender soever the credibility of any writer, his testimony is generally regarded, when it is opposed to the honour of the society to which he belongs: because, in this case, we conclude, that nothing but full conviction of the truth could have extorted such a testimony. The natural inference, then, from this assertion, is that as Boece, in other instances, appears abundantly zealous for the interests of the Church of Rome, he would not have ventured such an assertion, had he not known that, in his time, the truth of it was generally admitted. Had he been a presbyterian, his testimony would have been liable to exception. But his zeal for episcopacy cannot be doubted by any one who has looked into his work on the Lives of the Bishops of Morthlac and Aberdeen: a work expressly written in consequence of his attachment to Bishop Elphinston. Now, what temptation could a writer, who rigidly adhered to the whole hierarchy of the Church of Rome, have for asserting what he had reason to disbelieve, at the expense of the honour of that church of which he was a member? Others, it may be said, had done it before him. But this invalidates the objection from his want of credibility as an historian in other respects. He retained the assertion, because he saw no good ground for rejecting it as unfounded.

In the Breviary of Aberdeen, which was written before Boece's History, we have nearly the same account. There it is said, that before the time of Palladius, the Scots had " for teachers of the faith, and ministers of the sacraments, presbyters and monks; following only the rite and custom of the primitive church." Had it been supposed that there was any ground for doubting what is here asserted, how would it have obtained admission into the very first book printed in our country, as containing the liturgy of the church?

Martine, even while he asserts the antiquity of bishops in Scotland, pays great respect to the memory of the Culdees. This appears from a quotation which he makes in his *Reliquiae*. "To prove," he says, " that we had bishops in this kingdome very long since, even from near the time of our conversion to the faith, whom the Culdees elected, I shall set down a famous testimonie out of the MS. of the bishops and archbishops of St Andrews, in Latin, in the Life of William Wishart, bishop there. It is this: Quando ecclesia Scotica crescere bona fide, et in bona fruge adolescere coepit, Culdei semen evangelii mirum in modum multiplicatum cernentes, ex suo corpore episcopum crearunt, qui nullae certae sedi alligatus fuit, circa annum conversionis 62, i.e. reparatae salutis humanae 270. Cum vero unicus, qui sedem habere praecipuam incipiebat Sodorae in Argadia, non sufficeret, ut opinabantur, tunc plures ex eorum Culdeorum corpore episcopi sunt creati: Nec hoc

satis erat, quia postea ab eleemosynis ad certos annuos census
ecclesiastici transivere, tum episcopatus crescere, Abbatiae
fundari et donationibus ditari, dignitas etiam et honor, a
putativa illa sede apostolica, augeri a regibus optimatibusque
et populo in admirationem haberi coeperunt: tunc omnia
pessum ire.   Verum Culdei episcopum e suo corpore eligendi
potestatem in Scotia semper habebant, donec translatum fuit
ab iis jus illud ad clerum, quod primum in electione Sanctan-
dreani Episcopi Willielmi Wishart abrogatum fuit anno 1271,
aut eo circa."

The following things are admitted as facts by this ancient
writer: 1. That the seed of the word greatly increased by
means of the preaching of the Culdees.   2. That they elected
one, from among themselves, to be bishop over them.   3. That
this bishop had no fixed diocese.   When it is said that he had
his seat at Sodor, in Argyleshire, there is evidently a reference
to Iona, where it has been erroneously supposed that the
cathedral of Sodor was erected.   4. The Culdees are represented as the judges of the supposed necessity of an increase of
the number of bishops.   For *opinabantur* must refer to them,
in the same manner as *cernentes*.   5. It is admitted that the
Scottish bishops were at first supported merely by free gifts.
6. That the Culdees retained the exercise of their right of
choosing the bishops, till they were deprived of it at the time
of Wishart's election.

It is vain to say, that Fordun, and the other writers last
mentioned, lived too late to know anything certain as to the
original government of the Culdees.   When we find them
exhibiting a testimony in favour of a model directly opposed
to their own, we may be assured that this is not done wan-
tonly.   In this case, though we knew of no early records to
which they could have had access, we would be bound to
suppose, that it was from such documents that they had
formed their judgment.   How many chartularies and annals
might these writers have seen, which may have all perished

since their time!   But if we find that these later writers give
substantially the same testimony with others of a far earlier
date, who are of undoubted credit, especially if there has been
a succession of these : we are under a necessity of concluding,
that they acted both an honest and a judicious part, and of
admitting their testimony, as at least of the nature of cor-
roborative evidence.

Before leaving this important branch of our subject, it may
be proper to take notice of what has been advanced by Goodal ; whose account of the Culdees, according to Mr Pinkerton,
is " the best yet given."   He is at great pains to shew, that,
in a very early period, there were in Scotland a considerable
number of diocesan bishops living at the same time.   In order
to prove this, he refers to two passages in Bede, which we
have not yet considered.

" Bede," he says, " gives us a letter from Laurence Archbishop of Canterbury, directed to the bishops and abbots
throughout all Scotland in the year 604, Hist. ii. 4."   From
the confidence with which this is brought forward, I was
inclined to suspect that I might be mistaken in my preceding
conclusions : but, on looking into it, I found, not without
some degree of surprise, that it has no relation to the point
in hand. . The letter, indeed, bears this address : " To the lords
our dearest brethren, the bishops, or abbots, through all Scotland."   But the only judgment we can form, favourable to
this writer's integrity, is, that he had not read the chapter
that contains the letter to which he refers.   For Bede, speaking
of Laurence, says : " He not only watched over the church,
which was newly gathered from among the Angles, but also
over the ancient inhabitants of Britain ; and even exercised a
pastoral solicitude with respect to the Scots who inhabit Ireland, the island nearest to Great Britain."

He refers to another letter, but not more happily.   " Bede,"
he says, " has preserved to us a letter from Pope John in the
year 640, directed to five Scottish Bishops, and six Presbyters

by name, and one of these Segenus, Abbot of Hii, about the observation of Easter, and about Pelagianism, Hist. ii. 19."

This letter is addressed, indeed, Dilectissimis et sanctissimis Tomiano, Columbano, Cromano, Dinnao, et Baithano Episcopis, Cromano, Ernianoque, Laistrano, Scellano, et Segeno Presbyteris; Sarano, ceterisque Doctoribus seu Abbatibus Scottis; &c. But Bede evidently uses the term *Scottis* here, in the very same sense as in the passage last quoted. Accordingly, Smith observes in his notes, that Tomianus was Archbishop of Armagh, Dinnaus, Bishop of Connor, Baithanus, of Clonmacnois; Croman, Abbot of Roseree, and Segenus, of Hii. "The seats and titles of the rest," he adds, "I have not discovered." Thus, three, at least, of the bishops were Irish. This is admitted by Archbishop Usher, and by the Bishop of St Asaph.

Gillan claims a right to conclude, that, "because they confess they cannot find the sees of the other two bishops, they at least had their bishoprics in Scotland, especially" as it is granted, "that Segianus the priest was the same with Segenius, Abbot of Icolmkill." But it must be obvious, that the presumption lies entirely on the other side;—that, because three of these bishops were Irish, the rest were so. Nothing can be inferred from the circumstance of Segianus being joined with them. For it cannot be denied, that the connection of Hii with Ireland was not less than with North-Britain.

CHAPTER VI.

Of the principal Seats of the Culdees.—Of Abernethy.—Anti-
quity of this foundation.—Of St Bridget.—Whether Aber-
nethy was a Bishopric?—Of the University here.—Of the
Collegiate Church.—Property of the Abbey given to that of
Aberbrothoc.—Controversy on this head.—Temporal Lords
of Abernethy.

THE seats of the Culdees now claim our attention. They
had monasteries, or cells, in a variety of places in Scotland;
some of which afterwards became episcopal sees. Lloyd,
indeed, and other writers on the same side of the question,
wish it to be believed, that, wherever there was a bishopric,
the Culdee Abbot, and his monks, can only be viewed as the
dean and chapter of the diocese. With this view, it is asserted, that we do not find them at St Andrews, "till it had
been many years the see of a diocesan bishop." But it is
certain that, before the name of St Andrews was known, and
before the erection of any place of worship there, Abernethy
was a principal seat of the Culdees.

High antiquity has been ascribed to this religious foundation. The Pictish Chronicle carries it back to the third year
of Nethan I., or A. 458. But, as this erection is made coeval
with the time when St Bridget flourished, it is evidently
antedated when ascribed to Nethan I., King of the Picts.
For, it would appear, that she died about the year 520. That
a monastery had been erected here about the year 600, there
seems to be no good reason to doubt. Fordun says, that it
was founded by Garnard, the son of Dompnach, who began to
reign A. 587. But, according to the Register of St Andrews,
the honour of this foundation belongs to Nethan, Naitan, or
Nectan, II., who succeeded Garnard A. 598. The last account

seems preferable to that of Fordun: on this ground, that it may easily be conceived that, in the Pictish Chronicle, the one Nethan might be substituted for the other. As it seems probable that the place was denominated from a prince of this name, especially as *Abernethyn* occurs in ancient writings: may it not be supposed, that, in later times, without any intentional fraud, the Pictish sovereign, who first erected a religious house here, might be confounded with his predecessor of the same name, who had founded the town, or honoured it as a royal residence ?

As we learn from Bede, that Nethan, the third Pictish prince of this name, desired architects from the Angles of Northumberland for building a church of stone, Mr. Pinkerton hesitates whether this ought not to be accounted the epoch of the foundation of Abernethy. He adds, however : " But perhaps a wooden fabric might have been reared by Nethan II." The latter is certainly the most plausible idea : for we can scarcely suppose, that, in so rude a period, a Pictish king would propose to build a church of stone in a place which had not previously acquired great celebrity as a religious foundation.

After giving an account of the foundation here, Fordun says : 'Afterwards St Patrick there introduced St Bridget, with her nine virgins, into Scotland, as we learn from a certain chronicle of the church of Abernethy : and he gave to God, and to the blessed Mary, and to St Bridget and her virgins, all the lands and tithes, which the prior and canons have enjoyed from an early period. These nine virgins died within five years, and were interred on the north side of the said church."

Our historian, Leslie, seems to think that it was the same Bridget who has been so much celebrated both by the Irish and by the Scots. " St Bridget," he says, " was held in such veneration by Scots, Picts, Britons, English, and Irish, that you may see more temples erected to God in memory of her, among all these nations, than to any other saint. The Irish contend that they have her holy body at Down, where that of St Patrick their apostle is also preserved. Our countrymen claim the same honour to themselves; believing that they rightly worship it in the college of Canons at Abernethy." His language is materially the same with that of Boece.

Camerarius is at great pains to shew that the Bridget, who was contemporary with St Patrick, was a native of North Britain. His principal proof is, that by so many writers she is designed *Scota*, or a Scottish woman. This, however, from the period in which they wrote, is of no weight; as no candid person can doubt that, by foreign writers, the term was, in the middle ages, most generally applied to the inhabitants of Ireland. The idea of St Patrick introducing St Bridget at Abernethy, must therefore be rejected as a fable.

It is not quite improbable, however, that our ancestors might have a St Bridget of their own. The Irish, indeed, not without reason, charge our historians with such a want of moral honesty, that they could not secure their very saints against depredation. But the learned and candid Usher seems to think that our writers had confounded the Irish Bridget with another of the same name, of a later age, who, it is said, was educated at Dunkeld. Speaking of the account given by Boece of Kentigern, and Columba having resided for some time there, he shews that here there is evidently a gross anachronism: and that the story must regard another Columba, of whom we read in the life of St Cuthbert, Bishop of Lindisfarne, borrowed from what he calls the Histories of the Irish. There it is said, "St Columba, first bishop in Dunkeld, took Cuthbert when a boy, and kept and educated him for some time, together with a certain girl of the name of Bridget, of Irish extract. The age of Cuthbert," he adds, "indicates that this must have taken place soon after the year 640; and this Bridget apparently was that companion of St Monenna; and this Columba, the bishop, who, as we read, became celebrated in Scotland after the death of Monenna."

A ray of light, however faint, is thrown on this story, by what Bede relates concerning Cuthbert. He resided for some time, he says, with Trumwine, designed Bishop of Abercorn. Now, as we know that, in consequence of the inroads of the Picts, Trumwine found himself under the necessity of removing to Whitby, in England: if we can credit the history referred to by Usher, it may be supposed that Cuthbert found a retreat at Dunkeld.

It has been said, that "at Abernethy there is a very ancient church, which was built in an age that is beyond memory:" and that, while "its origin defies conjecture, it was certainly dedicated to St Bridget, by the command of the zealous Nectan."

That a saint of this name, whoever she was, had the honour of this dedication, can hardly be doubted; this being asserted in the Pictish Chronicle, formerly quoted,—a monument of antiquity, the credibility of which has scarcely been called in question. Although, as we have seen, the foundation of the church is antedated, by the substitution of one Nethan for another, this does not seem to be a sufficient ground for rejecting the evidence of this record with respect to the patroness, any more than for totally disregarding what is said as to the foundation.

It is evidently to this valuable chronicle that Camden refers, in what he says of Abernethy. I shall give his words as quoted by Sir James Balfour: "Or ever the river Ern hath joyned his waters with Tay in one streame, so that now Tay is become more spatious, he looketh upe a little to Aberneth, scatted at the feete of the Ocellian montanis, anciently the royall seate of the Picts, and a weill peopled citey, which, as we read in ane ancient fragment, Nectane King of the Picts gane unto God and St Briege, vntill the day of doome, togider with the bounds thereof, which lay from a stone in

Abertrent to a stone neigh to Carfull (I wold rather reid Carpull), and from thence als far as to Ethan."

Carpull is now written and pronounced Carpow, the name still given to a gentleman's seat here. Hence we may have some notion of the former extent of Abernethy, now reduced to a poor village. Carpow is about a mile east from the present town. The situation of Ethan, called Athan in the Pictish Chronicle, seems to be now unknown. The limits mentioned in this extract, may indeed denote only the extent of the territory annexed to Abernethy. But, according to tradition, the vestiges of streets and buildings have been discovered a great way to the east of the present town.

We have seen, that Fordun refers to the Chronicle of Abernethy. Innes also quotes the book of Paisley, as attesting the existence of the same chronicle. But it has not been seen for several centuries. We are, therefore, as much at a loss as to the age of the celebrated round tower, still standing at Abernethy, as we are with respect to its use. It seems most probable, that it had been built at the same time with the church by those architects who were employed by Nethan, when he resolved to erect a fabric of stone. The conjecture, now pretty generally adopted, is that these singular structures were meant for penitentiaries, though others view them as belfries.

Boece pretends that Abernethy was a bishopric, and indeed a sort of metropolitan see. For he says that Kenneth, the son of Alpin, "transferred to Kilrymont the pontifical seat of the Picts, which had been long at Abernethy: the latter being destroyed by fire and sword." The learned and ingenious editor of the last edition of Sibbald's History of Fife has made some remarks on this subject which deserve to be transcribed.

"Of the pretended bishopric of Abernethy," he says, "no traces are to be found in the registers of monasteries, or the earlier annalists; nor does there appear to have been any episcopal see, properly so called, north of the Forth, before the erection of the bishopric of St Andrews in the 9th century. It may be supposed that when the Culdees were accustomed to elect bishops, who had no fixed diocese, but exercised their functions wherever they came, Abernethy may have been the favourite residence of some of them. It was an ecclesiastical establishment perhaps as early as the beginning of the seventh century, and appears to have been a school for such learning as then obtained among the clergy. These circumstances might induce some of the bishops to reside there, and give them an influence over the clergy educated under their inspection, which tradition has magnified into a supremacy over all the churches of Pictland. That there were bishops among the Culdees in Pictland, we cannot doubt, though they were certainly (except in what immediately regarded the episcopal function) inferior in influence and power to the Abbot of Iona."

Such was the strength of the Culdean establishment at Abernethy, and so independent was it of any episcopal authority, that it subsisted long at this place after St Andrews became the seat of a bishopric. " It appears," as Sir James Dalrymple remarks, "that it still subsisted as a religious house in the reign of King Malcolm the third, from a charter of Ethelradus his son, of the church of Ardmore to the Keldees, where amongst the witnesses is *Berhcadh Rector Scholarum de Abernethy et eorum coetibus totius universitatis tunc de Abernethy*; and, even after the establishment of the popish orders there was a collegiate church here."

We learn from Fordun that Abernethy was converted into a priory of canons regular, A. 1273. Forbes, in his Treatise on Tithes, says that "a collegiate church was founded here by the Earl of Angus." It has been supposed that this assertion regards Archibald Earl of Angus, Lord of Abernethy, who gave the town a charter of privileges, Aug. 13th, A. 1476: and justly remarked that this " Earl might be a benefactor to the collegiate church, or restore it to a better state than it had been in for some time before; and on that account might be said to have founded it." But the collegiate church was undoubtedly erected long before. Sir James Balfour, though he has not mentioned his authority, has the following notice in his MS. Collections: "Abernethy, a collegiate churche, wherein eight prebends, foundit by Hen. Lord Abernethy." This seems to be the same person who is designed *Henricus de Abernyti miles,* as witness to a charter granted by Henry Bald, goldsmith in Perth, to the abbey of Scone. He lived in the reign of William the Lion: for this prince gives a confirmation of the charter referred to.

Fordun, who wrote about the year 1377, as he dedicates his Chronicle to Cardinal Wardlaw, then Bishop of Glasgow, calls Abernethy a "collegiate church." Did we understand his language in its strictest sense, it might seem to signify that it was so from the first. But most probably he meant nothing more, than that Garnard "founded and built" the house which, at the time when he wrote, was commonly designed "the collegiate church of Abernethy." Forbes indeed has said that collegiate churches began to be built after King Alexander the Third's time, when the erecting of monasteries was discouraged by the Popes usurping the right of patronage. But, from what we have already seen, it must be evident that this remark can apply only to their more frequent erection.

The Culdees, it would appear, manifested the same assiduity in the instruction of youth at Abernethy, as at Iona. They had most probably been engaged in this arduous and important work from the very foundation of the church there. From what has been already quoted, with respect to Berbeadh, the rector of the schools at this place, it is evident that they had been in a flourishing state in the time of Malcolm Canmore. They were then entitled to the honourable designation of a university. We may reasonably suppose that the members of this society continued to teach here till the time of the erection of the priory of canons regular: when this office would, in all probability, be claimed by them, for the increase of their own influence, and the diminution of that of the Culdees.

William the Lion, having built the noble abbey of Aberbrothoc, manifested his peculiar attachment to this erection by very liberal endowments. Among other donations, he gave to this abbey the church of Abernethy, with its chapels, lands, tithes, and oblations of every kind. This is evident from the very charter of erection.

While "the church of Abernethy, with its pertinents, viz. the chapels of Dron, Dunbule, and Errol, with the land of Belach, and of Petinlouer, and the half of all the tithes proceeding from the property of the Abbot of Abernethy," are conferred as "a free, pure, and perpetual almgift," on the abbot and monks of Aberbrothoc; the other moiety of these tithes, it is said, *habebunt Keledei*, the Culdees shall possess. The tithes also from the lands subject to the authority of the Abbot, as Mugdrum, &c., which they were wont to enjoy, are reserved for them. Although in the charter of renunciation, Laurence *de Abernethy* calls this *dominium* his, he admits that these tithes presently "do belong, and always had belonged, to the Culdees."

William must have granted this charter of donation between the years 1189 and 1199: for one of the witnesses is Hugh, the King's Chancellor. This was Hugh of Roxburgh, who died A. 1199, a year after he had been advanced to the Bishopric of Glasgow.

Simon, Bishop of Dunblane, granted a charter confirming this gift to the Abbey of Aberbrothoc, "at the *petition* of King William." In this, he mentions only one "moiety of the tithes arising from the money belonging to the Abbot of Abernethy." A similar confirmation, and in the same terms, was given by Jonathan, his successor; and also by Abraham,

Bishop of Dunblane, who was elected about the year 1220. As Jonathan was bishop before 1198, and this gift is confirmed by Simon his predecessor: perhaps we may venture to date it as early as 1190.

This donation, as might well be imagined, was keenly opposed by the suffering party. The controversy was carried on for a long time, perhaps nearly thirty years, by the Prior and Culdees, both before King William, and in the ecclesiastical court at Dunblane. One determination of the Bishop was not sufficient to quash it. The Register of Aberbrothoc contains two different decisions in this cause. As it appears that the first decision of Abraham was resisted by the Culdees, he entered on the second with more solemnity. For the sentence bears, that this controversy, which had been long agitated, both in the king's court, and in that of the bishop, was now finally settled " in his presence, and in his court, many noblemen having been appointed on the part of his Lord the King, for the purpose of hearing the cause." Among these was Brice, his majesty's chief justice, who affixes his name as a witness. Both parties agreed to submit to this sentence, and swore that they should never do anything to contravene it.

A few years, as would seem, after this decision, a different system was adopted with respect to the church of Abernethy. There was a partial restoration of the possessions which had been alienated in favour of the convent of Aberbrothoc. This appears from the deed in the register of this convent entitled, *Ordinacio Judicum delegatorum super ecclesia de Abirnethy.* It contains a good deal of curious information with respect to the ecclesiastical state of that age.

From this valuable paper we learn that letters had been addressed by Pope Gregory to W. and G. Bishops of Glasgow and Dunkeld: in consequence of a representation made to him, by the Bishop of Dunblane, of the deplorable state of his see. The names corresponding to these initials are, William, consecrated Bishop of Glasgow, A. 1233, and Galfrid, of Dunkeld. They were contemporary with Gregory IX., who was elected to the papacy in the year 1227. His rescript is dated in the eleventh year of the pontificate, or A. 1238; as near as we can infer from other dates, about forty years after the donation, made by King William, of the church of Abernethy to the Abbey of Aberbrothoc.

In this rescript, the Pope narrates the information which he had received from the Bishop of Dunblane; that his bishopric, in consequence of its having been, *olim*, some considerable time ago, vacant for more than a century, its property had been greatly dilapidated by secular persons; and that, though in process of time several bishops had been successively appointed, yet, from their simplicity or inattention, not only that part of the episcopal domains had not been reclaimed, but the remainder had been almost entirely alienated and wasted; whence, no fit person could be induced to take the charge of this diocese, so that, for ten years, it had been destitute of a pastor.

The Pope, therefore, appoints the two bishops, to whom his rescript is addressed, in conjunction with their brethren of St Andrews and Brechin, to make the necessary provision for that bishop who had been appointed, in consequence of their expectation that by this means the diocese might "be able to respire from the lake of misery." It is added, that the bishop, who had been nominated, found the see so desolate, that "he had not a place in the cathedral church where he might lay his head; that there was no college [of canons] there; but that in the church itself, which was unroofed, a certain rural chaplain celebrated divine service; and that the rents of the bishop were so slender, as scarcely to suffice for his maintenance for one half of the year."

Gregory therefore requires them "to repair to the cathedral itself; and, if they found matters to be as they had been represented to him, to assign to the bishop the fourth part

7

of the tithes of all the parish churches in the diocese, if this could be done without causing great offence; that at their determination, and that of other upright men, he might receive a competency for his own sustenance, and appropriate a sufficient portion for the dean and canons, whom the Pope willed and commanded them to appoint." He adds, that, "if this could not be done, the fourth part of the tithes of all the churches, which were detained by secular persons, being assigned to the bishop, they should transfer the episcopal seat to the monastery of canons regular of St John, in the same diocese; power being granted to the canons of said monastery to elect bishops in future, when the see should fall vacant."

In consequence of this papal rescript, these delegates, "having frequently convened all who had the right of patronage within the diocese of Dunblane, and the charge of attending to the increase of divine service there," at length concluded, that a partial restoration of the possessions, attached to the church of Abernethy, was necessary to the support of this see. Therefore, "with the advice of prudent men, they determined, between the Bishop of Dunblane on the one part, and the abbot and convent of Arbroath on the other, that the whole right, which the said abbot and convent had to the altarage of Abernethy, with the lands of Petenlouer, and of Belach, and with all their other just pertinents, should be ceded by them to the jurisdiction and disposal of the Bishop of Dunblane, and his successors; the monks of Arbroath retaining the moiety of the land of Belach, with all its pertinents, and all the teind-sheaves, which pertain to the said church of Abernethy; and, in like manner, all the rights and emoluments arising to them from the chapels of that church. The Bishop of Dunblane, and his successors, are laid under an obligation to provide from the profits of the foresaid altarage, that the said church of Abernethy be honourably served; that they shall take the charge of all burdens in relation to the bishop and his officials; and that he shall provide from the profits of said altarage, a vicar in the cathedral church of Dunblane, in name of the abbot and convent of Aberbrothoc, who, by his ministry, shall supply their place in this church, so that the church of Abernethy, for his [the bishop's] greater liberty, and for the protection of its liberty, shall be for ever held as a prebend and canonry of the church of Dunblane: and that the Abbot of Aberbrothoc shall be installed as canon in the same church, a proper place of residence being allotted to him among the canons of said church."

It thus appears, that the means formerly used, for the depression of the Culdees at Abernethy, had, in co-operation with other circumstances, threatened the dissolution of that diocese to which it belonged. Their adversaries were, therefore, in so far reduced to the necessity of retracing their steps.

As in the charter of donation, by King William, and also in that of Laurence de Abernethy, the abbot of this place is still mentioned in such a way as to suggest this idea, that the old frame of the monastery was not as yet completely dissolved; it does not appear that even the last decision of Bishop Abraham had this effect. There is no evidence that the Culdees were, in consequence of this determination, deprived of the moiety of tithes, reserved to them by King William, as arising from the property of the abbot; nor perhaps of those which they received from Mugdrum, &c.—For the tithes mentioned, as contested in the bishop's court, were due from Petkarry, Petyman, Malcarny, Pethorny, Pethwnegus, and Galthanim.

There seems to have been at Abernethy, at least the form of a Culdean monastery, till it completely merged in the regular canonry, in the year 1273, or about eighty years after the dilapidation of its revenues. I am inclined to think, that a considerable time before the Culdees were obliged to give

place to the canons, and probably some time during the
reign of William, after the alienation of great part of their
revenues, their religious establishment had been subjected to
a nominal degradation, from an abbey to a priory.   For,
whereas in the charter of King William, and in the confirmations by Bishops Simon, Jonathan, and Abraham, the superior
of the Culdees is called an Abbot; in the two sentences of
the latter he is only termed Prior.

Alexander II., who died A. 1249, confirms to the abbey of
Aberbrothoc, the church of Moniekyn [now Monikie], the
church of Gutheryn [Guthrie], and the church of Abirnethyn;
with the chapels, lands, tithes, and offerings of every kind.
This must be understood, it would seem, according to the
limitations fixed by the delegates appointed by Pope Gregory.

During the same reign, Matildis, Countess of Angus, gave,
as an almsgift, to the Abbey of Arbroath, the whole land lying
on the south side of the church of Monifod, i.e. Monifieth,
which the Culdees held during the life of her father.

When we consider the high life of Abernethy, as a seat of
learning, it may seem surprising that, in this respect, so little
notice is taken of it, in our ancient records, after the reign of
Malcolm Canmore.   In how different a light must its religious
men have been viewed in that early period, when we find not
only Berbeadh the rector of the university, but "Nesse and
Cormac, the sons of Makbeath, and Malnechte, the son of
Beelham, priests of Abernethy, and Malbryde another
priest, and Thuadel, and Augustine a priest of the Culdees,"
called to attest a charter of Edelred, the son of Malcolm,
along with his brothers Alexander and David, afterwards
king of Scotland, and Constantine Earl of Fife; a charter
granted, not to their own monastery, but to that of Lochleven!
One might naturally suppose, that their rector, at least,
would frequently appear as a witness in the deeds of succeeding ages.   But neither from the Register of Scone, though

this place was in the vicinity, nor in that of St Andrews, though the metropolitan seat, does it appear that one of the priests of Abernethy was accounted worthy to be enrolled as attesting a single deed. As Abernethy belonged to the diocese of Dunblane, had we the records of this bishopric, we might find some further vestiges of its ecclesiastical history. But Keith has observed: "The writs of this see have been so neglected, or perhaps wilfully destroyed, that no light can be got from thence to guide us aright in making up" even "the list of its ancient bishops." It was, however, undoubtedly the wish of the canons regular, who had obtained the superiority at the episcopal seats and in the monasteries, to keep the Culdees in the shade as much as possible. I am therefore inclined to think that they would not be acceptable visitors to those who had strained every nerve to eject them from their ancient possessions; while we may also suppose that they would themselves have little pleasure in the society of men whom they must of necessity have viewed as successful rivals.

In the first sentence of Abraham, Bishop of Dunblane, *Michael persona de Abirnythy*, and *Magister Willielmus de Abirnythy*, are named as witnesses.

The provost of the collegiate church of Abernethy is mentioned with respect in a charter granted by Archibald, Earl of Angus, A. 1476, to the burgh of Abernethy, which was to be held of him as superior, agreeably to a charter which had been granted to him and his successors by "James, King of Scots, of recent memory." He, who was at this time *Praepositus ecclesiae collegiatae de Abernethiae*, is designed *Venerabilis Vir Johannes Frizell*, i.e. Frazer. But we must certainly view him as one of the canons regular.

From the larger Register of Aberbrothoc, or that containing the Assedations, which in Macfarlane's MSS. is given as the second volume, we find that, A. 1328, William, Bishop of St Andrews, in consequence of a visitation held at that abbey, grants, with the consent of the monks there, to their abbot Bernard, who had been elected to the bishopric of Sodor, the use of all, *fructus garbales*, the *teind-sheaves* of the church of Abernethy, with the chapel of Dron for seven years, in order to indemnify him for his expenses in the support of the monastery during his incumbency there.

It also contains a protestation, in name of the abbot and convent of Aberbrothoc, against James Bonar of Rossy, before the lords of council, A. 1483, for claiming the tithes of Dunbolg of Abernethy, as if they had been heritable property.

David, Abbot of Arbroath, A. 1490, grants to John Ramsay of Kilgour, to his spouse, and to his sons, James and Colin, "for the term of Eleven years, the *teind-sheaves* of the church of Abernethy, in the diocese of Dunblane, of the chapel of Dron, and of that piece of land commonly called the Bellauth [f. *Bellauch*] on condition of the payment of £213 6s. 8d. Scots money, annually, to him and his successors."

The same tithes were afterwards given, A. 1501, to Robert Arnot and Peter Carmichael, for the term of thirteen years, for 360 marks Scots, to be paid annually.

History has not been equally silent with respect to the temporal superiors of this place. Besides Henry of Abernethy, already mentioned, we meet with different persons, who have a similar designation, and who seem to have been of the same family. *Orme de Abernethi* is one of the witnesses to a charter of William the Lion, concerning a resignation, on the part of the king, of Nar, one of the vassals of the Abbot of Scone. By the way it may be observed that, as many of the old Pictish race may be supposed to have settled about Abernethy, their ancient capital, it is highly probable that this family was Pictish. *Orm* was a designation common among the ancient Goths, whether Norwegians, Danes, or Angles, which at length passed into a surname. This, the learned Worm informs us, was the origin of his family name.

"Laurentius de Abernethi, son of Orm," says Keith, "gave Corbie, called also Birkhill, from a park of birks [birches] surrounding the house, to this monastery [of Balmerinach]; and in his charter is expressed the reason of his donation, viz. Because Queen Emergarda dying 3tio. Id Februarij, anno 1233, and being buried in the church of Balmerinach, *ante magnum altare*, had by her testament left him 200 merks sterling."

The same Laurence de Abirnet attests a charter of Alexander II., granting to the Abbot of Scone the wood of Kelcamsy for a forest. He is also one of the witnesses to a charter granted by Roger de Quenci, Earl of Winchester, constable of Scotland, confirming the donation of William de Len, also called de Lyn, to the Abbot and Canons of Scone. This may have been about the year 1231. The name of Reginald de Abernethy also occurs.

"I have seen," says Nisbet, "a charter of Hugh de Abernethy, of the lands of Owrebenchery to William de Federeth, exonerating him and his heirs from making any appearance in his court for these lands. This charter was granted in the reign of Alexander III. and the seal thereto appended was entire, having a lion rampant bruised with a ribbon. In the reign of Robert I. *Alexander de Abernethy, Dominus de eodem* (Sir Robert Sibbald's History of Fife), left behind him three daughters, coheirs; Margaret, married to John Stewart, Earl of Angus, who got with her the barony of Abernethy; Helen to Norman de Lindsay of Crawford, who got with her the barony of Balinbreich; and the third daughter, Mary, was wife to Andrew Leslie of Rothes, who with her got the barony of Downy in Angus. These three daughters were the mothers of three great families, Earls of Angus, Rothes, and Crawford, who have been in use to marshal the arms of Abernethy, as before blazoned, with their own."

But though Nisbet quotes Sibbald as his authority, he differs from him. For, according to Sibbald, Mary was the second daughter, heiress of Balmbriech, and married to Norman de Lesly. The third, he says, "was married to Lindesay de Cranfurd, who got with her the barony of Downie." It may be added, that William de Abernethy is mentioned by Prynne, vol. iii. p. 663.

The ancient seal of the College of Abernethy has been found within these few years. I have been favoured with the following account of it, from the records of the Literary and Antiquarian Society of Perth.

"The matrix in brass, or instrument for making casts of the common seal of the old collegiate church of Abernethy, was found in the year 1789, in a garden in Enniskillen, in the county of Fermanagh, in Ireland. It is now in the possesion of the Honourable James Drummond of Perth.

"Obverse. A shield of Arms. In a shield, Gules; a lion rampant, surmounted with bend dexter, argent. Legend, *S. Commune Collegii De Abernethe.*

"Reverse. An abbess (probably representing St Bridget) in a vail, holding a crosier in her right hand; and at her right side is a small figure of a bull, deer, or such other animal. Legend, *In Domo Dei Ambulavimus Cum Concencu.*"

CHAPTER VII.

Monastery of Culdees at Lochlevin.—Of St Serf.—Donations.—
Library.—Foundation at Dunkeld.—Reliques of Columba
transported thither.—Of the Primacy ascribed to it.—The
Memory of Columba long held in Veneration there—Monastic
Seal.—Culdees at St Andrews.—Of Regulus.—Of Constan-
tine.—Endowments of the Priory.—If originally the seat of
a Bishop?

BRUDI V., son of Derili, King of the Picts, about the year
700, bestowed the island of Lochlevin on St Serf, and the
Culdees residing there, and serving God. St Serf, or, as his
name is given in Latin, Servanus, was, if we may credit Wyntown, the Prior of Lochlevin, contemporary with Adamnan,
Abbot of Iona. Although not himself educated in that
island; in consequence of a visit from Adamnan, he seems to
have adopted the Columban rule. For Wyntown says, that
Serf

> ———— Arywyd at Incheketh
> The ile between Kyngorne and Leth,
> Of Yeolmkil the Abbot than
> Saynt Adaman, the haly man,
> Come til hyme thare, and fermly
> Mad spyrytuale band of cumpany,
> And tretyd hym to cum in Fyfe,
> The tyme to dryve oure hys lyfe.
>
> *Cronykil, B.V. ch. 12. ver. 1162, &c.*

In consequence of this *band of cumpany*, or bond of fellowship, between Adamnan and him, his followers lived as Culdees, and have still been distinguished by this denomination.
This priory, in an early period, was enriched by liberal
donations. "Successive kings," says a writer who has paid
considerable attention to this subject, "Macbeth, Malcolm

III., and Edgar, and his brother Ethelred, with the bishops Maldaw and Modoch, were all studious to endow the Culdees of Lochlevin. Macbeth gave the Culdees the lands of Kirkness, and also the village of Bolgy. Malcolm III., and his pious queen, granted them the town and lands of Balchristie. From Edgar they got Pitnemokin. Ethelred gave them the lands of Admore. Malduin, the bishop of St Andrews, granted them the church of Sconie: and from Fothald, the Bishop of St Andrews, they got the church of Hurkendorach. Reg. of St Andrews. David I. granted to the monks of Dunfermlin, 'Balchristie eum suis rectis divisis, excepta rectitudine quam Keledei habere debent.' MS. Charters, 104. A dispute ensued between the prior and canons of St Andrews, who came in the place of the Culdees, and the monks of Dunfermlin, about their respective rights to Balchristie. King William determined, that the monks of Dunfermlin should have Balchristie, subject to the rights which the Culdees had in it, during the reign of David I. Dalrymple's Coll. p. 283."

The writer of the register of the Priory of St Andrews has transcribed, from an old volume, "written" he says, "in the language of the Scots," the memorials concerning the rents and duties, payable from lands, churches, and otherwise, and the donations made to the church of St Servanus in the isle of Lochlevin. He professes to have done this, without the prolixity of the original, in order to prevent all vain and vexatious contentions in future times.

When this transcript was made is uncertain. As far as we may judge from the intention specified, it must have been during the existence of the Culdees: and, most probably, soon after the institution of canons regular at St Andrews, and the grant made of Lochlevin to them by David I. The deed immediately preceding in the Register is dated A. 1276. But we can determine nothing from this; as, in these registers, little regard is paid to the order of time. Some of the chartularies would seem to have been first formed by stitching together the loose parchments belonging to a monastery, without any attention to arrangement. When these were afterwards transcribed, the transcript was made according to the order in which they had been originally thrown together.

These memorials were published by Gillan, as an appendix to his remarks on Sir James Dalrymple's Collections; and afterwards by Crawfurd, who affixed them to his Lives of Officers of State, No. III., with the addition of the deed entitled *Perambulatio*. His copy, he says, was taken from the chartulary "belonging to the honourable family of Panmure." Mr Pinkerton has compendized this account in the appendix to the first volume of his Enquiry, pp. 467—469; where he also gives the contents of the Large Register of St Andrews, from a MS. in the Harleian Library, No. 4828. The copy given is from the Register of St Andrews, undoubtedly the smaller one, which has a place among the late learned Macfarlane's MSS. To these papers I shall subjoin an extract from the same register, giving an account of the donation of the village of Bolgyne, by Macbeth, to the Culdees.

Kellach, it would appear, was Bishop of St Andrews before the year 893. Sir James Balfour says, that he had seen a deed of this bishop, addressed to the religious Culdees of Lochlevin. But he has given no particular account of it. Maldnin, who was bishop about the year 1034, gave them the lands of Markinch.

None of our writers seem to have adverted to a singular and valuable relique of bibliography, with which the ancient record above referred to supplies us. This is a list of the books found in the Culdean Priory of Lochlevin, at the time that it was given up to the canons regular, or about the year 1150. This catalogue is valuable; not, indeed, on account of its extent: nor as containing the names of any works which have since perished, and thus exciting the vain regret of the antiquary, or of the collector: nor as giving us any high idea of the literary acquirements of these pious recluses; but as being perhaps unique in its kind, in the history of our country, and as exhibiting a fair state of the literature of the age. The list may also be viewed as furnishing a tolerably just specimen of the ancient conventual liararies. For, if we except those of Iona, Abernethy, Dunkeld, and St Andrews; considering the great antiquity of the establishment at Lochlevin, we may reasonably suppose that the library there would be as well stored as that of any other priory in that early age.

It is undeniable that there was a monastery of Culdees at Dunkeld long before it became an episcopal see. Alexander Myln, a Canon of Dunkeld, afterwards Abbot of Cambuskenneth, and last of all first president of the Court of Session after its erection A. 1532, wrote an account of the lives of the bishops of this see, still extant among the MSS. in the Advocates' Library. He says that Constantine, King of the Picts, "from his devotion for St Columba, at that time patron of the whole kingdom, founded and endowed an illustrious monastery" here, "about the year 729: two hundred and twenty-six, or, as some say, two hundred and forty years after the building of the church of Abernethy." Others carry down this event to the year 815. "In this monastery," Myln subjoins, "he placed those religious men called Keldees, having wives according to the custom of the oriental church, from whom they abstained, while they ministered in courses."

According to this writer, there was no bishop of Dunkeld before the reign of David I., about the year 1169: that is, more than four hundred years after the erection of the Culdee monastery. Goodall, however, shews that Cormac was bishop here in the days of Alexander I. In the charter of erection of this bishopric by David, there is an express exception of the rights that belonged to the abbey, *exceptis rectitudinibus quae ad Abbatiam de Dunkelden pertinent.* This not only proves, as Sir James Dalrymple has observed, "that there has been an Abbacie at Dunkeld before the erection of the bishopric," but that they "continued separate for some time, till the Keldees were chased out." Even Gregory, Bishop of Dunkeld, subscribes as a witness to this exception in favour of the abbey, over which he had formerly presided as abbot.

Mr. Pinkerton has referred to a remarkable passage, occurring in the most ancient and authentic records of Ireland, which seems to prove that the supreme ecclesiastical government remained attached to the Culdees, even after the accession of the Scottish princes to the Pictish throne. "Tighernac," he says, "and the Annals of Ulster furnish us with a bishop of Piktland much earlier [than 909, when Kellach is said to have been made Bishop of St Andrews]; for at the year 864, they say, *Tuahal Mac Artgusa, Archbishop of Fortren, and Abbot of Dun Callen, dormicit:* 'Tuahal, son of Artgus, Archbishop of Piktland, and Abbot of Dunkeld, died." This would lead us to suspect that after Hyona was destroyed by the Danes [A. 801], or after its power over the Piktish churches ceased, the Abbot of Dunkeld [a Culdee] was for a time regarded as supreme of the Piktish church. Certain it is that St Andrews had no title to be regarded as supreme church in Piktland, till erected into a bishopric."

Nearly the same idea is adopted by another writer. Having mentioned the dissolution of the monastery of Iona, in consequence of the barbarity of the Danish pirates, he says, that Dunkeld became the repository of the reliques of St Columba, adding: "A religious house was here built, upon the same system as the original establishment at Iona. In it, a bishop resided; over it, an abbot ruled. From the epoch of 848, the church of Dunkeld appears to have formed the primacy of Scotland for several ages, till it was supplanted, in its turn, by St Andrews." He then quotes the passage from the Annals of Ulster concerning the Archbishop of

Fortren, subjoining: " The annalist merely means to speak of the primate by the florid expression of archbishop. Under the year 872, the same annals state the death of Flavertach M'Murtach, the primate of Dunkeld."

It is of no consequence in regard to the point under consideration, whether Iurastach, the Abbot of Hii, carried the reliques of Columba to Dunkeld or not. This theory rests on the ground of a supposed error in the Ulster Annals, as if Ireland had been put for Scotland. The general idea seems well-founded, that Dunkeld was viewed as a second Iona. But it remains to be proved that, in this early period, there was a bishop, as well as an abbot, residing here. The only thing which seems to be offered in proof of this is the passage in the Annals of Ulster, quoted as under the year 865 [leg. 864], when we have an account of the death of Tuathal, Archbishop of Fortren and Abbot of Dunkeld. From what has been quoted above from the same work, this Tuathal seems to be viewed as "primate of Dunkeld." But with this it is not easy to reconcile what is said a few pages downwards: "The Ulster Annals, under the year 864, speak magnificently of the death of Tuathal, the Archbishop of Fortren, or Abernethy."

Could we for a moment suppose Fortren to mean the town of Abernethy (an idea not only different from that which has always been hitherto entertained, but not easily reconcileable with any of the notices concerning it in these annals), it must necessarily follow that this person could not be also the bishop connected with the monastery of Dunkeld : for he must have resided here, for " performing the functions of his office. We have no evidence, therefore, that this Archbishop of Fortren was any other than the Abbot of Dunkeld.

The remarks made by Mr Pinkerton have a great degree of verisimilitude. " The Abbot of Hyona," he says, " having such supreme power over the Piktish churches, certainly would not allow of any bishop's see, as the title was superior to his own, and [he who bore it] could not be controuled by him. Abernethy and Dunkeld were but abbacies, even in the eleventh century, long after St Andrews was a bishopric. Indeed, all our writers, ancient and modern, concur that St Andrews was the most ancient bishopric north of Clyde and Forth."

The author of Caledonia admits that Kellach, Bishop of St Andrews, "was the first bishop of any determinate see." When speaking of Tuathal, he finds it necessary to understand the language of the Ulster Annals figuratively; observing, as has been seen, that "the annalist merely means to speak of the primate, by the florid expression of archbishop." For he adds that, "in opposition to the claims of the register of St Andrews—Dunkeld long held the primacy of the united kingdom," i.e. of the Scots and Picts. Now, was this primate in fact a different person from the abbot? If so, the very foundation of the primacy ascribed to him is destroyed, and all analogy between Dunkeld and Iona obliterated. Why did the primacy belong to Dunkeld? Because, says the learned writer, "a religious house was here built, upon the same system as the original establishment at Iona." But who was primate in Iona? Was it any nameless bishop, who has been supposed to reside there for certain functions that no one but himself could perform? We have not been able to discover a single vestige of such a character. And can even those, who believe that an ecclesiastic of this description did reside there, merely because, according to their system, it ought to have been so, satisfy themselves that he was so completely the principal person in Iona, that the primacy centered in him, rather than in the abbot at the head of the Culdean college.

The only reasonable idea we can form is, that the Abbot of Dunkeld was called archbishop and primate, as holding the honours formerly conceded by universal consent to the Abbot of Iona. The author of Caledonia says that "the first bishop of Dunkeld who came out conspicuously on the stage of life was Cormac, who appeared under Alexander I. Yet it is certain that there were bishops at Dunkeld before the early age of Cormac." But how can this be certain, when there is no evidence, save of that supposititious kind which we have already considered? We can form no other conclusion, than that Cormac "was the first bishop who came out conspicuously," because he was the first who had been appointed to the episcopal office distinctly from the abbot, and as superseding his extensive authority.

From the faint vestiges of the history of these dark ages, it is evident that, even after the suppression of the Culdean establishment at Dunkeld, the memory of the Culdees was highly venerated there. This appears from various circumstances. Their successors still acknowledged Columba as their patron saint; and not only acknowledged him in this character, but ascribed a miraculous virtue to his reliques.

So late as towards the close of the fifteenth century, Bishop Livingston instituted a chaplainry, in honour of Columba as patron, at the altar of St. Martin, in the collegiate church of St Giles of Edinburgh. George Brown, one of his successors, seems to have consecrated a bell to the memory of the patron saint, and to have baptized it with his name.

Myln informs us that, "as in the year 1500, a most fatal pestilence raged throughout Scotland, and, according to the common report, the city of Dunkeld alone still continued uninjured; through the merits of its patron Columba, Bishop Brown ordered a great mass to be said at the great altar, at his own expense, in honour of their patron. At the end of the year, as the city, and the greater part of the surrounding country remained unaffected by the pestilence, he ordered that this mass should be perpetuated, and that ten pounds should be appropriated annually for this purpose. That those who celebrated this mass might be enabled to do it with due honour, and at the same time without fatigue, he chose seven vicars of the choir, who were to have a stipend of ten pounds. The service was to be honourably performed at seven altars of the church not yet founded, viz., those of the Saints Martin, Nicholas, Andrew the Apostle, of the Innocents, of All Saints, of Stephen the Protomartyr, and of John Baptist. Each of these vicars was, one day in the week, to celebrate mass in his turn as hitherto, at the second bell for matins: that devout ecclesiastics, seculars given to good works, and travellers, might joyfully assemble."

"Some," he elsewhere says, " in his ecclesiastical lands of Capeth, he visited, while labouring under the pestilence, and caused the sacraments of the church to be administered to them." The dreadful disease resisting this application, as would seem, the good bishop had recourse to another, and a more powerful, remedy. "But on a subsequent day he made holy water, in which he washed a bone of the blessed Columba, and sent it by his chancellor to be drunk by the patients. Many receiving this were completely cured. But one stubborn fellow replied to the chancellor: 'Why does the bishop send us water to drink? I would rather he would send me his best beverage.' He, however, with all the rest who rejected the water of St Columba, died of the plague, and were buried in one tomb below the said cemetery."

It may be viewed as a further proof of the great attachment still retained to Columba at Dunkeld, that so many of the bishops, most probably at their own desire, were interred in that island which bore his name, as having been consecrated to him. This is the island called Inch-Colm, or St Columba's Inch. We learn from Myln that a bishop of the name of Richard was buried in the church here A. 1173, or 1174; Richard de Praebenda, A. 1210; John Archdeacon of, Lothian, A. 1214; another of the same name, designed John of Leicester, is also mentioned, but viewed by Keith as the same person; Gilbert, A. 1236; Richard, the chancellor, who died A. 1250. According to Myln, A. 1272, the heart of

Richard of Inverkeithing was interred in the choir of St Columba's church in this island, although his body was buried at Dunkeld; and James Livingston, A. 1482-3. Galfrid, who died A. 1249, was buried in the old church of the convent at Dunkeld, dedicated to Columba.

To these observations we may add that, long after the extinction of the Culdees here, the monastic seal continued to exhibit the image of Columba as the patron saint.

The Culdean establishment at St Andrews next demands our attention. It is pretended by our ancient chroniclers, that Constantius having wasted the city of Patras, rather *Patrae*, Gr. Παηραει in Achaia, where the reliques of St Andrew were kept, Regulus was warned in a vision to take some of these, and carry them with him to a region towards the west, situated in the utmost parts of the earth; that he accordingly did so, and, after being long tossed at sea, was at length driven into a bay near the place where St Andrews now stands. According to some accounts, this took place about the year 365; while others make it somewhat later. In this quarter, we are told, Regulus lived devoutly, with his companions, in cells, for thirty-two years, occasionally travelling through the country, and building several churches. Three are particularly mentioned in the extracts from the Large Register. One, it is said, was at Fortevioth, one at Monechata, afterwards called Monichi, and another, beyond the Month, at Doldanha, in later times denominated *Chondrohedalium*. Hungus, son of Fergoso, King of the Picts, is represented as patronising Regulus and his companion, and as having given them some lands as a perpetual almsgift.

The Large Register of St Andrews, which contained this account, has disappeared for more than a century. The extracts, made from it, are however preserved in a MS. in the Harlein Library, No. 4628. They have been published by Mr Pinkerton, in the *Addenda* to his Enquiry.

The whole story, with respect to Regulus, has, it must be

acknowledged, greatly the air of a mere legend. It was very probably framed by the monks, after Kilrymont became the chief seat of ecclesiastical power, in order to give it more celebrity, and to wean the multitude from their attachment to religious places which had in fact a more early foundation : particularly from Iona, Abernethy, and Dunkeld. The very name of the Pictish prince, to whom the patronage of Regulus is ascribed, seems to betray the imposture. " He was fabricated," says Mr Pinkerton, " because a Hungus had founded St Andrews about 825 : and its priests wanted to pass Regulus for its founder in the fourth century."

This legend may be viewed as having more connexion with the history of the Culdees than what appears at first sight. Two circumstances suggest this idea. The first is, the conformity of the mode of life, attributed to Regulus and his companions, to that of the Culdees. They are described as living in cells, and as planting churches, just as the monks of Iona did. The second is still more striking. The very territory, said to have been given by an early prince of the Picts, of the name of Hungus, to Regulus and his brethren, and, as we know from history, actually given for a religious purpose, several centuries afterwards, seems unaccountably to pass into the hands of the Culdees. It is even recognised as theirs, without any kind of dispute, at the very time that their adversaries were abridging their power, and depriving them of their possessions. Now, if there ever was such a person as Regulus, he might, like St Servanus and others, be an associate of Columba, or of some of his followers. For, in this instance, little stress can be laid on the chronology of the Register, or of our early writers. With respect to the precious reliques of an Apostle, it is well known that the monks did not always need to go as far as to Patras for them. I am strongly inclined to suspect, that these had never been heard of at Kilrymont, till a noise had been made about the reliques of Columba at Dunkeld. Myln, as we have seen, asserts, with great appearance of truth, that Columba, the patron saint of Dunkeld, was acknowledged in the same character through the whole kingdom. It was therefore necessary that Regulus, who introduced the reliques of the apostle Andrew, to whom the saint of Iona must of course give place, should have a prior date.

According to the extracts from the Large Register, Hungus, king of the Picts, came to Kilrymont, and, perambulating great part of that place, presented it to God, and St Andrew, for the erection of churches and oratories. That such a gift was made by Hungus, is in the highest degree probable. For it appears indisputable, that, about the year 825, he founded a church at Kilrymont; which henceforth received the name of the Apostle to whom it was dedicated. Sibbald views this gift of the Pictish king as meant for the benefit of the Culdees. But we have more direct evidence. For, as Martine speaks of *Baronia Culedaiorum infra Cursum Apri*, or "the Barony of the Culdees below the Boar's Raik," the extracts bear, that this was given by King Hungus to St Rule. Yet we learn, from the same source of information, that this tract was afterwards taken from the Culdees; and given, first to the Bishop, and then to the Prior and Canons Regular of St Andrews: "so that," as Sir James Dalrymple observes, "this place appeareth to have been one of the ancient seats of the Culdees."

In the tenth century, such was their celebrity at St Andrews, that King Constantine III. took up his residence among them, and A. 943, died a member of their society; or, as Wyntown says, abbot of their monastery.

Nyne hundyr wyntyr and aucht yhere,
Quhen gayne all Donaldis dayis were,
Heddis sowne cald Constantine
Kyng wes thretty yhere: and syne
Kyng he sessyd for to be,
And in Sanct Andrewys a *Kylde*.

It is also believed that an Irish king attached himself to this religious body. For we learn from the Ulster Annals, that, A. 1033, Hugh Mac Flavertai O'Nell, King of Ailech, and heir of Ireland, *post penitentiam mort. in St Andrews eccl.* He has also been designed " King of A'cliath."

The Culdees at St Andrews seem to have had considerable endowments. But it is not easy to form an accurate judgment as to the extent of these, by reason of the mistakes of copyists with respect to the names of places, as well as the change of these names in the lapse of ages; and also, because we cannot certainly distinguish between the original possessions of the Culdees, and those lands, which, in the way of superadded donation, were given to their successors the canons regular. Another difficulty arises from the impossibility of determining, whether certain lands belonged to the Culdees of Lochlevin, or to those of St Andrews. After the exclusion of this religious order, though there was a priory of canons regular at Lochlevin, distinct from that at St Andrews, the former evidently depended, in some way, on the latter: and some modes of expression occasionally occur in ancient deeds, which rather induce the idea, that, during the power of the Culdean establishments, the priory of St Andrews was dependent on that of Lochlevin.

Sibbald, having given an account of the lands which were held by the Culdees of Lochlevin, says: " Besides these mentioned above, the excerpts of the Register show, that there were other lands in this shire [of Fife, which] belonged to them. Terrae quas tenent Keledei, Kinkel, Kinnadin Fihe, Kinnadin Egu, Lethin, Kerin, Kerner, Kynninis Rathmatgallum, Syreis, Baletoch, Kaletuise, Baleocherthin, Pethkenin, Kingorg."

By these he undoubtedly means the lands which belonged to the Culdees of St Andrews. Some of them are particularly mentioned, as their property, in the small Register; as Kinkel, which was confirmed to them by a charter of Mal-

colm IV.   It is probably the same place which is elsewhere
called Kinakelle.   Kymninis is frequently mentioned; and
the lands of Lethin are, in a variety of places, specified as
still the property of the Culdees, *Quas Keledei habent*.   Syreis
is undoubtedly the town of Ceres, Pethkenin the Petkenin of
the Register.   Kerner may be Kernes: and Kingorg the
same with Chindargog.

In order to shew that the Culdean priory at St Andrews
" formed originally the residence of a bishop," it has been
observed, that, " under the year 872, the Ulster Annals state
the death of Bishop Colman, the Abbot of St Andrews."
This is not in the extracts given by Mr Pinkerton, though it
occurs in Johnstone's : and even the latter gives it with evident hesitation.   His extract is in these words : " Bishop
Coleman, the Abbot of Androis (f. St Andrews) died."   At
any rate, it must be viewed merely as complimentary language ; or, as the Author of Caledonia observes, concerning
Tuathal, when designed Archbishop, as "a florid expression."
Besides, this writer has himself ascribed the foundation of
the bishopric of St Andrews, to Grig, who did not begin to
reign till the year 883.   It may be added that, though Keith
has given from different writers no fewer than seven lists of
the Bishops of St Andrews, the name of Colman does not
appear in one of them.

CHAPTER VIII.

*Of the Culdees of Brechin.—Whether they merely constituted
the Episcopal Chapter?—Of those at Dunblane.—Of the supposed Foundation at Muthel.—Of that of Monimusk.—Culdees at Portmoak.—Scone.—Kirkaldy.—Culross.—Mailros.*

THAT Brechin was at an early age a distinguished seat of
the Culdees, appears from what we find in the Pictish
Chronicle : "This is he who gave the great city of Brechin to
the Lord." In this manner does the ancient writer point out
our Scottish king Kenneth, commonly reckoned the third of
that name, who began to reign in the year 970.

In a work lately published it is said : "That there was a
bishop established among the Culdees at Brechin, before the
erection of the bishopric by David I., is certain from his
charter of erection, which was granted *Episcopo, et Kelledeis,
in ecclesia de Breichen.* Dalrymple's Coll. p. 219. [leg. 249."]
But, undoubtedly, the mode of expression used proves
nothing more than that from this time there was a bishop
here. When David granted a charter, erecting Brechin into
a bishopric, it may naturally be supposed that he had
previously fixed on one to fill this station : and that he gave
him the title, as was frequently done, before his actual
instalment. At any rate, from an ancient charter, granted
before the erection of the bishopric, it may be presumed that
the Culdees here had only an abbot among them. For I will
not carry the matter so far as Sir James Dalrymple does,
who, in the very passage referred to, reasons thus : " In the
charter of Balchristin,—amongst the witnesses is Leodus
Abbas de Breichen ; which is a clear evidence that at that
time Brechin was not erected into a bishopric, and that Leod
was abbot there."

"At Brechin," says our industrious and learned antiquary, Goodall, "the Culdees continued yet much longer," than they had done at Dunblane, "to be the dean and chapter. Bricius, their prior, is a witness to some of Turpin's charters; and after him Prior Mallebride attests divers charters by the Bishops Turpin, Ralph, Hugh, and Gregory. The designation given him by the bishops is *Prior Keledeorum nostrorum,* 'Prior of our Culdees,' or 'Prior of Brechin;' and sometimes only Prior. The Culdees, like other chapters of episcopal sees, gave confirmations of charters granted by their bishops, some of which are still extant," &c.

From what is here said, one would naturally conclude that it appeared from ancient writs that the prior and Culdees formally constituted the chapter of Brechin; and of course, that the Prior was the Dean. But this was not the case. To what dependence soever on the bishop the Culdees may have been reduced, it is evident that they had not been absolutely cast into the mould of a mere chapter. For, in the charter of Ralph, Bishop of Brechin, *De Procurationibus,* besides the designations, *Gregorio Archidiacono,* and *Matheo Decano de Brechyn,* distinct mention is made of Mallebride as *Priore Keledeorum de Brech.* This Matthew is, in another charter of the same Ralph, designed *Decano nostro;* and in one of Turpin, *Matheo Decano de Brechyn.*

In Turpin's charter, *De Decima Retis,* the witnesses are thus mentioned: *Hugone Epō Sti Andree, Bricio Priore Keledeorum de Brech., W. Archid. Sti Andree, et Matussale Decano, Andrea Capellano, et Matheo Sacrista ecclæ de Brechyn, et insuper Gillebryd Comite de Angus, et Dorenald Abbe de Brech.* According to the construction, this Matussal was at this time Dean, while Matthew, afterwards advanced to this dignity, was only Sacrist. This must have been before the year 1187; for in this year Hugh, Bishop of St Andrews, died. Here, and in several other instances, the Prior of the Culdees takes place of the Dean.

All that can fairly be inferred from the language of these deeds, is, that the bishops here were willing that the Culdees should retain their ancient right of election, in conjunction with others. For, even in both the charters given by Goodall, the Prior and Culdees, though introduced as having a seat in the chapter, are expressly distinguished from the rest of the members: *Prior, et Keledei, ceterique de Capitulo Brechynensis ecclesiae.* In several others, their prior is mentioned as peculiarly as if he had no connection with the chapter. The bishop, therefore, must have used the phrase, *Keledeorum nostrorum,* "our Culdees," not as if they had formally constituted his chapter, but because they were the Culdees residing within his diocese, and connected with this see.

Maitland has fallen into a series of blunders, when speaking of the abbey of Trinitarian or Mathurine monks here; which, he says, "probably, by its antiquity, owes its erection to King David I., who established the bishop's see in this place." His proof is: "For about the year 1178, Dovenaldus, Abbot of Brechin, granted to the Abbot of Aberbrothocke, Terram de Ballege le Grand, which King Alexander confirmed by charter; and, anno 1219, I find one John to have been Abbot of Brechin." There could be no Mathurines or Red Friars at Brechin A. 1178: for this order was instituted during the papacy of Innocent III., who was not elected till the year 1198. This Dovenaldus of whom he speaks was evidently a layman. His name occurs in several charters. In that to which Maitland must have referred, the land is denominated *Balegille grand,* and the donor, *Douenaldus Abbe de Brechyn.* In the charter of confirmation immediately following the name is *Douenaldus Abb.* There can be no doubt that Abb or Abbe was his surname. We have seen him conjoined in a preceding extract with the Earl of Angus: and they are evidently distinguished from the clergy mentioned before. In the charter immediately preceding that concerning *Balegille grand,* Morgund Abbe confirms the gift of fewel from his forest, which his father, John Abbe, had made to the abbey of Arbroath; which confirmation his father, and his paternal uncle, and his brother John, attest. The father of John had been Malis, who was proprietor of the forest of Edale, most probably what is now written Edzel, the name of a parish not far from Brechin, whence one of the principal branches of the family of Lindsay took its title. This appears from a charter of confirmation by King William, in which the donor is designed Johannes *Abbas* filius Malisii. This is probably the origin of the surname of Abbot, which still exists in Angus.

The names of two Culdees are recorded in a charter granted by Turpin, in which he gives some lands in the village of Struncatherach, i.e. Strickathrow. Besides Brice, Prior of Brechin, mention is made of Gillesali *Kelde*, and Machalen *Kelde*.

Concerning the foundation at Dunblane, I scarcely need any other testimony than that of Keith, who was so zealous for the rights of episcopacy. "Formerly," he says, "there was a convent of Culdees here, and continued so to be, even after the erection of the bishopric, which owes its foundation to King David II. towards the end of his reign. St Blaan was superior of this convent in the time of King Kenneth III., and from him the see derived its name [*Britan. Sancta*]."

Here there is undoubtedly a mistake. Keith must have meant to speak of David I., who erected Dunblane into a bishopric. Mr Chalmers says that "St Blaan was the patron, as he was the chief of this religious establishment" of Culdees: "being a bishop here about 1000 A.D." He refers to Keith's Catalogue, p. 100. But Keith has not mentioned St Blaan as a bishop, and still less as bishop of Dunblane. He could not, indeed, consistently do so; as he says that St Blaan lived in the reign of Kenneth III.; whereas the bishopric owed its foundation to David I., who did not begin to reign till the year 1124. In the Aberdeen Breviary he is said to have been consecrated to the episcopal office; but no mention is made of Dunblane, nor of any other place of residence. Camerarius makes him bishop of Sodor; adding that the city of Dunblane in Scotland received its name from him. Lesley also speaks of him as a bishop, but takes no notice of his see.

It has been supposed that there was also a Culdee establishment at Muthil. "We find," says Crawfurd, "the Abbots and Priors of the Culdees at Brechin, Muthill, Dunkeld, and Abernethy, all frequently witnesses to the deeds or grants of the bishops: and getting churches or tithes from them, together with the *Curae Animarum.*" On the supposition that such an establishment subsisted at Muthil, perhaps it could only be viewed as a cell belonging to the monastery of Dunblane. Goodall observes that Michael, parson of Muthil, and Macbeath his chaplain, are conjunct witnesses with Malpol, whom he seems to view as Prior of the Culdees at Dunblane. They attest a confirmation by William, Bishop of Dunblane, of the "gift of the church of Kincardine to the monks of Cambuskenneth, to be seen in their charter, fol. 80." But from the inscription of a charter, quoted by Crawfurd, Malpol appears as "Prior of the Culdees of Muthil" *Carta Simonis Episcopi Dunblanen. Monialibus de North-Berwick, Ecclesiae de Logy-Athry. Testibus, Malpol Prior Keledeiorum de* Methyl, *et Michael, et Malcolmo, Keledeis de* Methyl. The quotation is certainly inaccurate. The charter, he says, is in the Earl of Marchmont's family archives. But I have no opportunity to examine it. On looking, however, into the charter referred to by Goodall, I find the witnesses thus designed: *Archidiacono Ionatha capellano meo,* that is, chaplain to W. Bishop of Dunblane; *Cormac Malpol, priore Keldeorum* persona *de Mothell, Michaele et eius capellano Mackbeth,* &c. As Crawfurd has given such Latin as even monks would not have written, I strongly suspect that, in the Marchmont charter, Malpol must be designed as here; and that Crawfurd has left out the word *persona* between *Keledeiorum*, and, according to his orthography, *de Methyl*. If so, the only proof, as far as I have observed, of a Culdee establishment at Muthil, falls to the ground.

This charter was granted towards the close of the twelfth century. Before the Reformation Muthil was the residence of the Dean of Dunblane.

The power of the Culdees was also considerable in that diocese, of which the see was originally at Mortlach, but afterwards, in the reign of David I., translated to Aberdeen. For, notwithstanding the great additions made to this episcopate on occasion of the change of its seat, bishop Nectan did not prevail in his attempt to expel the Culdees. They still continued at least at Monimusk. We learn from the Chartulary of Aberdeen that "Edward, successor to Nectan, was the first bishop who instituted canons at Aberdeen, by the authority of the apostolic seat." Hence Sir James Dalrymple concludes "that no sort of churchmen but the Culdees can be supposed to be established there before that time: nor," he says, "needed churchmen to be expelled by papal authority, to make way for the Chanoins, if they had been of the Romish institution. It is certain," he adds, "that the Culdees were at Monymusk, in the diocese of Aberdeen, which afterwards became a popish priorie."

Malcolm II., A. 1010, having defeated the Danes at Mortlach, soon after founded a religious establishment there, in token of gratitude for his victory. Some of our writers call this a bishoprie; others view it as only a religious house, which became the residence of a bishop. Sir James Dalrymple has given the deed of foundation from the Chartulary of Aberdeen. But by some writers this deed is considered as a monkish forgery. I shall give it, in a note, as extracted from the Chartulary itself:[1] where it appears with some slight variations as to orthography.

[1] Malcolmus Rex Scotorum omnibus probis hominibus suis, tam clericis quam laicis, salutem : Sciatis me dedisse, et hac charta mea confirmasse, Deo

How soon after the foundation at Mortlach the Culdees were settled at Monimusk, we cannot pretend to determine. It is certain, however, that they were here about a century after, during the episcopate of Robert of St Andrews. Their most liberal donor was undoubtedly Gilchrist, Earl of Mar, who lived during the reign of William the Lion. His donations will be more particularly mentioned when we come to consider the suppression of this order: and his charter will be found in the Appendix, extracted from the register of St Andrews.

The same lands were afterwards confirmed to them by another Earl of Mar, of the name of Duncan. It is evident that he was later than Gilchrist. For he assigns, as one reason of the donation, his desire of the prosperity of his lord King Alexander. This was the second of the name, the son of William, who is referred to as deceased: for he speaks of his granting this donation "for the soul of his lord King William." But Gilchrist, in his charter, expresses his wish "for the safety and prosperity of his lord King William, and of all who are dear to him." This Duncan designs himself

et Beate Marie et omnibus sanctis, et episcopo Beyn de Morthelach, ecclesiam de Morthelach, ut ibidem construatur sedes episcopalis, cum terris meis de Morthelach, ecclesiam de Cloveth cum terra, ecclesiam de Dulmeth cum terra, ita libere sicut eas tenui, et in param et perpetuam elemosinam. Teste meipso apud Forfare octavo die mensis Octobris, anno regni meo sexto. Registr. Aberdon. Fol. 47.

It does not seem to have been observed by our ecclesiastical writers that this Cloveth in Mar is counted among our monastic establishments. Pope Adrian, in a bull of confirmation granted by him to Edward, who was bishop of Aberdeen in the reign of David I., speaks of both Cloveth and Mortlach as monasteries.—Monasterium de Cloveth, villam et Monasterium de Murthlach, cum quinque ecclesiis et terris eisdem pertinentibus. This seems strongly to confirm the idea that Mortlach had at first been only a religious house. Boece says that this Edward was the first who instituted canons regular in the church of Aberdeen. Eduardus vero primus omnium regularis vitae viros (quos vocauit Canonicos) veluti confratres ad diuina cum sacellanis exequenda primus omnium in Aberdonen. ecclesia instituit. Aberdon. Epise. Vit. Fol. 3 b.

the son of Morgrund; and there is a codicil to this deed by William, Earl of Mar, the son of Duncan, and of course the grandson of Morgrund, addressed to Peter, who was bishop of Aberdeen from the year 1247 to 1256. This Morgrund seems to have been the son of Gilchrist. He is undoubtedly the same person to whom William the Lion granted the renewal of the investiture of the Earldom of Mar. This curious deed is given by Selden, from a charter in his possession. It is dated A. 1171, at *Hindhop Burnmuthae*, apparently some place in the south of Scotland. Morgrund, as the name is here given, is called the son of *Gillocherus*. There can be no reason to doubt that this is the same person; and that the name had been written in this manner by some southern scribe, to whom Gilchrist was not familiar, and written by the ear; or that in the original deed there may be that abbreviation on the latter part of the name which is common in ancient manuscripts.

The first deed of confirmation, by John, Bishop of Aberdeen, is indeed said to be granted *ad presentationem et petitionem Gilchrist Comitis*. Now, John was not elected till the year 1200, that is twenty-nine years after Morgrund succeeded to Gilchrist. But it would seem that the language merely refers to the presentation, by his son Morgrund, of the deed of donation formerly made by Gilchrist; or perhaps the episcopal confirmation had still been withheld on account of some demur.

The donation of Duncan is confirmed by a charter issued by Alexander II. Duncan also gave them the lands of Kindrouth, formerly a parish by itself, but now annexed to Crathy; of Auchatandregan, and of Alien, apparently Ellon. This donation is confirmed by the deed of Gilbert, who was chosen Bishop of Aberdeen A. 1228, and died A. 1238.

Nor were the Earls of Mar the only benefactors to the Culdees at Monimusk. Colin, designed *Hostiarius*, or *Durward*, confirms to them the possession of the lands of Lorthel, or rather Lochel. This is repeated by Philip de Monte. Thomas, whose designation is given more fully, as he is called *Hostiarius Regis,* gave them the church of Afford, or Alford, with all its pertinents, and certain duties from Feodarg, and some other places specified. Roger, Earl of Buchan, gave them annually certain duties out of the lands of Feodarg, after the example of his grandfather Garnach. Although in some of these deeds the name of Culdees does not appear, but only that of Canons, we certainly know that the Culdees still continued there. For they are expressly mentioned under this name by William, who was elected Bishop of Aberdeen A. 1345, and died A. 1351. In the charters of Thomas Hostiarius and Roger, Earl of Buchan, they are designed by their ancient name. It might appear, indeed, that both Culdees and Canons Regular had for a long time held distinct establishments at Monimusk. For Pope Innocent IV., who came to the pontifical chair A. 1242, grants confirmations of the lands given to the prior and convent of Monimusk, designing them, *Ordinis Sancti Augustini.* Yet John, elected to the bishopric of Aberdeen A. 1351, in his deed of confirmation of the charter of Gilchrist, expressly mentions the Culdees as living at Monimusk. I am inclined, however, to think that there is either a mistake in the language of the papal bull; or, that the pope did not wish formally to recognise a society which did not claim his patronage.

They had also an establishment at Portmoak, in the vicinity of Lochlevin. A religious house was founded here, some time in the ninth century, by Eogash, king of the Picts, as Spotiswood denominates him, that is Hungus, most probably the second of his name. This writer says that it was consecrated to the Virgin Mary. But this may have been a secondary consecration in a later age.

There was a similar foundation at Dunfermline. Of this the following account has been given by a writer of great research : "The splendid abbey of Dunfermlin owed its inconsiderable foundation to Malcolm Ceanmore; its completion to Alexander I.; and its reform to David I. The monastery of Dunfermlin was dedicated, like the other Culdean establishments, to the Holy Trinity. Here the Culdees, with their abbot, discharged their usual duties, during several reigns; and David I., who lived much with Henry I. of England, upon his accession introduced among the Celtic Culdees thirteen English monks from Canterbury." Spotiswood mentions that this place " was formerly governed by a prior: for Eadmerus, speaking of the messengers that were sent by —— King Alexander [I.] in the year 1120, to Radulph, Archbishop of Canterbury, for procuring Eadmer to be bishop of St Andrews, says, *Horum unus quidem monachus, et Prior ecclesiae Dunfermelinae, Petrus nomine.*" He conjectures that " it was then an hospital;" especially as it is designed in some old manuscripts, *Monasterium de monte infirmorum.* " But it is evident that this is merely a monkish play upon the name of the place: like *Mons rosarum* for Montrose, properly *Munross.* As Gaelic *Dun* denotes a hill, and *fiar* crooked: it might afford a tolerable foundation for monkish ingenuity. The fact seems to be, that it continued as a priory till the time of David I., who, A. 1124, raised it to the dignity of an abbey. He wished, perhaps, by giving greater honour to the place, to reconcile the Culdees to the introduction of his English monks.

It has been supposed, with great appearance of reason, " that when the fatal stone was transferred by Kenneth, the son of Alpin, from Argyle to Scone, a religious house would be established at this ancient metropolis:" and asserted, on certain grounds, that " a Culdean church was here dedicated, in the earliest times, to the Holy Trinity, like other Culdean establishments. There can be no doubt that there was such an establishment before the reign of Alexander I. For in a charter of his, A. 1115, by which its form was changed, it is described as "a church dedicated in honour of the Holy Trinity." And in the Chronicle of Mailros, under this year, it is said: "The church of Scone is delivered up to Canons."

"Some have conjectured," as we learn from Martine, "that there was a company and colledge of" Culdees "at *Kirkcaldie*, which, they say, was, and should be, called *Kirkculdee*, and that the old name was *Cella Culdeorum*. It has been also said that the place was named *Kil-celedic*, which was changed during the Scoto-Saxon period to *Kirkceledic*."

Brudi, son of Derili, King of the Picts, according to Wyntown, about the year 700, "founded a religious house at Culross." Several circumstances induce us to view this as a Culdean establishment. It is natural to think that it would be similar to that which, as we have already seen, the same prince founded at Lochlevin. It was to this place that St Serf retired; and here he resided for many years, as we learn from Wyntown:

> And oure the wattyr, of purpos,
> Of Forth he passed til Culros :
> Thare he begowth to red a grownd,
> Quhare that he thowcht a kyrk to found.

From Culross he passed to Lochlevin, where he remained for several years. He afterwards returned to Culross, where

> He yhald wyth gud devotyowne
> Hys cors til hallowed sepulture,
> And hys saule til the Creature.
> *Cronykil*, B.V. ch. 12. ver. 1178. 1333.

As we have had occasion to take notice of the religious association between him and Adamnan, it is most probable that he conformed to the Columban rule here, as well as at Lochlevin; and that the church erected at Culross which bore his name was on the same establishment.

It may be observed, however, that the Breviary of Aberdeen takes notice of two saints of this name; the one a

Scotsman, contemporary with Palladius, who made him a bishop; the other, a foreigner, who was distinguished by many miracles, in the time of Abbot Adamnan. The latter is said to have resided in the island Petmook. This is undoubtedly meant for Portmoak, which, from its vicinity, has in various instances been confounded with the island of Lochlevin, called St Serf's Isle, where he in fact resided, and which was afterwards dedicated to him.

It has not generally been observed, that Mailros has a claim to be reckoned one of the ancient seats of the Culdees, the most ancient indeed on the main land. "The name," we are told, "is supposed to be Gaelic, compounded of Mull and Ross, 'a bare promontory,' remarkably descriptive of a little peninsula about a mile to the east" of the modern village "formed by the windings of Tweed, which is still called Old Melrose, and famous for its ancient monastery, one of the first seats of the religious Culdees in this country." It is afterwards subjoined : "The monastery of Old Melrose was probably founded about the end of the sixth century. Bede gives us an account of its situation on the bank of the Tweed, and likewise of its abbots. This place was a famous nursery for learned and religious men, and probably continued till the other one at the present Melrose was founded by King David."

"Old Melros," says a lively and celebrated tourist, "is now reduced to a single house, on a lofty promontory, peninsulated by the Tweed : a most beautiful scene; the banks lofty, and wooded, varied with perpendicular rocks, jutting like buttresses from top to bottom. This was the site of the antient abbey of Culdees, mentioned by Bede to have existed in 664, in the reign of the Saxon Oswy. This place was as celebrated for the austerities of Driethelmus, as ever Finchal was for those of St Godric. The first was restored to life after being dead an entire night. During that space, he passed through purgatory and hell, had the beatific vision, and got very near to the confines of heaven. His angelic guide gave him an useful lesson on the efficacy of prayer, alms, fasting, and particularly, masses of holy men ; infallible means to relieve the souls of friends and relations from the place of torment."

The account given above of the establishment of Culdees at Mailros, corresponds with the general tradition of the country. It is also supported by the character of the person to whom the foundation of this religious house has been with great probability ascribed. This is the celebrated Aidan. Bede, indeed, has not expressly said, that it was founded by him. But, speaking of Eata, under the year 664, he says, that he "was abbot of the monastery which is called Mailros." This Eata, he adds, "was one of the twelve young disciples of Aidan, of the nation of the Angles, whom he received, when he entered on an episcopate, to be instructed in Christ." Now, from the general tenor of his history, it appears that, before the mission of Aidan, there were no monasteries in that quarter. Eata was succeeded by Boisil, "a priest," says Bede, "distinguished for his virtues, and of a prophetic spirit." Upon his death the celebrated St Cuthbert was made abbot. After living many years at Mailros, he was made bishop of Lindisfarne. Aedilwald was abbot, A. 696. He was afterwards bishop of Lindisfarne ; and was one of Bede's contemporaries. In the Chronicle of Mailros, he is denominated Ethelwald.

Aidan himself, we certainly know, was a Culdee ; and hence we might conclude, that he would prefer this establishment to every other. But the language of Bede incidentally affords a clear proof that he did so. When we read of the "twelve disciples of Aidan," or "young men" committed to his charge, no doubt can remain, that he meant to instruct them according to the rule of Iona ; as he adhered to the very number which had the sanction of Columba, himself representing the abbot as their head.

"This place," says Milne, "was a famous nursery for learned and religious men, who were filled with zeal for propagating the Christian religion, particularly among their neighbours the Pagan Saxons."

"This convent," he subjoins, "has been inclosed with a stone wall, reaching from the south corner of the Tweed to the west corner of it, where the neck of land is narrower; the foundations of the wall are still to be seen. At the entrance to the convent, about the middle of this wall, there has been an house, built likely for the porters, called yet the Redhouse. The place where the chapel stood is still called the Chapel-know, and places on Tweed at this place still retain their names from the monks there, as the Haly-wheel, [i.e. holy-whirlpool, or eddy] and the Monk-ford. I do not think there has been any great building about it; for, as Bede acquaints us, their churches then were all of oak, and thatched with reeds."

Speaking of Colmsly, he says: "There has been a chapel here, the ruins of which are yet to be seen: It has been dedicated to Columba, abbot of Hii, from whence the place seems to take its name, as it is likewise called Cellmuir, from the chapel in the muir."

Nennius," he elsewhere remarks, "a British historian, who lived, as some say, in the year 620,—or rather, as the Bishop of Carlisle places him, anno 853,—speaks of the noble and great monastery of Melrose, which was ruined likely then after the destruction of the churches and monasteries by the Pagan Danes, who burnt the churches and houses wherever they came." But although Milne here quotes Sir James Dalrymple's Collections, he takes no notice of what the author has justly observed, that the passage referred to in Nennius is "a manifest interpolation." This he proves, from its being said that "Wedale is a village now subject to the Bishop of St Andrews;" whereas there was no bishop of this designation when Nennius wrote.

In this interpolated passage, it is pretended, that Arthur obtained a signal victory over the Pagans of this district, by means of a cross consecrated at Jerusalem. "The fragments of this cross," it is said, "are still held in great veneration at Wedale."—*Cujus fractae adhuc apud Wedale in magna veneratione servatur.* Wedale, Anglice : *Vallis doloris,* Latine : Wedale est villa in Provincia Lodonesie, *nunc* vero jurios episcopi sancti Andreae Scotiae, VI. milliaria ab occidentali parte, ab illo quondam nobili et eximio Monasterio de Meilros. Gale, vol. i. 114.

Sir James conjectures, that "this interpolation has been made before the last erection of the abbacie of Melross, and after the time of William the Conquerer, and Malcolm the Third." When Wedale is spoken of as a village, that of Stow is undoubtedly referred to; for Milne uses both terms as applied to the same place, p. 65. But Wedale, in its larger signification, has been applied to the valley itself. Stow, according to the sense of the word in Anglo-Saxon, might signify the place or village of Wedale. Different places in England are thus denominated; and the term enters into the composition of the names of others, as Walthamstow, &c.

"The monastery of Melrose," Mr Pinkerton says, "was apparently ruined by the Danes about the year 800, if not by Kenneth III. about 850. Chron. Pict. It remained in ruins till refounded by David I. 1136." The latter part of this account receives confirmation from the silence of the Chronicle of Mailros, as to any abbots, or even monks, belonging to this monastery, during the period referred to : and still more, from the express language of Simeon of Durham. He relates that Aldwin, Turgot, and some others leaving the monastery of Girwy, "came to what was formerly the monastery of Mailross, but then a solitude; and being delighted with the retirement of that place, began to serve Christ there. But when Malcolm King of Scots, to whom this place belonged, was informed that they had taken up their residence there, he subjected them to great injuries and persecutions, because, observing the rule of the gospel, they would not swear fealty to him. In the meantime the venerable bishop Walcher, by letters and precepts, desired, admonished, and adjured them " to return to Girwy, having threatened to excommunicate them "in the presence of the most sacred body of St Cuthbert, if they did not return to live under this saint." They at length obeyed: "being more afraid of excommunication than of the wrath of the king, which threatened them with death."

From the Chronicle of Mailros, it appears that this Walcher, who was bishop of Durham, was killed A. 1080, that is, fifty-six years before the foundation of the new monastery.

CHAPTER IX.

Of the Monasteries of Crusay and Oronsay.—Of Govan ;—Aber-
corn ;—Inchcolm ;—Tyningham ;—Aberlady ;—and Cold-
ingham.—Of the First Missionaries to the Orkney Islands.—
Churches and Chapels dedicated to Columba.

BESIDES these places, a variety of others might be mentioned.
In Crusay, and Oronsay, two of the western isles, monasteries
were founded by Columba, which, like other Culdean
establishments, were at length given to the canons regular.
The isle of Oronsay "is adorned," says Martin, "with a
church, chappel, and monastery. They were built by the
famous St Columba, to whom the church is dedicated.
There is an altar in this church, and there has been a modern
crucifix on it, in which several precious stones were fixed.
The most valuable of these is now in the custody of Mack-Duffie,
in black Rainmused village, and it is used as a catholicon for
diseases." Pennant views it as more probable that the
monastery was founded "by one of the lords of the isles, who
fixed here a priory of canons regular of Augustine, dependent
on the Abbey of Holyrood, in Edinburgh." But the settlement of canons regular here, in a late age, so far from being
a proof that this monastery was not originally peopled by
Culdees, is a strong presumption that it was.

In the Statistical Account, this monastery is given to a
different order of monks; although I suspect, erroneously.
"There was," it is said of Colonsay, "a monastery of Cister-
cians in this island. Their abbey stood in Colonsay, and its
priory in Oronsay. The remains of the abbey were, with
Gothic barbarity, torn asunder not many years ago, and the
stones put into a new building. The walls of the priory are
still standing, and, next to Icolmkill, is one of the finest
religious monuments of antiquity in the Hebrides.

Dr Smith has observed, that "Adamnan, besides the chief monastery of Iona, mentions several more in the Western Isles; such as that of Achaluing, in Ethica; Himba, or Hinba, and Elen-naomh; also Kill-Diun, or Dimha, at Lochava or Lochow."

According to Colgan, Columba founded the monastery of Govan on the Clyde. But the accounts of this foundation vary so much, that no certain judgment can be formed. "The church of Govan," it is said by another writer, "appears to have been originally mortified by King David I. to the church of St Mungo at Glasgow. The deed of mortification is entered in the chartulary of Glasgow." Fordun gives an account quite different from both these; but such as shews the conviction of his age that this was a very ancient foundation. "Contemporary with St Columba," he says, "was St Constantine, King of Cornwall, who, having renounced an earthly kingdom, began to fight under the heavenly King, and came to Scotland with St Columba, and preached the faith to the Scots and Picts. He founded a monastery of brethren near Clyde, over whom he presided as abbot. He converted the whole country of Kintyre, where he himself suffered martyrdom for the faith, and received burial in his own monastery at Govan."

It has also been said that Columba and his successors extended their jurisdiction over the monastery of Abercorn. This monastery, we are told "was one of the most ancient in Scotland." It is several times mentioned by Bede, though he gives no particular account of it. Towards the end of the seventh century it was the residence of a bishop Triumvin. At this period the territory of the Northumbrians extended to the Frith of Forth; but in the year 648, Aegfrid their king was defeated and slain by the Picts, on which Triumvin left Abercorn; and from that time it is uncertain whether the monastery continued, as there seems to be nothing recorded in history with respect to it. To this old religious establishment we must refer the names of many places, such as Priestinch, St Serf's Law, Priest's Folly, &c.

"About the year 1170 a dispute arose concerning the patronage of the church of Abercorn, between John Avenale, or Avonale, Lord of Abercorn, and Richard, second Bishop of Dunkeld. The latter succeeded, as was to be expected in these times of increasing church power. In the year 1460, the whole lands belonging to the Bishop of Dunkeld on the south side of the Forth, consisting of Abercorn, Cramond, Preston, and Aberlady, were erected into one barony, to be called the barony of Aberlady."

It seems highly probable that the monks here were Culdees. As the lands of Abercorn, with those of Cramond, belonged to the bishopric of Dunkeld, originally a Culdean establishment, we may reasonably conjecture that they were an early donation, made perhaps because the same rule was observed here as at Dunkeld; especially as the church of Cramond was dedicated to Columba. A charter, dated A. 1478, contains the grant of a sum "to be levied from different tenements in Edinburgh, the Canongate, and Leith, for the support of a chaplain, *divina celebranti et in perpetuum celebraturo annuatim*, at the parochial altar of St Columba, situated within the parish church of St Columba of Nether Crawmond." This opinion gains strength from the probability that this monastery was founded by Oswald, King of Northumbria, who, as he had received his education among the Culdees, still retained the warmest attachment to the society.

There is reason to think that some of the Orkney Islands were subdued to the Christain faith by the Culdean missionaries. We learn from Adamnan, that while Columba resided at the court of Brudi, King of the Picts, there was at the same time there the *regulus*, or petty prince of the Orkneys. Columba, knowing that Cormac, one of his disciples, with some of his companions, had been searching for some island as a place of religious retirement, solicited Brudi, that, if Cormac should land in any of these islands he would earnestly recommend him to the protection of this prince, lest any violence should be done to him or his associates in his territories. Adamnan adds, in the style of writing common in his time, that "the saint said this, because he foreknew in spirit, that after some months the same Cormac would go to the Orkneys; which accordingly took place afterwards: and, in consequence of the recommendation of the holy man, Cormac was delivered from imminent danger of death in these regions.

Although we have no subsequent accounts of the success of these missionaries, there is ground to conclude, from collateral evidence, that they settled in some of these islands. For Wallace, in his account of the Orkneys, has supplied us with an authentic record of Thomas, Bishop of the Orkneys, dated A. 1403, which throws considerable light on this subject. In this "we are told," as Mr. Pinkerton has observed, "that when the Norwegians conquered the Orkneys they found them possessed, *duabus nationibus*, scilicet *Peti et Pape*, by two nations, the Pets and Papas." The reasoning of this learned inquirer on this subject is so convincing that I shall make no apology for transcribing it.

"The first of these nations," he says, "was palpably the Pikts, called *Pets* by the Scandinavians, as Saxo's *Petia*, or Piktland, and the name *Petland fiord* for Piktland frith, in Icelandic writings may witness. The Papas, by the usual confusion of long tradition here called a nation, were clearly the Irish papas or priests, long the sole clergy in the Pikish domains; and who, speaking a different language from the Pikts, were by the Norwegian settlers regarded, not as a distinct profession only, but as remains of a different nation. Thus Arius Frodi [De Islandia, p. 11], who wrote about 1070, tells us that the Norwegians who colonized Iceland found there Irish *papas*, who were driven out, but left their Irish books, *bœer Irscar*, behind them. *Papey*, one of the Orkneys, in all likelihood derives its name from being a chief residence of the Papas."

Barry adopts the same theory, adding: "There are several places here which still retain the name of *Papay* or *Paplay*, which, when viewed with attention, seem to have something strikingly peculiar. They are all in a retired situation, distinguished for the richness of their soil and the variety of their natural productions. When all these circumstances are considered, along with some venerable ruins which some of them contain, we are almost compelled to believe that they once were the abode of men of that sacred character."

There are other more minute circumstances which confirm the idea that these islands were formerly inhabited by the followers of Columba. The church of Burness, in the island of Sanday, was dedicated to St Colm. In the foundation of the cathedral church of Orkney, confirmed by Cardinal Beaton, on the application of Lord Robert Stewart, Bishop of Orkney, A. 1544, the sub-chantor, Sir Matthew Strange, is designed prebendary of St Colm. He also subscribes the deed as *prebendarius Sancti Columbae*. Malcolm Halcro, another of the witnesses, is designed, *archidiaconus Zetlandiae, ac prebendariae* [prebendarius ?] *Sanctae Trinitatis*.

It is not certain, however, that this church was dedicated to the apostle of Iona. For, as a learned writer has observed, "Keith has another St Colm, a bishop and confessor, in Scotland, A.D. 1000, under the 6th of June." He subjoins: "In Dempster's Menologia, under the 6th of June, there is 'Kirkue Colmi Oread. apostoli;' and in Dempster's Nomenclature of Scottish writers, there is 'St Colmus Epis. Oread. 1010 A.D.' The St Colm's Kirk, in the isle of Sanday, in Orkney, was, perhaps, named from this St Colm, who was the apostle of the Orkneys, at the end of the tenth century." Camerarius mentions, under the sixth of June, Columba, confessor and presbyter. He views the island called Inchcolme, in the Frith of Forth, as named from him; but says that he was "a different person from Columba, the holy abbot."

The writer lately quoted, who has paid so much attention to the antiquities of Scotland, justly remarks: "The numbers, and distances of the churches which were dedicated to Columba, are proofs in confirmation of Bede, and Adamnan, and Innes, of the extent of his authority, and of the influence of his name. There are Kilcolmkill, the oldest church, and burying ground, in Morven; Kilcolmkill, in South Cantire; Kilcolmkill, in Mull; Kileolmkill, in Isla-Island; Kilcolmkill, on the north-west of the same isle; Kilcolmkill, in North-Uist; Kilcolmkill, in Benbecula; Kilcolmkill, in Skye; Kilcolmkill, in Sutherland; Colmkill, in Lanark; there are Columbkill-isle, in Loch Erisport, in Lewis; Columbkill Isle, in Loch Columkill, whereon there are the remains of a monastery, dedicated to St Columba; Inch Colm, in the Frith of Forth, on which a monastery was founded by Alexander I., A.D. 1123, and dedicated to St Columba; Eilean Colm, a small island in Tongue parish; there was formerly St Colm's Kirk in the island of Sanday, in Orkney. There is St Colm's Isle in the Minch, on the south-east of Lewis, which, with St Mary's Isle, and some other Isles, are called the Shiant Isles; and, in Gaelic, *Eileanan Sheanta*, which means the blessed or consecrated islands. The parish church of Lonmay, in Aberdeenshire, was dedicated to St Columba. There is the parish of Kirkcolm, in Wigtonshire. In the parish of Caerlaverock, there was a chapel dedicated to St Columba; to him was dedicated one of the chaplainries which was attached to the Cathedral of Moray," &c. We have formerly mentioned the chapel at Colms-lee, from the name of Columba abbreviated, and Anglo-Saxon *leag*, a field, pasture, or *lee*.

It appears that this saint was held in great veneration at Kilwinning also; where there was a monastery of peculiar celebrity in times of popery. It was not founded, indeed, till the year 1140, when the power of the Culdees was on the wane; and it was possessed by monks of the Tyronesian order, who were brought from Kelso. But there are still vestiges of the regard that was here paid to Columba. "The fairs," we are told, "in all the towns and villages connected with the monastery, were named after some particular saint, who was afterwards accounted the protector, or particular saint of the place; such as, St Anthony, St Colm or Columba, St Margaret, St Bride or Bridget. The days on which these fairs are held are still called after the saint whose name they bear; as Colm's day, Margaret's day," &c.

Martin mentions more churches in the Lewis islands as dedicated to Columba. Besides "St Columkil, in the island of that name :—St Collum in Ey, St Collum in Garten;" also St Columbus's [Columba's] Chapel, in Harries. He gives a particular proof of the strong attachment of the inhabitants of Benbecula to the memory of Columba. "There is a stone," he says, "set up near a mile to the south of Columbus's church, about eight feet high, and two feet broad. It is called by the natives the Bowing-stone; for when the inhabitants had the first sight of the church, they set up this stone, and there bowed and said the Lord's prayer."

There was also a chapel dedicated to Columba in the isle of Troda, which lies within half-a-league of the northernmost point of Skye, called Hunish. In Hadda-Chuan, also, that is, Hadda of the ocean, which is about two leagues distant from Hunish-point, there is another chapel dedicated to the same saint. "It has an altar in the east end; and there is a blue stone of a round form on it, which is always moist. It is an ordinary custom, when any of the fishermen are detained in the isle by contrary winds, to wash the blue stone with water all round, expecting thereby to procure a favourable wind, which the credulous tenant, living in the isle, says never fails, especially if a stranger wash the stone. The stone is likewise applied to the sides of people troubled with stitches, and they say it is effectual for that purpose. And so great is the regard that they have for this stone, that they swear decisive oaths on it."

"Kirkubrith, in Galloway," says Hay, "belonged to the monastery of men in Iona."

Sir James Dalrymple has given a charter of William the Lion, in which he makes a donation of several churches and chapels in Galloway, belonging to the monastery of Iona, to the canons of Holyrood-house. Those mentioned are, the churches of Kirchecormach, of St Andrew, of Balenecros, and of Cheleton. Whether Kirchecormach be an error for Kircuthbert, I shall not pretend to determine. Different saints of the name of Cormac appear in the Scottish calendar. But there was a church, dedicated to Cuthbert, in Kirkcud- bright; and another, also within the burgh, called St Andrew's Kirk, which seems to be the second mentioned in the charter.

It does not appear that this alienation was immediately directed against the Culdees. For the Cluniac monks seem to have been previously settled here: and it has been said that these churches were taken from them, because, accord- ing to their constitutions, they were not permitted to perform the functions of a curate. If, however, William had been as partial to the Culdees as to the canons regular, he could easily have found priests of the former description to supply these charges, without alienating, from the abbey of Icolm- kill, churches which had been so many ages under its juris- diction.

Perhaps we ought also to reckon the abbey of Inchcolm, an island in the Frith of Forth, as a Culdean settlement. This abbey, indeed, was founded by Alexander I., about the year 1123; and the religious men, whom he placed in it, were canons regular. But it was dedicated to St Columba, Abbot of Iona, and had been formerly possessed by one of his followers

Veneration for the memory of Columba is assigned, by our writers, as the very reason of the royal foundation. It is said that the king, when attempting to cross at the Queen's Ferry, being overtaken by a violent storm from the south, urged the mariners to run into the isle Aemonia; where at that time lived a certain hermit, who, devoted to the service of St Columba, diligently attended to the duties of religion, contenting himself with such slender support as he could derive from the milk of one cow, and from the shell-fishes on the sea-shore. The king and his company, being confined here for three days by the storm, were supported by these means; and because, from his youth, he was attached to St Columba, and had vowed to him, when in danger of perishing by the storm, that, if he arrived safely at this island, he would erect some monument worthy of his memory, he afterwards founded and endowed the abbey here.

Kentigern, or St Mungo, who had been viewed as the founder of the s e of Glasgow, might with propriety be numbered among those who adorned the name of Culdee; as, for many years, he was the disciple of St Servanus, at Culross. The famous Baldred, or Balthere, was the disciple of Kentigern. He inhabited a cell in Tyningham, in Haddingtonshire, where a monastery was afterwards erected. This was burnt by Anlaf, King of Northumbria, A. 941. Two arches of elegant Saxon architecture, the sole remains of the ancient church, give additional beauty to the lawn which surrounds the seat of the Earl of Haddington.

Baldred, according to Simeon of Durham, died in the year 606-7. Three places contended for the honour of retaining his dust,—Aldham, Tyningham, and Preston. Aldham is the same with Whitekirk. In the account of lands belonging to the abbey of Holyrood-house, "the barony of Aldhamrie, alias Whitkirk," is mentioned. In Latin it was denominated *Album Fanum*, and *Alba Capella*. This place was greatly celebrated in times of popery. Hither many pilgrimages were made. It was under pretence of a pious expedition to Whitekirk, in order to perform a vow which she had made for the safety of her son, that the queen-mother cozened Crichton the Chancellor, and carried off James II., in a chest, to Stirling.

Such was the credulity of these times, that it was believed that the body of the saint was in all these places : and this, of course, afforded an irrefragable proof of the doctrine of transubstantiation. Camerarius gravely says, that, "for the termination of the dispute between these parochial churches, it was at length effected, by the prayers of the saint himself, (for nothing is impossible with God,) that each of them should enjoy this treasure." Major asserts the doctrine, as supported by this fact.

The Breviary of Aberdeen contains some particulars with respect to Baldred, which I have not met with anywhere else.

"This suffragan of Saint Kentigern," it is said, "flourished in Lothian, in virtues and in illustrious miracles. Being eminently devout, he renounced all worldly pomp, and, following the example of John the Divine, resided in solitary places, and betook himself to the islands of the sea. Among these, he had recourse to one called Bass, where he led a life without all question contemplative and strict, in which, for many years, he held up to remembrance the most blessed Kentigern, his instructor, in the constant contemplation of the sanctity of his conduct.

In this work, we find a miracle ascribed to the worthy Baldred, that must have rendered him an estimable acquisition to a people living on a rocky coast. "There was a great rock between the said island [the Bass] and the adjacent land, which remained fixed in the middle of the passage, unmoved by all the force of the waves, giving the greatest hinderance to navigation, and often causing shipwrecks. The blessed Baldred, moved by piety, ordered that he should be placed on this rock. This being done, at his nod the rock was immediately lifted up, and, like a ship driven by a favourable breeze, proceeded to the nearest shore, and henceforth remained in the same place, as a memorial of this miracle, and is to this day called St Baldred's coble or cock-boat."

Here a different account is also given of the ubiquity of the saint's body. We are informed that the inhabitants of the three parishes which were under his charge, as soon as they knew of his death, assembled in three different troops at Aldhame, where he breathed his last, severally begging his body. But, as they could not agree among themselves, they, by the advice of a certain old man, left the body unburied, and all separately betook themselves to prayer, that God himself, of his grace, would be pleased to signify which of these churches was to have the body of the saint. Morning being come, a thing took place that has not often had a parallel. They, being all assembled, as before, in their different troops, found three bodies, perfectly alike, and all prepared with equal pomp for interment. Each of the companies, of course, departed well pleased; and each parish erected a monument over that body of the saint which had fallen to its share.

It has been conjectured that the Culdees had a seat at or near Aberlady, in the same county. "There are still visible," it is said, "the vestiges of a small chapel on the north-west corner of the churchyard." The same account is given by Mr Chalmers. "There appears to have been here," he says, "in early times, an establishment of the Culdees: And Kilspindie, the place of their settlement, near the village of Aberlady, on the north-west, is supposed to have derived its name from the Culdees; *Cil-ys-pen-du* signifying, in the British speech, the cell of the black heads; and the word is pronounced *Kilyspendy*. The cell of the Culdees near Aberlady was, no doubt, connected with the Culdee monastery of

Dunkeld. When David I. established the bishopric of Dunkeld, he conferred on the bishop of this diocese Kilspindie
and Aberlady, with their lands adjacent, the advowson of
the church, and its tithes and other rights."

Coldingham has also been numbered among the original
seats of the Culdees. "Certainly," says the learned Selden,
referring to the language of Bede, " I cannot but suspect that,
in *Coludi urbs*, the name of the ancient Culdees lies hid, or is
more obscurely exhibited; as having been ennobled, above
other places, by the residence of a greater number of this
society, or perhaps by their more solemn convention."

This was undoubtedly the most ancient nunnery in North
Britain. It is supposed that it was founded during the reign
of Oswald, who died A. 643. In the year 670 it was under
the government of Ebba, who was not less distinguished by
her virtues, than by her royal descent.

It does not appear, however, that any stress can be laid on
the name, as indicating that this was originally a seat of the
Culdees; for in this case, according to analogy, the initial
syllable would most probably have been *Kil* or *Cil*. But
there seems to be as little ground for asserting that "the
prefix is plainly from the Saxon *Col-den*, the Cold vale." Nor
does this etymon derive much support from what is added :
"This kirktown is the *Urbs Coldona* [1. *Coldana*] of Bede,
saith Gibson, in his *Explicatio nominum locorum*, subjoined to
his Saxon Chronicle. The coincidence is decisive, as *Coldana*,
and Coldene, or *dean*, are the same in substance." This is not
precisely what Gibson says. Explaining the name *Coludesburh*,
which occurs in the Chronicle, he says : " *Urbs Coldana*, et
Coludi urbs, Bed." If *Coldana* is used by Bede, I have not
been so fortunate as to find the place. *Coludi urbs* occurs in
three places. By Alfred it is rendered, as in the Saxon
Chronicle, *Coludes burh*. The phrase, *Coldana et Coludi*,
appears in the margin of Ptolemy, among the *Aequipollentia;*
and to this Gibson might possibly refer. But the Κολανια of

Ptolemy could never be viewed by our Scottish topographer as the same with the modern Coldingham; as he has himself placed it in Lanarkshire. *Coludi*, or *Coludes*, must be viewed as the original name of Coldingham; and surely there is no great resemblance between either of these and *Col-den*. Although "between the church and the sea there is a place called Cold-mill," it will not prove that the monastery was designed from the bleakness of its situation. If it stood there in the Saxon period, it was most probably denominated *Coludes myln*.

While Ebba resided here, "there was in the same monastery," as we are informed by Bede, "a man of the Scottish race, called Adamnan, who led a life entirely devoted to God in continence and prayer, so that he never tasted food except on the Lord's day and on Thursday; frequently spending the whole night in prayer." He, we are told, informed the abbess of a revelation which had been made to him, that the judgment of God was shortly to come on the monastery, because of their corruptions. It was afterwards consumed by fire.

The name of this devotee is another circumstance on which Selden rests his supposition. The hypothesis, indeed, is not liable to the charge of anachronism. For that Adamnan who is here mentioned resided at Coldingham between the years 671 and 679, when the monastery was burnt. He, who had the same name, was this very year made Abbot of Hij, and died A. 703. As we learn from Bede, that many of the inhabitants of Coldingham, among whom was his co-presbyter Aedgils, left it on account of that destruction: Adamnan might be one of these; and, being a Scotsman, might go to Hij, where he had most probably received his education. The austerity of his life might point him out as the most proper person for filling the vacancy at Hij.

This Adamnan has by Camerarius been called Abbot of Coldingham. But although there were monks as well as nuns there, in this early age, the Abbess, like Hilda at Whitby,

seems to have had the supreme authority. Other writers call
him a monk ; and this seems to have been the only character
which he had at Coldingham. But although he had received
no higher designation, even from writers of an earlier age,
it would not amount to a proof that, after he retired from
this place, he had not been advanced to greater dignity.
Bede, indeed, does not say that Adamnan, Abbot of Hij, was
the same person. But his silence on this head affords no
evidence that he was not, but rather the contrary. Trithe-
mius, Usher, and Smith, view him as a different person.
Bale, Possevin, and others, consider him as the same.

It may be added, that the celebrated Ebba, mentioned
above, must have had her education among the Culdees.
She was the daughter of Edilfrid, king of Northumbria, who
being slain in battle, was succeeded by Edwin, king of the
Deiri. In consequence of his succession, Ebba and her
seven brothers were either exiled, or found it most safe to
betake themselves to Scotland. The illustrious Oswald,
afterwards king of Northumbria, was one of them. It was
in consequence of his education among the Culdees, as we
have seen, that he afterwards applied to the elders of the
Scots for a spiritual instructor to his subjects.

According to the Aberdeen Breviary, she and her brothers,
while in a state of exile, were received and kindly nourished
by Donald Brek, king of Scots. Fordun dates this event in
the reign of his father Eugenius IV. Bede seems uncertain
whether it was among the Scots or Picts that they received
protection. "During the life of Edwin," he says, "the sons
of Edilfrid, with a great company of noble youths, were in a
state of exile among the Scots *or* Picts, and were there instructed in the doctrine of the Scots, and received the grace
of baptism."

It is also said in the Breviary, as above referred to, that
Ebba was buried "in her own monastery, called *Colludi*." It
would also seem, that from her the promontory of St Abb's

Head derived its name.   It is said that, when seeking refuge
in Scotland, she was driven in on some part of the coast near
this headland; and afterwards, when chosen abbess, that,
from gratitude for her preservation, she built a church or
chapel on the promontory, at her own expense.

CHAPTER X.

It is evident, notwithstanding the partial accounts we have of these remote transactions, that, from a very early period, the Culdees vigorously opposed the errors, and resisted the encroachments, of the Church of Rome. But even while the more candid writers, who favoured or adhered to the Romish interest, mention this opposition; such was their conviction of the blameless character of the men, that they could not withhold their praise.

Bede, when speaking of the difference between the Scottish Church and the Church of Rome, as to the mode of observing Easter, calls that of the latter "the canonical observation;" and says, that Oswald, king of the Angles, having applied *ad majores natu Scottorum*, "to the Scottish elders," that they might send him a bishop for the instruction of his people, soon after "received bishop Aidan, a man of the greatest meekness, piety and moderation, and animated with divine zeal, although not entirely according to knowledge. For he was accustomed to observe Easter Sunday after the manner of his own nation, from the fourteenth to the twentieth moon. For, after this mode, the northern province of the Scots, and the whole Pictish nation, celebrated Easter ; persuading themselves that, in this mode of observation, they followed the writings of that holy and praise-worthy father Anatolius : which, whether it be true, every intelligent person can easily discern."

Afterwards, speaking of Aidan, in reference to the same diversity of celebration, he says : "But, during the life of Aidan, this difference with respect to Easter was patiently endured by all; as they were fully sensible that, although he could not observe Easter in a way contrary to the custom of those who sent him, he nevertheless laboured, that all the works of faith, piety, and love, should be diligently practised according to the custom common to all saints: for which cause he was deservedly beloved of all, even those who differed from him in sentiment with regard to Easter; and was held in veneration, not only by persons of inferior rank, but also by the bishops themselves, by Honorius, Bishop of Canterbury, and Felix, Bishop of the East Angles."

Goodall labours to overthrow this proof of the independence of the Scottish Church; but in a very unfair manner. "If enquiry be made," he says, "upon what foundation all these things are asserted, there will nothing be found but ignorance or fable. For it is a strange inference, that, because the Scots in old times observed the feast of Easter by another cycle than that which the Church of Rome had adopted, therefore they entertained the same opinions with the modern Presbyterians, who utterly condemn any celebration of that festival as highly superstitious." But, who has asserted that the Culdees " entertained the same opinions with the modern Presbyterians," as to the observation of festival days ? The question is not if they adhered to some rites, for which the modern Presbyterians can discern no authority from the word of God. For it is admitted that a variety of human inventions had been too generally introduced long before the age of Columba. Nor is it of consequence to inquire from whom our forefathers originally received such rites ? But the proper question is,—Ought not their rigid adherence to their own modes, in what way soever they had been introduced, to be viewed as a clear proof of their independence as a church ; and particularly, of their refusing to give any subjection to the usurped authority of the Church of Rome?

"Whereas it has been alledged and maintained," says Goodall, "that the disputes which the Culdees had with some bishops and canons, were, on account of differences about religious tenets, it will appear, by examining into the instances alledged, that it was not so, but merely such disputes as the bishops and canons had pretty frequently among themselves, about money, lands, and privileges."—"They differed no more in religion from the rest of the Church of Rome than Black Friars do from White."

That the Culdees had disputes about matters merely secular, as well as those who formally adhered to the Church of Rome, no reasonable person will deny. But it must be observed that their disputes about these things, according to all the accounts transmitted to us, were chiefly in later ages.

From the common influence of corruption, it is natural to think that, as this was more generally diffused, especially in consequence of the increase of the power of Rome, their zeal would appear more ardent with respect to their secular privileges, than as to those of a superior description. But it will not follow that they never had any other grounds of difference with the Church of Rome. The certainty of their having disputes with respect to "money, land, and privileges," will not destroy the evidence which we still have, that they differed as to various points both of doctrine and worship.

There is another consideration, however, which more especially demands our attention. Although it were true that latterly the Culdees had no disputes, save with respect to "money, lands, and privileges," we could be at no loss to perceive the reason of this. Their enemies knew that they had a far more certain prospect of success by attacking them on these points than merely by opposing their peculiarities. They had every reason to fear that the Culdees, if allowed to retain their temporal emoluments, especially as they were the favourites of the vulgar, would fight it out with them to the last. They, therefore, like men who had some portion of the wisdom of the serpent at least, called in the aid of princes and peers, of popes and bishops; knowing that the arm of power is an argument that cannot easily be answered. They reduced the Culdees to the necessity of either disputing about "money, lands, and privileges," or of depriving themselves of the possibility of continuing their disputes on more important grounds. They seem to have applied the same national proverb to this refractory fraternity, which tradition ascribes to the successors of the Culdees, at a later period, as practically applied to friars of every order, whether "black" or "white:" "Ding doon the nests, and the rooks will flee away."

Before proceeding to consider the proofs, yet extant, of the difference between the Culdees and the Church of Rome, as to particular points of faith or practice, it may be observed that George Con, although a bigoted adherent to the interests of this church, even since the Reformation, has given them a very honourable testimony. "Among the Culdees," he says, "was seen that pure pattern of the Christian life, which, withdrawn from the noise of the world and the society of men, was wholly employed in the contemplation of heavenly things: such as it appeared among the Egyptians, Greeks, and Assyrians, during that and the following ages, in the lives of those illustrious servants of God, who were called Anchorites and Ascetics."

The celebrated Alcuin, who flourished in the eighth century, nearly at the same time with Bede, in his epistle addressed *To the very learned Men and Fathers in the Province of the Scots*, appears as a witness that our countrymen did not acknowledge auricular confession. "It is reported," he says, "that none of the laity make confession to the priests." But, although he argues against their sentiments, he gives the following character of the men. "We hear many commenda-

tions of your wisdom and piety, both on account of the holy
lives of the monks, who, free from the bustle of worldly cares,
resign themselves to the service of God; and of the religious
manners of the laity, who, in the midst of temporal occupa-
tions, continue to lead virtuous lives."

Although Bromton complains that Colman would not renounce the sect of the Scots, yet he gives a very honourable testimony to him, and to his predecessors, Aidan and Finan, as men
of wonderful sanctity, temperances, humility, and spirituality.

That they opposed auricular confession further appears
from what the famous St Bernard, Abbot of Clairvaux, says
concerning Malachy, Bishop of Armagh, in the twelfth
century: " He anew instituted the most salutary use of
confession."   On this subject Toland has made the following
observations: " They rejected auricular confession, as well as
authoritative absolution: and confessed to God alone, as
believing God alone could forgive sins: which made I know
not whom to exclaim most grievously against such, and to
say, 'that if they could conceal their sins from God, they
would no more confess them to him than to the priest.'   A
very shrewd egregious discovery! but laughed at by the Irish
laity, who, notwithstanding their native simplicity, could
discern this sanctified trap laid for their private and public
liberty, with all the subtlety of hypocritical priests."

The Scottish clergy had received the ridiculous rite of the
tonsure.   But it is no inconsiderable proof of their independence on Rome, that it was not till the eighth century that
they could be prevailed on to adopt the Roman mode; although
so early as the time of Augustine, the papal legates had
introduced the latter into Britain, and had persuaded the
Anglican clergy to receive it.   This, indeed, appears to have
been one of the very important changes designed in their
legation.   But the more frivolous the thing itself, which the
Romanists wished to impose on the clergy in Scotland, the
greater is the proof of their spirit of resistance.

It has been supposed, from the language of Bede, that, "without the ceremonies used by the Romanists, they baptised in any water they came to." This is confirmed by the complaint which Lanfranc, Archbishop of Canterbury, makes concerning the Irish Christians, who were taught by Culdees. "Infants," he says, "are baptised by immersion, without the consecrated chrism."

It has been inferred, from the language of Bernard, that "confirmation was quite in disuse, if at all ever known," among the Irish Culdees. For in his life of Malachy he says that he "anew instituted the sacrament of confirmation."

They seem also to have opposed the doctrine of the real presence. We read of Bishop Sedulius, who, about the beginning of the eighth century, went to Rome in company with Fergustus or Fergus, a Pictish bishop. Sedulius is claimed both by the Scots and by the Irish. He subscribes himself, in a council held at Rome, A. 721, *Britanniæ episcopus, de genere Scotorum*. But it is immaterial whether he belonged to Scotland or to Ireland ; as the doctrines and forms of both churches were so similar. He left a commentary on all the epistles of Paul, which has been printed. On 1 Cor. xi. 24. *Do this in remembrance of me*, he says: "He has left his memorial to us, in the same manner as anyone, who was about to go a great distance, should leave some pledge to him whom he loved ; that as often as he saw it he might be able to recollect the benefits and the love of his friend."

The Culdees, it would appear, withstood the idolatrous worship of the Roman Church. "It is to be observed," says Sir James Dalrymple, "that the common practice of the Culdees was to dedicate their principal churches to the Holy Trinitie, and not to the Blessed Virgin, or any Saint." "There is a charter by Malcolm IV. to the abbey of Dunkeld, in which the church is designed that of the Holy Trinity." It seems highly probable that the church of Brechin, which has been generally viewed as a remnant of Pictish architecture, had a similar dedication ; as the principal market held there is still called Trinity, by corruption, Tarnty Fair.

It is admitted, indeed, that this was their established mode of dedication. "The monastery of Dunfermlin," says a learned writer, in a passage formery quoted, "was dedicated, like the other Culdean establishments, to the holy Trinity." Speaking of Scone, he says : "A Culdean church was here dedicated, in the earliest times, to the Holy Trinity, like other Culdean monasteries." Spotiswood says that the abbey of Scone was dedicated "to the Holy Trinity, and St Michael the Archangel." But there can be no doubt that he is here to be corrected from the more full and interesting account given us by Sir James Dalrymple. He has, indeed, inserted from the Chartulary of Scone, the charter of Alexander I. erecting the abbey. This bears that there was a church here, formerly dedicated to the Holy Trinity. But a reason is assigned for the change of the dedication, as well as of the mode of service ; a reason perfectly consonant to the spirit of the times.

The words are : "I, Alexander, by the grace of God King of Scots, son of King Malcolm and Queen Margaret, and I, Sibilla, Queen of Scots, daughter of Henry, King of England, being disposed to decorate the house of God, to exalt his habitation, give and deliver up the church, dedicated in honour of the Holy Trinity, to God himself, and St Mary, and St Michael, and St John, and St Laurence, and St Augustine." It is added that it was "for extending and exalting the worship and honour of God, that canons were introduced from the church of St Oswalds, *ad serviendum Deum canonice.*

"Here," says Sir James, "is a new order of ecclesiastics, and a new form of worship introduced, upon pretence of enlarging and exalting the worship and honour of God, as if it had not been established formerly in purity at Scone ; and chanoins regular of St Austine, serving God by their profession, brought from the church of Oswalds in England, a place famous for its religion; as if the Scots and their predecessors, before this time, had not been servants of God after the right rule, and their churches famous for professing the true religion; or that they had not served God canonically, albeit according to the canon of the holy scriptures, because not according to the rule of St Austine."

This new erection seems to have taken place A. 1114, or 1115: and it was the first instance of the introduction of canons into the Scottish church. For it was from Scone that canons were brought to St Andrews, in the year 1140.

This exactly tallies with the account given of the Irish, while under the religious direction of the Culdees. Toland observes, that " in their public worship, they made an honourable mention of holy persons deceased; offering a sacrifice of thanksgiving for their exemplary life and death, but not by way of propitiation for sins." For he says: " They neither prayed to dead men, nor for them. And though naming particular men on such occasions gave a handle for erecting them afterwards into tutelary saints, yet at that time the Irish were as far from addressing themselves to saints as to angels. For they were persuaded, (to use the words of Claudius), that, ' while we are in the present world, we may help one another either by our prayers or by our counsels; but when we come before the tribunal of Christ, neither Job, nor Daniel, nor Noah, can intercede for any one, but every one must bear his own burden,' which is plain sense and scripture. But that which is plain nonsense, and nowhere authorised in scripture, I mean the service for the dead, the Irish never practised till they were obliged to do it by the council of Cashel, convoked by order of Henry the Second, in the year 1172. And it is certain that nothing does more contribute to harden the ignorant sort in a vicious course of life, than this mummery; when they observe such things said and done at burials, with relation to their deceased pro-

fligate companions, as may persuade them they are upon a
level with the best, for all their past wickedness."

Toland, when speaking of the Irish, says that Claudius was
" one of their most celebrated divines."   He flourished in the
year 815, and is said to have been Bishop of Auxerre ; according to others, of Turin.

Gillan has made an effort to prove that there was no
superstition in dedicating churches to saints.   " If Sir James
[Dalrymple,]" he says, " will be at the pains to consult, but
very superficially, the writings of the ancient fathers and
ecclesiastic historians, he will find that no sooner did Constantine encourage and embrace the Christian religion, but stately
churches were dedicated all the Christian world over to saints
and martyrs.   And what superstition or idolatry can there
be in consecrating a church to the service and worship of
God alone, and calling it by the name of a saint, both to
preserve the memory of that saint, and to distinguish it from
other churches ?"

But the learned writer has chosen a very unlucky æra for
the commencement of these dedications.   Any one who con-
sults ancient writers, although superficially, if he does it coolly,
must see that, as "the mystery of iniquity" had been working
long before, it made very rapid advances from the time of
Constantine ; and that the power which he lent the church,
and the pomp with which he surrounded her, proved her
greatest snares, and did more real injury to the interests of
religion than all the cruel persecutions of the heathen emperors had been able to effect.   It has also been generally
acknowledged by protestant writers, that the dedication of
churches to saints and martyrs, however innocently meant
by pious Christians, was the great inlet to the worship of
demons, or departed men.

Although Bede has said, that " Ninian's episcopal seat was
distinguished by the name and church of St Martin the
Bishop," it does not follow that the church was thus dedicated

by Ninian himself. At any rate, Bede says, in the very same place, that he had been regularly trained up at Rome.

Gillan adds, that "Sir James had been at needless trouble to bring charters to prove that churches were dedicated to the Blessed Trinity." Undoubtedly he has not. For, from what we have already seen, it appears that the Romanists were by no means satisfied with this kind of dedication. Therefore they altered it, as not being sufficiently conducive to the honour of the catholic church.

They were also enemies to the doctrines of works of supererogation. "They were so far," says Toland, "from pretending to do more good than they were obliged [to do], much less to superabound in merit for the benefit of others (but such others as should purchase these superfluities of grace from their executors the priests,) that they readily denied all merit of their own; and solely hoped for salvation from the mercy of God, through faith in Jesus Christ: which faith, as a living root, was to produce the fruit of good works, without which it were barren or dead, and consequently useless: for, as Claudius observes, from some other sage, 'The faithful man does not live by righteousness, but the righteous man by faith.' This excellent sentence, culled out of numberless testimonies to the same purpose in the oldest writers, comprehends at once and decides the whole controversy."

Sir James Dalrymple has understood a passage in an ancient deed, respecting a dispute between the Culdees and the canons of St Andrews, as proving that the former celebrated divine ordinances in a manner different from that of the Church of Rome. Goodall observes that he has misunderstood the sense; as the language merely signifies that inquiry was to be made "if these Culdees had sung or said mass, while they were not at liberty, *sic ligati*, as lying under ecclesiastical censure." Goodall has undoubtedly given the genuine meaning of the passage.

But there is a proof of this difference, as to the mode of

administering divine ordinances, which cannot easily be set aside. In the Extracts from the Register of St Andrews, it is said: "The Culdees celebrated their office, after their own manner, in a certain very small corner of the church." This, as Sir Robert Sibbald remarks, "insinuates that their way of performing the divine service differed from the Roman way, which at that time [in the reign of Alexander I.] came to be followed by many of the other clergy."

They are represented in these extracts as having been, for a long time, chargeable with this offensive conduct. "After the death of any of the Culdees, their wives, or children, or relations, appropriated the possessions which they had held, and even the offerings made at the altar, at which they did not serve. Nor could this evil be cured till the time of King Alexander [I.] of blessed memory, a great friend of the holy Church of God."

Dr Ledwick, although he opposes the idea that the Culdean constitution had any favourable aspect towards presbytery, views this passage as a clear proof of their resistance to the Romish innovations. "The Register of St Andrews," he says, "informs us that the Culdees, relaxing in discipline, were deprived of their possessions; but King Alexander restored them conditionally, that they should be more attentive in attending divine service, which they neglected, except when the king or bishop was present; performing, however, their own office in their own way in a small corner of the church. This account is obscure, merely because the truth is not related. For the registry acquaints us, when Alexander began the reform in the church of St Andrews, there was no one to serve at the altar of the blessed apostle, St Andrew, or to celebrate mass. This shews that the Culdees, who were settled there, paid no respect to these holy relicks, or to the mass, but chose rather to forfeit their church and property than desert their principles; preferring their ancient office with integrity of heart, in a corner, to the possession of the choir and its superstitious pageantry. Their office was Gallican, and very different from the Roman. We are sure it was not the mass, which Pope Gregory [Epist. 63. l. 7.] confesses was the work of a private person, and not of apostolic authority. The Anglo-Saxons accepted the Roman office, but the British and Irish retained their primitive forms."

This appears to be a just view of the narrative. For the weight of the charge seems to rest here, that they did not worship canonically. It is not asserted, that they did not continue to perform divine service regularly. Their crime was, that they performed it, not at the altar, but in a corner of the church; not with pomp, except when they were obliged to conform on special occasions; not after the Roman pattern, but after their own manner. The character given to Alexander also deserves our attention. He was "a great friend of holy church;" that is, according to the spirit of the writer, he was zealous for the Romish rites, and warmly attached to their keenest abettors.

The mode of expression used, as to the condition on which the Culdees were to enjoy the privileges restored to them, corresponds to the rest of the narration. It does not signify, as it has been rendered: "on this express condition, that the service of God should be restored in the church;" but, "that in the church itself a proper form of divine service should be constituted," or "set up." The religion, to be framed for the service of God, is explained of service at the altar of the blessed Apostle, and celebration of the mass, nay, the celebration of it there,—at the altar, and in no other part of the church.

Wyntown, like a good catholic, speaks as if there had been no religion at all at St Andrews, before the blessed change made by Alexander the First.

11

Saynt Androwys cytè he come til :
Thare in hys devotyoune
He *ordanyd to be relygyowne,*
And stedfastly that to be done.—
Wyth consent of Dawy yhyng
Hys ayre, nest for to be kyng,
Hys brodyr, and Erle of Huntyngtown,
At Sanct Androwys *religyowne*
Fra thine to be gave his gud will.
                    Cronykil, B. vii. c. 5. ver. 70.

It was to be at St Andrews *fra thine,* that is, from thenceforth. The term *relygyowne,* as used by Wyntown, seems
strictly to denote "a religious order," or "a religious foundation for a monastic order." But it is evidently used to the
exclusion of the Culdees, as if they had been totally unworthy of so honourable a designation.

I have no doubt that their practical opposition to celibacy
was one great cause of the persecution carried on against
them, how much soever it might be veiled. As the Roman
system gained ground, that bond, which the allwise God
instituted as honourable in men of all characters, came to be
reckoned quite inconsistent with the sanctity of the clergy.

We have a pretty clear proof of this in Myln's Lives of the
Bishops of Dunkeld, formerly referred to. Speaking of the
Culdees in the monastery of Dunkeld, he says : " They were
religious men, although they had wives, according to the
custom of the oriental church ; but when it pleased the
supreme Moderator of the whole of Christendom, crescenteque
Principum *devotione* et *sanctitate,* and the devotion and
holiness of princes being on the increase, David the holy
king,—having changed the monastery, erected it into a
cathedral church, and having rejected the Culdees, *repudiatis
Kelledeis,* appointed a bishop and canons, and ordained the
monastery to be henceforth a secular college." Here a popish
writer plainly enough owns that the Culdees were repudiated

by David, with the consent of the Pope; because their living in wedlock was, in consequence of the increase of devotion, deemed unworthy of the sacred character. They were themselves divorced, because they would not agree to divorce their wives.

The zealous friends of the Roman interest did not consider the Culdees as properly brethren. Robert, formerly prior of Scone, was elected Bishop of St Andrews about the year 1126. He chose rather to continue without the exercise of his function, than to acknowledge the Culdees as his clergy. "In his church," says the Register of St Andrews, "he neither had, nor inclined to have any power, till the Lord should procure for him that society which he wished for divine service. He had resolved not to associate himself to priests of other churches, lest, differing in sentiment, the fabric might be ruined ere it was well founded." It is in this manner that the Culdees are spoken of.

Is it said that Robert was unwilling to acknowledge them as his clergy, because they did not profess celibacy? This, so far from being an objection, is a confirmation of what we mean to prove,—that the Culdees would not submit to the Romish authority. Robert, indeed, was chosen bishop for the express purpose of bringing the Scots to a closer conformity with Rome. He was a native of England, and having been a canon *Sti Oswaldi de Nostellis*, near Pontrefact in that country, was far more attached, than our countrymen, to the Romish rites.

The celebrated St Bernard, formerly mentioned, describes the Irish Christians, who were Culdees, as if they had been wild beasts, because they did not comply with the Roman innovations. In his life of Malachy, when relating that he was made Bishop of Connor, he says that "he came not to men, but to beasts, absolute barbarians, a stubborn, stiffnecked, and ungovernable generation, and abominable; Christians in name, but in reality pagans." The grounds of this severe crimination immediately follow : "They neither pay tithes, nor first-fruits, they do not enter into lawful marriage, [not being married by the clergy,] they do not go to confession; no one can be found who applies for the prescription of penance, nor any one who will prescribe it." Elsewhere he says, as we have formerly seen, that Malachy "anew introduced the most salutary use of confession, and the sacrament of confirmation."

CHAPTER XI.

*The judgment of the adherents of Rome concerning the Culdees.
—Of the Synod of Streoneshalch.—Of Colman and Adam-
nan.—Government not the only ground of difference with the
Romanists.—Charge brought by Richard of Hexham against
the Scots.—Character given of the Culdees by Dr Henry.—
Of the Synod of Cealhythe.—Their Character as given by
Gibbon.—Of Clemens, Samson, and Virgilius.—Speech of
Gilbert Murray.*

THIS hostility between the Culdees and the Romanists was
of a very ancient date.   If, on some occasions, the warm
adherents of Rome seemed unwilling to fraternize with the
Culdees, they were only returning a compliment which had
been paid to themselves several centuries before.   The dislike
was indeed mutual.   Bede gives an extract of a letter from
Laurence, who succeeded Augustine, as Bishop of Canterbury,
A. 605, to the Scots, who inhabited Ireland, in which he says:
"When the see apostolic—sent us to these western parts to
preach to the pagan nations, and we happened to come into
this island, which is called Britain, we held both the Britons
and Scots in great esteem for sanctity before we knew them;
believing that they conducted themselves according to the
custom of the universal church.   But becoming acquainted
with the Britons, we thought that the Scots had been
better.   We have, however, learned from Bishop Dagan,
who came into this aforesaid island, and from the abbot
Columban in France, that the Scots no way differ from the
Britons in their behaviour.   For Bishop Dagan, coming to
us, not only refused to eat with us, but even to take his
repast in the same house in which we were entertained.   This
Dagan, it is said, came from the monastery of Bangor, in Ire-

land, to be Bishop to the Scots.   It is evident that he treated
the votaries of Rome, not excepting the Bishop of Canterbury
himself, as if they had been actually excommunicated.   He
viewed them as men with whom he was not so much as to
eat; nay, as even communicating pollution to the place
where they did eat.

Bede, afterwards speaking of Caedwal, King of the Britons,
who "bore the name and made a profession of Christianity,"
when describing his hostility to the Angles, says: "Nor did
he pay any respect to the Christian religion, which had newly
sprung up among them; forasmuch as, even to this day, it is
customary with the Britons to view the faith and religion of
the Angles as of no account, and to hold no more communion
with them than with the heathen."

It is evident that the pertinacity of the Culdees greatly
piqued the Romanists, who deemed it the highest presumption in men, living in such distant regions, to pretend in any
thing to differ from those who pleaded the transmission of
the keys from the apostle Peter.   At a synod, held at *Streoneshalch*, now Whitby in England, A. 662, called for the purpose of settling the controversy about Easter, the Roman
clergy urged the authority of Peter: but Bishop Colman,
and the Culdee presbyters, good simple men, reason as if the
authority of John the apostle had been of as much weight
as the other.   Wilfrid, however, a Northumbrian abbot, who
"had gone to Rome to learn the ecclesiastical doctrine,"
brought back with him, if he made no other acquirement,
the lofty tone of the mistress of nations.   Thus he replies to
Colman: "As for you and your companions, beyond a doubt
you sin, if, having heard the decree of the apostolic see, yea
of the catholic church, and the same confirmed from the holy
scriptures, you refuse to obey it.   For, although your fathers
were holy, do you think that their small number, in a corner
of the remotest island, is to be preferred to the catholic church
of Christ throughout the world?"

Notwithstanding the supposition with respect to the sanctity of their predecessors, he seems not very willing to admit it. For he had previously reminded them, in reference to Columba and his followers, whose sanctity Colman had said was confirmed by signs from heaven, that many in the day of judgment should say to our Lord, that in his name they had prophesied, &c., to whom he should reply, that he never knew them. Although King Oswy decided in favour of Wilfrid, Colman was not convinced; but, "perceiving that his doctrine was rejected, and his *sect* (as Bede expresses it) despised, he left his bishopric at Lindisfarne, and, having carried his adherents with him, returned to Scotland.

We learn that this Wilfrid, afterwards being made a bishop, "by his doctrine introduced into the churches of the Angles a great many rules of the catholic observance. Whence it followed, that the catholic institution daily increasing, all the Scots, who had resided among the Angles, either conformed to these, or returned to their own country."

About forty years after, another attempt was made to subject the Scots to the Roman authority with respect to Easter, by a person of such respectability and estimation among them, that, if any one could have prevailed, he must have done it. This was no other than the celebrated Adamnan, whose conversion, and attempts to proselytize his adherents, are thus narrated by Bede: "Adamnan, presbyter and abbot of the monks who were in the island of Hij, being sent ambassador by the nation to Aldfrid, King of the Angles, and having tarried for some time in that province, witnessed the canonical rites of the church. Being earnestly admonished by many, who were more learned, that he should not, with a handful of adherents, and those situated in an extreme corner of the world, presume to live in opposition to the universal custom of the church, either in relation to the observation of Easter, or any other decrees whatsoever: he changed his mind, so that he most willingly preferred those things which he had seen and heard in the churches of the Angles to the custom which he and his people had observed. Returning home, he was at pains to bring his own people who were in Hij, or who were subject to that monastery, into that path of truth, which he had himself become acquainted with, and embraced with his whole heart. But he could not prevail. He then sailed to Ireland, and preaching to the people there, and declaring, by modest exhortation, the lawful time of Easter, reduced many of them, almost all, indeed, who were free from the dominion of those of Hij, to the catholic unity."

Bede then informs us, that, returning from Ireland, where he had canonically celebrated this festival, he made another attempt at Hij; "most earnestly recommending to his own monastery the catholic observation of Easter; not more successfully, however, than before." But the good abbot died before the return of this solemnity; which the venerable historian views as a very happy circumstance; "the divine goodness," he says, "so ordering it, that this man, who was a great lover of peace and unity, should be snatched away to eternal life, before he should be obliged, on the return of the time of Easter, to engage in a far hotter contention with those who were unwilling to follow him in the way of truth."

With what warmth does this candid and worthy writer express himself on a subject of so little importance; as they differed only as to the particular day on which this festival should be celebrated! But this trivial difference of the Scots swelled into a crime, being viewed as gross disobedience to the holy apostolic see.

"It appears," says Toland, "that as low as the 10th century, the famous contest about the celebration of Easter, a question in itself unnecessary and insignificant, was still kept on foot in these islands; as Usher judiciously observes out of the anonymous writer of Chrysostom's Life." This is not stated with sufficient accuracy: for the good bishop seemed to view the proof as extending only to the middle of the ninth century.

The friends of episcopacy are anxious to have it believed, that whatever difference the adherents of Rome had with the Culdees, they had none with respect to the form of government. Bede, when giving an account of the ordination of Ceadda by Wini, with the assistance of two British bishops, says, that, "except Wini, there was not then any bishop canonically ordained in all Britain." This the learned Selden understands, as referring to the mode of ordination at Hij by presbyters. I confess that I cannot go so far as Selden : for Bede seems especially to have in his eye what was denominated the *quartadeciman heresy*. But we are not hence to conclude, that the Romanists were satisfied with the ecclesiastical government of the Scots. We meet with several vestiges of the contrary. The fathers of the synod of Vernon in France, A. 755, speak of those "bishops who wandered about, having no parish ; neither," say they, "do we know what kind of ordination they had." This has been understood of the Scots bishops ; especially as express mention is made of them in the second council of Cabilon, or Chalons, A. 813. "There are," it is said in their Acts, "in certain places Scots, who call themselves bishops, and contemning many, without the licence of their lords or superiors, ordain presbyters and deacons ; the ordination of whom, because, for the most part, it falls into the Simonian heresy, and is subject to many errors, we all, with one consent, decree, that it ought to be invalidated by all possible means."

In like manner we find, among the works of Peter of Blois, a letter written about the year 1170, and attributed to Richard, Archbishop of Canterbury, in which he complains that "in these days certain false bishops of Ireland, or pretending the barbarism of the Scottish language, although they have received from no one imposition of hands, discharge episcopal functions to the people." He enjoins all his clergy that, throughout their dioceses, they should "take care to prohibit the episcopal ministrations of all belonging to a barbarous nation, or of uncertain ordination."

Bede testifies that the monastery of Rippon being given by King Aldfrid to those "who followed the Scots," they, "being left to their choice, would rather quit the place than receive the catholic Easter, and other canonical rites, according to the custom of the Roman and apostolic church." It seems highly probable, that, among "the other canonical rites," there might be a reference to their peculiar mode of ordination.

Notwithstanding all these marks of discrepancy between the Culdees and the Church of Rome, it is surprising that any, who call themselves Protestants, should not hesitate to assert that the points in which they differed "did not at all affect the faith." While the friends of the Reformation, in other countries, have manifested a laudable eagerness to shew that, during the darkest ages of the anti-Christian dominion, there were still some to "contend for the faith once delivered to the saints," a *nubes testium*, in their successive generations refusing to join with others, who, according to the language of inspiration, "wondered after the beast;" it is affecting to observe that, among a people so highly distinguished as we have been, any should be found, who are determined at all events to affirm, that all the errors and corruptions of the Church of Rome were greedily and universally adopted by their ancestors as soon as they were introduced.

The account which we are able to give of the points in which they differed is indeed very imperfect. But when the extreme difficulty of discovering the genuine doctrines of those who opposed the Romish innovations is considered, as all the memorials of these passed through the hands of prejudiced writers; when we reflect on the gross falsifications of history with respect to other witnesses for the truth, especially the Waldenses and Albigenses, who have been generally dressed up by popish historians, like those prepared for an *Auto da Fé;* we rather have reason to wonder that so many hints have escaped from these writers, which throw light on the true character of the Culdees.

It has been seen that they agreed with the ancient Britons in faith. Now, from the testimony of Bede, which, in this instance, cannot reasonably be called in question, we learn that the controversy about Easter was by no means the only cause of discord between the Romans and them. For he says that Aldhelm, Abbot of Malmesbury, "by the order of a synod of his nation, wrote an excellent book against the error of the Britons, according to which error, as they do not celebrate Easter in the proper time, they hold a great many other things contrary to ecclesiastical purity and peace."

A charge, somewhat of a similar nature, is exhibited against them in the Register of St Andrews. It is there said, that "those, who are called Culdees, lived more according to their own opinion and the tradition of men, than according to the statutes of the holy fathers." At first view, things might here seem to be opposed, which are in themselves virtually the same; "the tradition of men," and "the statutes of the holy fathers." But they are meant to be viewed as directly contrary. For by "the tradition of men" we are to understand that which was transmitted to them by their own predecessors, as adhering to the Culdean doctrines and mode of worship. To these they were so attached, because they accounted them scriptural, that they would not, like the votaries of Rome, implicitly receive what was imposed on them as the doctrine of unerring fathers, many of whom had been canonized as saints.

The crimination brought by Richard of Hexham, against our ancestors, has been keenly argued by former writers on this subject. "The Scots," he says, "for a long time differing from the Cis-alpine, nay, almost from the universal church, seemed too much to favour the destestable memory of Peter of Lyons, and his apostasy : but, by the inspiration of divine grace, they all unanimously received, with great veneration, the mandate of Pope Innocent, and his legate." Sir James Dalrymple had inferred from this passage, that the writer meant to charge the Scots with attachment to the doctrine of the Leonists or Waldenses, who strenuously opposed the errors of the Church of Rome. Gillan has asserted that the ancient writer refers only to the adherence of the Scots, for about eight years, to the anti-pope Anacletus. But he does not seem to have invalidated Sir James's observation, that it cannot easily be conceived, that, if Richard referred merely to their adherence to the anti-pope, he would not only have compared the Scots with the Leonists, condemned heretics, but exhibited this charge against them exclusively ; as all the French and English were equally attached to the schismatical Anacletus. Here the ancient writer undoubtedly takes the opportunity afforded by their present conduct, of giving vent to an old grudge.

Gillan seems to triumph in the proof of the complete subjection of the Scots, said to have been given by their cordial reception of the legate. I am far from saying that they were nowise subjected to the papal authority, even before this time. But there are very different degrees of subjection : and it is well known that it has been always considered as a strong proof of the extreme reluctance of our forefathers to submit to the claims of the Roman see, that we have not the slightest evidence that a legate had been ever received in Scotland, or even sent thither, before this time, A. 1125, when John of Crema appeared in this character. It cannot be denied, that in a far earlier age, legates had been sent to countries of less note ; because it was known that they would be made welcome.

But even the reception given to this deputy affords no great proof of the strength of papal authority in this country. He came no farther than to Roxburgh, which was long the

very border of the Scottish territory.   Had he reckoned himself a welcome visitor, especially considering the novelty of
the thing, he would in all probability have ventured a little
farther.   Prudence must have dictated this, in order more
firmly to establish that subjection which had hitherto been
refused.   But this very principle seems to have suggested a
course directly the reverse.   John of Crema was not certain
as to the ground he was treading on.   It was as really debate-
able ground to him as ever it had been between the adverse
kingdoms.   He therefore acted like a man who wished to
rest satisfied even with the semblance of subjection.

It is said, indeed, that "all unanimously received him with
great veneration."   But it plainly appears from the narrative,
that we are to understand the all of the Scottish nation as
acting merely by proxy.   He was received, in the manner
described, by the priest-ridden David, and by a few of the
courtiers and bishops, who wished in all things to conform to
Rome.   The legate seems wisely to have judged, that it was
not expedient to put the unanimity of the Scottish nation
fairly to the test.   "I am sure," says Gillan, "the style is
high enough, *rogando mandamus.*"   But is this an argument
of any weight, in judging of papal pretensions?   Has it ever
been doubted, that it was still the policy of Rome to talk in a
lofty tone: or suppposed, that we were to form an estimate
of the real power of the Vatican from the noise made by its
thunder?

Here it may not be improper to subjoin the character given
of the Culdees by two late historians, each of them celebrated
in his line, both distinguished for industry and learning; and
although antipodes in their views respecting religion, giving
a similar testimony on this subject.

"Ever since the violent disputes," says Dr Henry, "between
the Scots and English of the Roman communion, about the
time of keeping Easter, and the retreat of the Scotch clergy
out of England, there had been a violent animosity between

the churches of England and Scotland.   This animosity was
very strong in this century, as appears from the fifth canon
of the council of Ceal-hythe, A.D. 816; which decrees, that
no Scotch priest shall be allowed to perform any duty of his
function in England.   The Scots and Picts were instructed
and governed by their own clergy; who, being educated at
home, and having little intercourse with foreign nations,
retained much of the plainness and simplicity of the primitive
times in their forms of worship.   These clergy were called
Kuldees, both before and after this period: a name which
some derive from the two Latin words *Cultores Dei*, and
others from the *kills* or cells in which they lived.   They were
a kind of presbyters, who lived in small societies, and
travelled over the neighbouring countries, preaching, and
administering the sacraments.   In each of these cells there
was one who had some kind of superintendancy over the rest,
managed their affairs, and directed their missions; but
whether or not he enjoyed the title and authority of a bishop
in this period is not certainly known.   The council of Ceal-
hythe seems to have suspected that he did not; for the chief
reasons assigned by that council for refusing to keep communion with these Scotch Culdees were,—That they had no
metropolitans amongst them,—paid little regard to other
orders,—and that the council did not know by whom they
were ordained, *i.e.* whether they were ordained by bishops or
not.   The rectors or bishops of the several cells of Kuldees
were both chosen, and ordained, or consecrated, by the
members of these societies; which was probably the very
thing with which the council of Ceal-hythe was dissatisfied.
When the cells or monasteries of Scotland came to be
enlarged, better built, and better endowed, they were long
after this possessed by these Kuldees or secular clergy, who
had the privilege of choosing the bishops in those places where
bishops' sees were established."

The other testimony referred to, is that of an elegant

writer, who, although very sparing of his praise to ecclesiastics, could not withhold the following tribute from the Culdees. It is, indeed, given with that drawback which might be expected from a writer of his principles. "Iona," he says, "one of the Hebrides, which was planted by the Irish monks, diffused over the northern regions a doubtful ray of science and superstition. This small, though not barren spot, Iona, Hy, or Columbkill, only two miles in length, and one mile in breadth, has been distinguished, 1. By the monastery of St Columba, founded A.D. 566; whose abbot exercised an extraordinary jurisdiction over the bishops of Caledonia. 2. By a classic library, which afforded some hopes of an entire Livy; and, 3. By the tombs of sixty kings, Scots, Irish, and Norwegians, who reposed in holy ground."

It is not without sufficient grounds, that David Buchanan has given the following testimony to the noble resistance made by the Culdees to the Roman corruptions. "About the end of the seventh age, men from Scotland, given to ambition and avarice, went frequently to Rome for preferment in the church; and seeing it lay much that way then, they did their best to advance the design of the Romish party, wherein all the skill of worldly men was employed, both in Rome and among the Scots of that party. Many men went to and fro, between Rome and Scotland, to bring the Scots to a full obedience unto Rome, and conformity. By name, there was one Boniface sent from Rome to Scotland, a main agent for Rome in these affairs; but he was opposed openly by several of the Scots Culdees, or divines, namely, by Clemens and Samson, who told him freely, ' That he, and those of his party, studied to bring men to the subjection of the pope, and the slavery of Rome, withdrawing them from obedience to Christ;' and so, in plain terms, they reproached him and his assistants with this, ' That they were corruptors of Christ's doctrine, establishing a sovereignty in the Bishop of Rome, as the only successor of the apostles, excluding other bishops; that they used and commanded clerical tonsure; that they forbade priests' marriage, extolling celibacy; that they caused prayers to be made for the dead, and erected images in the churches;' to be short, 'That they had introduced into the church many tenets, rites, and ceremonies, unknown to the ancient and pure times, yea, contrary to them.' For the which and the like, the said Clemens, and those that were constant to the truth with him, were excommunicated at Rome as heretics, as you have in the third volume of the *Concels*, although the true reasons of their excommunication be not there set down."

Petrie gives materially the same account. "Many did preach and write against him [Pope Zachary] and his superstitions, as Adalbert, a French bishop, Samson, a Scot, Bishop of Auxerre, and Virgilius, an Irishman, Bishop of Juvavia; as Nauclerus and Aventine do record. Boniface dilateth them unto Pope Zachary; and as *Bern. Lutzenbury in Catal.* writeth, the Pope, in a synod at Rome, condemneth them, depriveth them of their priesthood, and excommunicateth them before they were heard; and when they sought to be heard, and plead their cause in a synod, Boniface denied access unto them, and said, ' Excommunicated men should not be admitted into a synod, nor have the benefit of the law.'— One Clemens did reprove Boniface, 1. That he did so advance the authority of the Roman bishop, seeing all teachers are equally successors of the apostles. 2. That he condemned the marriage of priests. 3. That he did speak too much for the monkish life. 4. That he appointed masses for the dead, and other new rites unknown in the church heretofore. *Avintin. Annal. lib. 3. et Epist. Zachar. ad Bonifac. in tom. 2. Concil.*"

Usher, in his *Sylloge*, has given a letter written by Boniface, Archbishop of Mentz, to Pope Zachary, concerning Adalbert and Clement. Of the latter he says: " But another heretic, named Clement, contends against the catholic church, denies the canons, and reproves the proceedings of the churches of

Christ, and refuses the explanations given by the holy fathers, Jerome, Augustine, and Gregory. Contemning the rights of synods, he expressly affirms that he can be a lawful Christian bishop after having two sons born to him in adultery." He is also charged with heretical doctrine as to the descent of Christ into hell, and predestination. But it is evident that his great heresy was, that he did not submit to the absolute authority of the church, and the infallible decisions of the fathers. When he is accused of having sons born to him in adultery, all that can be meant is, that they were born to him in marriage, a state not lawful for one in holy orders. He acknowledged them as his sons, and vindicated his conduct. Had he called them only nephews, and his wife a spiritual sister, he might probably have escaped without any accusation.

Flacius Illyricus, in like manner, assigns the opposition of Clement to the corruptions of Rome as the real reason of his condemnation. Nor did his enemies stop here. He was given over to the secular power, and devoted to the flames.

An ecclesiastical historian, who has been generally celebrated, both for industry and for impartiality, gives the following eulogy of him. " As to Clement, his character and sentiments were maliciously misrepresented, since it appears, by the best and most authentic accounts, that he was much better acquainted with the doctrines and true principles of Christianity than Boniface himself; and hence he is considered by many as a confessor and sufferer for the truth in this barbarous age." His learned translator adds this note. " The great heresy of Clement seems to have been his preferring the decisions of scripture to decrees of councils and the opinions of the fathers, which he took the liberty to reject when they were not conformable to the word of God."

Flacius gives a similar testimony concerning Samson. "The intimate companion of Clement," he says, " Samson, a Scotsman, was among those bishops who accused Boniface of being the fabricator of falsehoods, the troubler of peace and of the Christian religion, and the corruptor of it both by word and by writing. Although prepared to demonstrate his assertions from the word of God, he was not admitted to a fair trial, but excommunicated without being heard, &c. John of Mailros, a Scotsman, and Cladius Clement, sprung from the same nation, flourished at the same time. Concerning John of Mailros, Antoninus relates that he displeased the Romans, because, adhering to the Greeks, he impugned the papal dogmas."

Sir James Dalrymple has referred to a speech made by Gilbert Murray, a young Scottish clerk, in the presence of a cardinal, who acted as the Pope's legate, A. 1176. It is given by Petrie from an old MS. Register of Dunkeld; and deserves our attention, not only because of the honourable allusion made to the clergy of Iona, and the proof which it affords of the general reception, in that early period, of the account given of them by Bede as perfectly authentic; but also as demonstrating the high sense of independence that the church of Scotland has always retained, and the conviction, which then generally prevailed, of the obligations that the Church of England lay under to her sister-church, how much soever she might wish to forget them.

Malcolm, surnamed the Maiden, and his brother William, having given homage to Henry I. for the lands which they held in England, he thought of extending the claim of subjection to the church. With this view, he and William, King of Scotland, having met at Norham, with some of the clergy, he urged that they should acknowledge the Archbishop of York as their metropolitan. But at this time they prevailed to get the business delayed. Next year, however, he renewed his attempt. Hugo, Cardinal of St Angelo, having been sent from Rome, summoned all the Scotch bishops to appear before him in Northampton. When they were assembled there, with many of their clergy, he used a great deal of art to cajole them into a compliance with the claims of the Archbishop of York. The bishops, it is said, were silent, lest they should offend the legate. But young Gilbert rose up, and made the following address, as recorded in the register formerly referred to.

" It is true, English nation, thou mightest have been noble, and more noble than some other nations, if thou hadst not craftily turned the power of thy nobility, and the strength of thy fearful might, into the presumption of tyranny, and thy knowledge of liberal science into the shifting glosses of sophistry; but thou disposest not thy purposes as if thou wert led with reason, and being puffed up with thy strong armies, and trusting in thy great wealth, thou attemptest, in thy wretched ambition and lust of domineering, to bring under thy jurisdiction thy neighbour provinces and nations, more noble, I will not say, in multitude or power, but in lineage and antiquity; unto whom, if thou wilt consider ancient records, thou shouldst rather have been humbly obedient, or at least, laying aside thy rancour, have reigned together in perpetual love: and now with all wickedness of pride that thou shewest, without any reason or law, but in thy ambitious power, thou seekest to oppress thy mother the Church of Scotland, which from the beginning hath been catholique and free, and which brought thee, when thou wast straying in the wilderness of heathenism, into the safe-guard of the true faith, and way unto life, even unto Jesus Christ, the author of eternal rest. She did wash thy kings, and princes, and people, in the laver of holy baptism: she taught thee the commandments of God, and instructed thee in moral duties; she did accept many of thy nobles, and others of meaner rank, when they were desirous to learn to read, and gladly gave them daily entertainment without price, books also to read, and instruction freely; she did also appoint, ordain, and consecrate thy bishops and priests: by the space of thirty years and above, she maintained the primacy and pontifical dignity within thee on the north side of Thames, as Beda witnesseth.

"And now, I pray, what recompense renderest thou now unto her, that hath bestowed so many benefits on thee ? is it bondage ? or such as Judea rendered unto Christ, evil for good ? It seemeth no other thing. Thou unkinde vine, how art thou turned into bitterness ! We looked for grapes, and thou bringest forth wilde grapes; for judgment, and behold iniquity and crying. If thou couldest do as thou wouldest, thou wouldest draw thy mother the Church of Scotland, whom thou shouldest honour with all reverence, into the basest and most wretched bondage. Fie for shame ! what is more base, when thou wilt do no good, to continue in doing wrong ? Even the serpents will not do harm to their own, albeit they cast forth to the hurt of others; the vice of ingratitude hath not so much moderation; an ungrateful man doth wrack and massacre himself, and he despiseth and minceth the benefits for which he should be thankful, but multiplieth and en-largeth injuries. It was a true saying of Seneca, (I see) The more some doe owe, they hate the more; a small debt maketh a grievous enemy. What sayest thou, David ? it is true, They rendered me evil for good, and hatred for my love. It is a wretched thing (saith Gregory) to serve a lord, who cannot be appeased with whatsoever obeysance.

"Therefore, thou Church of England, doest as becomes thee not : thou thinkest to carry what thou cravest, and to take what is not granted. Seek what is just, if thou wilt have pleasure in what thou seekest. And to the end I do not weary others with my words, albeit I have no charge to speak for the liberty of the Church of Scotland, and albeit all the clergy of Scotland would think otherwise, yet I dissent from subjecting her, and I do appeal unto the Apostolical Lord, unto whom immediately she is subject; and if it were needful for me to die in the cause, here I am ready to lay

down my neck unto the sword.   Nor do I think it expedient
to advise any more with my lords the prelates ; nor, if they
will do otherwise, do I consent unto them : for it is more
honest to deny quickly what is demanded unjustly, then
[*i.e.* than] to drive off time by delays, seeing he is the less
deceived, who is refused betimes."

The historian adds : " When Gilbert had so made an end,
some English, both prelates and nobles, commend the yong
clerk, that he had spoken so boldly for his nation, without
flattering, and not abashed at the gravity of such authority ;
but others, because he spoke contrary unto their minde, said,
A Scot is naturally violent, and *In naso Scoti piper.*   But
Roger, Archbishop of York, which principally had moved
this business, to bring the Church of Scotland into his see,
uttered a groan, and then with a merry countenance laid his
hand on Gilbert's head, saying, *Ex tua pharetra non exiit illa
sagitta ;* as if he had said, When ye stand in a good cause, do
not forethink what ye shall say, for in that hour it shall be
given unto you.   This Gilbert was much respected at home
after that.   And Pope Celestin put an end unto this debate ;
for he sent his bull unto King William, granting that, neither
in ecclesiastical nor civil affairs, the nation should answer
unto any forain judge whatsoever, except onely unto the
Pope, or his legate specially constituted.   So far in that
Register of Dunkel."

Archbishop Spotswood has certainly given a more natural
interpretation of these words, *Ex tua pharetra,* &c., " Meaning," he says, " that he was set on to speak by some others of
greater note."   Mackenzie, however, seems to be mistaken in
ascribing the other interpretation to the translator.   " But
Mr Petrie," he says, " the ecclesiastical historian of the Presbyterian party, thinks, that by this expression the Archbishop
of York was against all set-forms."   Petrie undoubtedly gives
this as the gloss of the chronicler.   For he subjoins : " So
far in that Register."

The appeal made by Murray to the Pope, may perhaps be viewed as a proof that the Church of Scotland acknowledged complete subjection to Rome. But this seems to have been the first instance of an appeal being formally made to the papal see. As it was the act of a single person, it is to be observed, that even he had the highest sense of the liberty and independence of his mother-church. He doubtless thought that they were shut up to it, and considered it as the least of two evils. From the power of England, from the partiality of the papal legate, and, perhaps, from the disposition of others to submit, he saw that the only question was, as to the form of their dependence; and that it was better to submit to a distant authority, than to one at hand, that would intermeddle in every ecclesiastical matter; to an authority by this time almost universally recognised, than to the newly-invented claim of a sister-church, nay, of a see, that had originally been supplied by missionaries from Scotland. He must also have seen, that, by submitting to the see of York, the Church of Scotland would inevitably be subjected to a double yoke; that see being itself completely under the papal dominion.

This appeal, however reluctantly made, seems to have had its full effect. For, although the legate was previously devoted to the English interest, it is evident, that both he and his master were so well pleased to have a formal recognition of the papal authority in Scotland, that they paid no further regard to the vamped-up pretensions of the Church of England.

This Gilbert, it is said, was a son of the family of Moray, or Murray, afterwards designed of Bothwell. His conduct was ·so generally approved, that he was soon after made Dean of Murray and great Chamberlain of Scotland. On the death of Adam of Mailros, he was promoted to the bishopric of Caithness. He died A. 1245, and was afterwards canonized.

CHAPTER XII.

VARIOUS were the means employed for suppressing the Culdees, who were viewed with so jealous an eye by the votaries of the papal chair, and who had all along presented so powerful a barrier to its influence. This was first attempted in an artful manner. "It is observable," says Sir James Dalrymple "that the Romish church did advance very warily, and by slow steps, endeavouring to gain the Culdean abbots to their partie, by promoting them to bishoprics to be erected, and by preserving to the Culdees (possessed of parochial churches) their benefices for their life-time, and making the suppression of these churches in favours of the new-erected Romish abbacies only to take place after the incumbent's death; and frequently these concessions bear the consent of the presbyter or churchman incumbent, with the reservation of his own right during life-time."

In the passage quoted, as well as in p. 286, Sir James gives several proofs of the annexation of parish churches, formerly occupied by Culdee presbyters, to the newly-erected abbeys.

The learned Dr Ledwich gives a similar account. "It was not easy to eradicate a reverence founded on solid piety, exemplary charity, and superior learning; or to commit sudden violence on characters where such qualities were found. The Roman emissaries were therefore obliged to exert all their cunning to remove these favourable prejudices, and where force could not, seduction often prevailed. The alternative of expulsion or acquiescence must ever strongly operate on human imbecility: in a few instances the latter was chosen: thus, about the year 1127, Gregory, Abbot of the Culdean monastery of Dunkeld, and Andrew his successor, were made bishops, the first of Dunkeld, the other of Caithness.—The same policy was followed in Ireland. The president of the Culdees was made præcentor; he was to have the most honourable seat at table, and every respect from his corps. Such little distinctions, while they flattered and saved appearances, were fatal to the Culdees; many breaches were made in their rights, and at last, they lost all their privileges, their old institute, and retained barely the name of their pristine celebrity."

An increase of the number of the episcopal sees seems, indeed, to have been one of the measures adopted for the overthrow of the Culdean influence. The idea may excite a smile from those who affect to speak contemptuously of this religious body. But there can be no doubt that their influence, among the lower classes especially, had been great. How much soever the testimony of Boece may be despised, when he pretends to narrate the history of a very early period; he certainly deserves attention, when speaking of things almost within his own observation. "The name," he says, "acquired such a degree of authority among the vulgar, that all priests, almost to our own times, were commonly designed, without distinction, Culdees, that is, worshippers of God." David L., who seems to have been determined to depress this order, and who pursued a variety of measures which had this tendency, added at least four bishoprics to those which had been erected before his time; and it is by no means improbable, that this was one thing that he had in view in extending the power of the prelacy.

In connexion with this, I may add, that the description

of the prelates invested, from this time forward, strongly corroborates what has been said. Sir James Dalrymple has made some observations on this head, which I shall give in his own words. "Other methods perhaps were taken to subvert the antient, and to introduce the Romish religion into this kingdom, viz. that used in England, to make the Saxons depend entirely upon Rome for their conversion, and to hinder conformity with the British Scots or Picts; that first their bishops were chosen forreigners, at least of forreign education. It is observed in Chr. Sax., that from Austine, the first Archbishop of Canterbury, there was no Saxon admitted to be archbishop there, till Brightwaldus anno 690; and just so the Norman kings of England would not admit of the Saxons to be bishops there, till the reign of Henry the Second. Our Scots kings Alexander and David have followed this patern, in choising Turgot, Eadmar, and Robert (instructed in the Romish religion in England) to be Bishops at St Andrews. John, Bishop of Glasgow, also appears to be a forreigner, and probably educat at Tours in France, whence he brought monks to Selkirk, and where he retired when he was dissatisfied with the manners of the Scots. It is said that he was consecrate by Pope Paschasius. It is plain that Robert, the first prior of St Andrews, was bred in England with the prior of St Oswald's," &c.

But the great plan devised for the overthrow of the Culdees, was the introduction of Canons Regular. These had been erected by a permanent order of the eleventh century. Being patronised by the Pope, they were devoted to the interests of the Church of Rome, and zealous for the extension of the authority of their ghostly father. They acquired credit with the superstitious, as having more appearance of sanctity than the Culdee Presbyters; especially as they lived in celibacy, while the honest Culdees laid no claim to the gift of continence. They affected far greater pomp in their worship. No sooner were these canons introduced at St Andrews, than matters assumed an appearance of what was deemed religion in those days, which had been quite unknown before. Their prior at St Andrews "wore, in all public meetings, and in solemn services upon festival days, the pontifical ornaments, viz. a mitre, gloves, ring, cross, crosier, and sandals or slippers, as the bishops; and in parliament had the precedence of all abbots and priors." The very design of their introduction into those places, where the Culdees had formerly had the power, was the establishment of this species of religion :—ut in dicta ecclesia religio *constitueretur*.

Wyntown, when speaking of the zeal of David I., commonly called the Saint, in furthering the injunctions of his brother Alexander as to the establishment of those canons, gives such an account of the aspect of matters before, as if the country, because of the more simple forms of worship, had been absolutely in a state of heathenism.

> All thus illumynyd he thys land
> Wyth kyrkis and abbays rycht pleasand,
> And othir stedis of renowne,
> Seculare, and of religyowne,
> That, or Malcolm hys fadyre
> Had weddyd Saynt Margret his modyr,
> Rwyd and sympil all tyme wes,
> Bot lyk a blynd wild bethynes.
> *Cronykil*, B. vii. c. 6 v. 125.

In some instances, where canons regular were introduced, the Culdees were tolerated, if they would not consent to live according to the canonical rule. This was the case at Loch-levin. St Serf's Isle, which formerly belonged to the Culdees, was annexed to the priory of St Andrews, to the end that a monastery of canons regular might be instituted there, with the reservation; Et Keledei, qui ibidem inventi fuerint, si regulariter vivere volueri[n]t, in pace cum eis, et sub eis, maneant. Thus they were subjected to the canons. And it is expressly required, in addition, that if they made resistance they were to be expelled from the island.

It has been supposed that the Culdees were expelled from Dunkeld as early as the year 1127, when David I. made Gregory, who had been abbot of their monastery, bishop of this see. David—mutato Monasterio, in ecclesiam cathedralem erexit: et *repudiatis Kelledeis*, episcopum et *canonicos* instituit, secularemque collegium in futurum esse ordinavit.

But Dalrymple concludes, with apparent reason, that they continued there for some time after the erection of the bishopric; and that, "although the chanoins might get into the cathedral, yet the Culdees did retain their other possessions." In support of this opinion, he refers to what he calls the large charter of David I. to the abbey of Dunfermline, which contains an exception with respect to the rights pertaining to the abbey of Dunkeld: Exceptis rectitudinibus quae ad Abbatiam de Dunkelden pertinent.

We have formerly spoken of the change of the religious foundation at Abernethy. The precise time of their suppression at Brechin cannot easily be determined. There is extant a charter of William the Lion, confirming one of David I. This is addressed to the bishops and Culdees of Brechin; *Episcopis et Keldeis in Ecclesia de Breichen*. But it appears that they had been superseded, or at least that canons had been introduced into the chapter instead of them, before the time of Robert Bruce, or soon after he came to the throne. For a charter, granted by Robert, in the second year of his reign, is addressed, *Episcopo et Canonicis de Breichen*.

William Malvoisin, Bishop of St Andrews, was a keen adversary of the Culdees. This enmity might perhaps be owing to his being educated abroad; if he was not, as some assert, a native of France. He had most probably resolved to attempt the total extinction of this respectable society. But before he would begin his great attack at St Andrews, he seems to have deemed it most prudent to try his power at Monimusk, which was within the bishopric of Aberdeen, and subject to Malvoisin as metropolitan. He might be induced to adopt this plan of procedure, partly from the remoteness of the place, as being situated in the wilds of Mar. Here he might have a more flattering prospect of success, in endeavouring to crush the power of the Culdees, than in a more populous country, where their influence was greater. Besides, if he failed here, his disgrace would be less, than if he had been defeated in the very seat of his power. He might also have a more plausible pretence for attempting their reduction here; because the seat of the bishopric having been changed, the Culdees might seem to have less ground for maintaining their claim to elect the bishop. But, in all probability, his most powerful excitement was, that, whereas the Culdees had been gradually declining in most of their monasteries, here they had received an accession of strength, as to both numbers and wealth, in consequence of the liberal donations of some of our nobles.

Notwithstanding the comparative obscurity of the place, this part of their history is of considerable importance. For it affords a striking display of the difficulties which their adversaries met with in their warfare against them. It has also been grossly misrepresented, and generally misunderstood. It is, therefore, necessary to examine it with more attention than it might otherwise seem to claim.

Sir James Dalrymple quotes an ancient writing, entitled, *Conventio inter Dominum Williclmum Episcopum Sancti Andreae et Keldeos de Monymusk;* in which it is conceded, he says, "that they should live in communnion after the manner of the Keldees," and have one oratory, one refectory, and one dormitory, "as they presently possessed it;" the half carrucate of land being secured to them, which they had from the donation of Robert, of good memory, Bishop of St Andrews; their ancient alms being also secured, and the offerings which they, and their predecessors had, from the time of Bishop Robert to the present day: "and that they submitted to the disposal of the B.[ishop]: and that there might be 12 Keldees there, and Britins the 13th, whom they were to present to the bishop, that he might be their magister or prior: and after his dimission or decease, the Keldees might choise three of their Con-keldees by common consent, and present them to the bishop or his successors, who was to choise one out of the three to be prior or magister in all time coming; and that they should not exceed the number formerly mentioned, nor substitute any person; and that they should resign, in favours of the bishop, the lands which they got from Gilchrist, Earl of Marr, and claime no right to them afterward, without the bishop's consent; and that the bishop and his successors were obliged to help and maintain the Keldees as their own, with power to him to add dew clauses, until this agreement was confirmed by the K[ing]'s authority: and Magister Britins and Andraes did swear to the agreement for themselves and the Culdees, and the seals of the parties and delegates were appended. In implement of this transaction, William Bishop of St Andrews, with consent of his archdeacon and chapter, granted to the Keldees a charter in the terms of the above agreement, with some 'additions: That the" oratory should be without a cemetery, so that the bodies of the Keldees, and of the clergy, or of the laics dwelling with them, might receive ecclesiastical sepulture in the cemetery of the pariochal church of Monymusk: "and that the prior was to swear fidelity to the bishop: the lands of Dulbechot and Fournathy, gifted by the Earl of Marr, were to be resigned to the bishop; and that, when the bishop came to reside at Monymusk, the Keldees should receive him with a solemn procession."

Hence Sir James argues, that Bishop Robert, who was elected to this see A. 1122, "was not able to subdue the Culdees of Monymusk, but obliged to make an agreement with them;" and that his successor, Malvoisin, who died A. 1237, although he "encroached farther upon them," still left them some of their peculiar privileges.

This deed of settlement was made in consequence of a reference to the papal chair. Yet did the Bishop of St Andrews, " in opposition to a solemn promise, suppress those Culdees; and place canons regular in their room at Monymusk, which became thenceforth a cell of the priory of St Andrews."

Goodall has made several remarks on the inferences deduced by Sir James Dalrymple from this deed. "The chartulary," he observes, " has a notable piece of a sentence, which Sir James has not given us; for in the article about the election of a prior, when a vacancy happened, 'the Culdees were to elect three of their fellow Culdees, by common consent, and present them to the bishop, or his successor, who was to make choice of one of the three at his will and pleasure, and that person was to swear fealty to the bishop' [here Sir James stops, but the chartulary proceeds] as Founder of the Culdees' House."

I have examined the chartulary, and find that it contains the words omitted by Sir James. If he withheld this clause, because he viewed it as tending to overthrow his hypothesis, undoubtedly it was not consistent with that candour which he has almost uniformly manifested. But, in making the quotation referred to, it does not appear that he transcribed from the chartulary itself, but from the MS. "Collection of Mr James Law of Bogis," to which he refers. Whether the deed might not be so fully extracted in that collection, I cannot pretend to say.

At any rate, Sir James has no reason for apprehension from anything contained in this deed. Nor had Goodall sufficient reason for adding: "So it is plain, the bishops founded the convents of the Culdees, and the Culdees elected the bishops, whenever they resided about the bishop's see; although not at places like Monymusk, where there was no bishop."

The following remarks naturally occur from the tenor of

this deed and are of considerable importance in the question.

1. An attempt had previously been made to change the form of the institution at Monimusk. It appears that, after the translation of the episcopal seat to Aberdeen, the bishops had wished to reduce the convent to a mere hospital; and even to represent it as having never held any higher place. For the inscription of the deed, as it stands in the chartulary of Aberdeen, is: *Commissio impetrata per Dominum Episcopum Sti Andree contra destruentes hospitalia, aut in aliam naturam convertentes, et specialiter ad reformand. hospitale sive Kildey de Monymuske, et processus super eodem.* It is perfectly clear, from the very strain of the inscription, that the innovating party wished to exhibit the Culdees as men worthy to be classed with the destroyers of hospitals, because they attempted to convert an hospital to another use than that which, as they pretend, was originally designed by the founder. They had even framed a new word for their purpose; a word which, as far as I have observed, occurs nowhere else. This is *Kildey*, which they use as if it had been synonymus with *Hospitale*. This was "a commission—for reforming the Hospital or Kildey of Monymusk." We see in what sense the Bishop of St Andrews might design himself the "Founder of the Culdees' House," and pretend a right to require that the prior should do homage to him in this character. He might be called its Founder, in the same sense in which an usurper, who has destroyed an ancient city, blotted out its very name, and built a new one on its ruins, claims this title. He had exerted himself to the utmost to change the nature of the institution, and had tried to make the very language of his country bend to his humour: as if it had been possible, by the mere witchery of a word, at once to deprive all his contemporaries of the power of recollection; or to persuade them, that what had existed for centuries as a monastery, had never been more than an hospital.

2. The limitation of their number on this occasion seems to imply that they had previously been more numerous. It is probable, indeed, that thirteen was the usual number in one house. But, unless they had exceeded this number here, or had different houses, we cannot easily conceive why they should henceforth be restricted to one oratory, one refectory, and one dormitory. Why this limitation, if they had not formerly enjoyed greater privileges? As it is certain, that Gilchrist, Earl of Mar, built a new monastery for them, it would appear that they henceforth meant to occupy two houses at Monimusk.

3. We discern the reason of their being said to act as canons. Before the change of the seat of the episcopate, they, like the Culdees in other places, had the sole power of electing the bishops. Since the translation of the see, canons regular had been instituted at Aberdeen, to whom their rights were transferred. The Culdees of Monimusk, however, asserted their claim; and seem either to have presented themselves as electors at Aberdeen, or to have made an election of their own. For the first article of the complaint, as it had been stated to the ghostly father at Rome, and as it is echoed back by him, is, that "certain Culdees, *se canonicus gerunt*, carry themselves as if they were canons." This, however, might rather apply to some who did not reside at Monimusk; because those residing there are designed *quidam alii*, "certain others." Finding that all right of taking any part in the election was denied to them, on the pretence that they were not canons; whatever aversion they might have to the change of their mode of life, they appear, at their own hand, without consulting either bishop or pope, to have erected themselves into a canonry. This, at least, is the obvious sense of the second article of complaint, as it stands in the chartulary of Aberdeen, unless it be viewed as the language of exaggeration, used in order to call forth the fulminations of the papal chair, because of their sacrilegious

intrusion. *Quidam alii Aberdonensis Dioces. infra villam de Monimuske pertinentem ad ipsum quandam canoniam regularem, eodem renitente, contra justitiam, construere non formidant, in ecclesie sue prejudicium et gravamen.* " Certain others of the diocese of Aberdeen, in the village of Monimusk, belonging to him [the Bishop of St Andrews], are not afraid iniquitously to erect a certain regular canonry, notwithstanding his opposition, to the prejudice of his church."

4. We have here a proof of the power, and at the same time a strong presumption of the ancient right, of the Culdees. From the interference of the Bishop of St Andrews, it is evident that the Bishop of Aberdeen had found them too strong for him. But even he, who seems in this instance to have claimed the dignity of primate, found it necessary to solicit the aid of the papal authority.

5. The manner in which the continued enjoyment of certain dues is expressed, clearly shews, that they had been long settled in that quarter. They are allowed to hold these, *libere et quiete, juxta quod ab antiquis temporibus retro usque ad hec tempora habuerint,* " freely and peaceably, in the same manner in which they have enjoyed them from ancient times even to the present day."

6. There is pretty good reason for concluding from this very deed, that the keen adherents to the Church of Rome did not consider them as good Romanists. We have already adverted to the different charges exhibited against them. They speak of them as men who were not actuated by a due regard to the authority of their superiors, who were " not afraid, contrary to justice, to erect a certain regular canonry." If the charge be not exaggerated, this was undoubtedly a bold step. The very term certain, *quandam canoniam,* seems to contain a proof that, even in this erection, the Culdees did not strictly conform to the papal ideas of a canonry.

They are represented as non-descripts, as a sort of anomalous species, for which the Church of Rome, notwithstanding the great compass of her religious nomenclature, could find no proper designation. They are not even allowed the name of monks, although observing the rule prescribed by one of the saints in her own calendar. For it is said : *Non licebit eisdem Kildeis, vitam seu ordinem monachorum vel canonicorum regularium, sine consensu, ipsius Episcopi vel successorum, ibidem profiteri in perpetuum.* "It shall never be permitted to these Keldees to profess, either the monastic order, or that of canons regular, without the consent of the bishop, or of his successors." They were Culdees, yet neither monks nor canons regular. In what light then did the Church of Rome view them, if neither as monks nor as canons ?

7. Taking it for granted that, according to the statement given in the Register of Aberdeen, they did erect a "certain regular canonry" at Monimusk; as it appears that it was not of such a description as to please the keen abettors of the Romish interest : one thing highly offensive in the conduct of the Culdees, was their proceeding to take this step without the consent of the bishop. They had in former times claimed a superiority over bishops, whom they viewed as deriving their power from them. When, therefore, about to found a monastery in any place, they did not think of asking the sanction of those whom they had themselves invested with ecclesiastical authority. Those of Monimusk retained their old mode of procedure; and thus showed that they were not reduced to that canonical or implicit obedience, which was now become the great test of sanctity.

8. There is great ground to think, that, in the agreement with respect to one refectory, and one dormitory, more is included than has yet been mentioned. We know that it was a charge exhibited against the Culdees of St Andrews, that their wives, children, and relations, claimed and made use of the offerings presented at the altar as their own. May it not be supposed, that, in the article with respect to one refectory, &c., there is a secret thrust at some of the Culdees

at Monimusk, who neither ate nor slept in the monastery, but with their families in their own houses?

It may seem unaccountable, that, while the papal delegates allow the possession of a distinct oratory, refectory, and dormitory to the Culdees, they should preclude them from having any cemetery, save that which belonged to the parish church of Monimusk. This exception might appear to have proceeded from mere caprice, or from some strange perverseness. But we have here, I apprehend, a striking instance of their consciousness of the very high popularity of the Culdees. The Bishop of St Andrews and his adherents knew that if there was a distinct cemetery belonging to this society, that of the parish, which the bishop considered as his, would be unfrequented: and this one very considerable source of emolument to his canonical friends would be dried up. Hence, in the agreement, only the fourth part of the funeral oblations is appropriated to the Culdees, though formerly they had the whole.

This is illustrated by a prior convention between the canons regular of St Andrews and the Culdees there, in the time of Roger, the predecessor of Malvoisin; in which the canons appropriate to themselves, besides other offerings, all those made at the time of death, except when the Culdees are to be interred; to whom a right is reserved of being buried where they choose. If we can suppose that the same oppression was carried on in this early period as in later times, we need not wonder that the canons wished to secure to themselves these mortuary gifts. Before the reformation, the priest claimed, not only what was called the *Corspresent*, but a cow, and the uppermost cloth which had covered the deceased.

Goodall also says: "Another cause of quarrel was, that it seems, by a pretended gift from the Earl of Mar, they had possessed themselves of some lands that belonged to the bishop, without his consent; and by this deed of agreement, bound themselves not to do the like afterwards, either by that earl's or any other man's gift."

The Culdees seem to have been doomed, like many worthy men, not only to be oppressed by their contemporaries, but to be traduced by those in succeeding ages, who, from their profession, ought rather to have appeared as vindicators of their character. It is evident that this quarrel was picked by William Malvoisin, that he might have a pretext for ejecting the Culdees. It was the good bishop who pretended a right, which, there is reason to think, he could never have established in any way but by the arm of power. The matter of dispute is, in the deed of compromise, called "a certain canonry, or canonical parish, belonging to him." This must have been the church of Lorthel, with the lands annexed, tithes, &c. For it is to this that the charter, granted by Gilchrist, expressly refers. Now, this gift was confirmed to the Culdees by John Bishop of Aberdeen, in two distinct deeds. In another, he confirmed to them the gift of the church of Afford by the same earl. This John was elected about the year 1200, perhaps somewhat earlier.

This was previous to the time of Malvoisin. For he was not Bishop of St Andrews till the year 1202. He did not enforce his claim on this "canonical parish," till nearly twenty years after his instalment. Can it be at all imagined, that neither he, nor his predecessor Roger, would endeavour to prevent all these confirmations, had they entertained the idea that they had any rightful claim ? But the gifts of the Earl of Mar seem to have been the great sources of the temporal support of the Culdees; and therefore, in order to their suppression at Monimusk, these must be wrested from them.

Spotiswood is chargeable with great inaccuracy, when he says that Gilchrist, Earl of Mar, in the reign of William the Lion, built at Monimusk "a priory for the *canon-regulars* of St Andrews, after which the Culdees were turned out of their possessions." Nothing can be more clear, from his own charter, than that the earl was peculiarly attached to this religious community. He expressly "grants and confirms to God, and to the church of St Mary of Monimusk, *et Keledeis ibidem servientibus et servituris*, "and to the Culdees serving, and to serve, there," the church and lands afterwards specified, "in perpetual alms to them, for the safety and prosperity of his Lord King William, his son, and those who were dear to him," &c. He adds: "I will, and enjoin, that the foresaid Culdees shall possess the foresaid church, with all its pertinents, as freely, and quietly, fully, and honourably, in perpetual alms, as other canons, or monks, or other religious men whatsoever, in the whole kingdom of Scotland hold any church or alms, by the donation of baron or earl." But, indeed, how can it for a moment be supposed that Gilchrist built a priory here for canons regular; when it is well known that the very matter of controversy between the Culdees and the Bishop of St Andrews, was the pretended gift of lands to them by Gilchrist?

Let it not be supposed, however, that Gilchrist was the founder of the Culdean establishment at Monimusk, though he built a monastery for them. For it is said, in the second charter given by John Bishop of Aberdeen, that "G. Earl of Mar, gave the church of Lorthel," &c., to his monastery, which he constructed at Monimusk, in the church of St Mary, in which the Culdees formerly were." While John confirms to them the possession of this monastery, and the lands connected with it, that they might hold it as any other religious house did in Scotland; he adds, that they shall "not be subject to any other house, or do homage to any other than to himself and his successors; and that they shall give such subjection as the other religious houses throughout Scotland, constituted in episcopates, owe to their bishop." The first clause might seem to secure them against the usurpations of the canons regular; and the second might be meant to guard against such high pretensions as, he knew, the Culdees had formerly made.

It is worthy of remark, however, that John seems unwilling to express himself entirely in the style of Gilchrist. The bishop, who could be no stranger to the predilection of the Court for canons, bears, as far as possible, to this side in his language. Gilchrist speaks only of Culdees; John, of *Canonici, qui Keledei dicuntur,* of "canons, who are called Culdees;" and towards the close, he merely calls them, prefate Canonici, "the foresaid canons," dropping their proper designation entirely.

It appears from the vestiges of ancient history which yet remain, that a variety of means had been used for subduing them at Monimusk. The first attempt, as we have seen, was to reduce them to the rank of hospitallers. But, as they persisted in contending for their rights, and were supported by Gilchrist Earl of Mar, by Gartenach and Roger, Earls of Buchan, and other men of rank: Malvoisin, how anxious soever he was entirely to suppress the society, found it necessary to compromise matters. He allowed them to live according to their own rule, if they would acknowledge him as their founder, and give up those lands which rendered them too powerful.

This plan must have been long in contemplation. For the Pope appointed arbiters in the thirteenth year of his pontificate; which corresponds to A. 1211, or 1212. But it does not seem to have been observed, that this scheme was not carried into effect till more than seven years after. This appears from the ancient writing, which contains the Convention. It would even seem that the papal bull was expressed indefinitely, to be put in force, or not, as occasion should require. For, in this, he specifies no names; but merely nominates his "beloved sons, the Abbots of Mailros and of Dryburgh, and the Archdeacon of Glasgow." Now, one of the persons who acted was not in office at the time of the appointment. Adam was elected Abbot of Mailros, A. 1219. As Robert, Archdeacon of Glasgow, died A. 1222, it is evident that the arbitration must have been made by them between the years 1219 and 1222.

But even the business of the compromise did not subdue the spirits of the Culdees. Disgusted at the humiliating restrictions to which they were subjected, some of them left their monastery, and preferred living in other religious houses, whether of their own description, or not, we cannot pretend to determine, or perhaps acting as curates in parishes. For, in the register we have a letter addressed by the Bishop of St Andrews "to all abbots, priors, archdeacons, officials, and all rectors of churches; also to all his subjects, whether clergy or laity, throughout his diocese." He begins as if he had been as zealous for the strict observance of the Culdean rule, as of that of the canons regular: with great solemnity reminding those to whom he writes, that "it is certain that those, who, under pretence of religion, have left the secular habit, deprive themselves of any right to return to the world; and that he who presumes, by his own temerity, to depart from any place of religion, deserves, like the dog returning to his vomit, and the sow that has been washed to her wallowing in the mire, to be had in abomination both by God and by man." "Therefore," he adds, "moved by the just intreaty of our beloved sons, the Prior and Culdees of Monimusk, we require of you all, by these presents, that you presume not to admit any of the brethren of the said place, who have assumed the religious habit there, and have professed themselves, to reside among you, without the licence of the Prior and Culdees, and letters of recommendation given to them; or to admit them to fellowship; but rather that you hold such an one as a heathen man and a publican, until, reduced by repentance, he return to his proper residence and society, to give satisfaction for his offences, and, according to the institutions of their own rule, receive canonical discipline."

This keen adversary of the Culdees died A. 1233, and was succeeded by David, who continued in the see till the year 1250. There is a charter of his in the register, confirming the grant of some lands to this priory. But it does not mention the Culdees; being addressed to " the prior of Monimusk, and the canons there serving God, and to serve him for ever." This designation, however, does not imply that by this time they were canons regular. It might rather seem, that the attempt was renewed to convert the priory into an hospital. For the expressed design of the gift is, " for the sustentation of the poor, and of pilgrims that flocked thither." The only witness, whose name is mentioned, is Adam de Malkarviston, undoubtedly the same who was provost of the Culdean church of St Mary in the city of St Andrews, and who was cited to Inverkeithing, A. 1250.

The register also contains posterior charters, granted in favour of the church of Monimusk, by Adam, Gilbert, and Peter, Bishops of Aberdeen. But in none of them are the Culdees named. The phraseology is, " the canons residing there." It does not appear that these were canons regular. But the bishops use the name canons, as applicable to the Culdees, because they professed to observe a religious rule; while they avoid the name which these monastics preferred, as wishing it to be buried in oblivion.

We have also a rental of the priory of Monimusk for the year 1260, which was about forty years after the agreement between the Culdees there and Malvoisin. Perhaps it must, therefore, be viewed as giving the state of the priory, after it had assumed more of the canonical form.

Goodall asserts, that " there is not one syllable of the first article of that agreement which is given us by Sir James Dalrymple, p. 281, viz. " That the Culdees of Monimusk should live in communion, after the manner of Culdees." But undoubtedly, this is at least taken for granted in the deed; nay, it is the very thing conceded by the bishop on the terms

there stipulated.   They are acknowledged by the name of
Culdees; they are to have a prior of their own, only so far
subject to the bishop, with respect to nomination, that a list
of three must be given in to him, that he may fix on one of
them; and they are allowed their original number of twelve
monks beside the prior, and to have one oratory, one refectory, and one dormitory.   This is farther confirmed by the
circumstance, that, as has been seen, the same bishop, in
another deed, acknowledges their peculiar rule of life: as he
requires the wandering Culdees to "return to their own house
and companions;" and says, that they should receive canonical
discipline according to the institution of their own rule."
This strongly resembles an agreement on his part, "that they
should live in communion after the manner of Culdees."

Sir James Dalrymple, according to Goodall's estimation,
"has forgotten to give the main foundation of this controversy, which was, that these Culdees would needs be canons
regular, and would erect themselves into a canonry, not only
without the consent, but against the declared will of the
bishop their patron and founder."   After the most attentive
examination of all the ancient writings I can find on the
subject, I do not perceive that there is any proper ground for
this assertion.   The mistake has probably arisen from the
ambiguity of the term canon.   By this time, in most of our
cathedrals, the chapter consisted of those ecclesiastics denominated canons-regular, who generally followed the rule of
St Augustine.   The Culdees claimed the right to act as the
chapter, or, in other words, to elect the bishop.   On this
ground, as also because they observed a certain rule of their
own, they were frequently designed canons in a general sense.
But, while they asserted their ancient right to choose the
bishops, they manifested no inclination to renounce their
peculiar rule.

The complaint made by the Bishop of St Andrews properly
includes two charges, the one limited, the other general.   The

first is, that, quidam se Canonicos gerunt, "certain" of the Culdees "act as canons." There is nothing here which shews that they " would needs be canons regular." Did they mean to renounce their own rule for that of St Augustine or Benedict? No; the obvious meaning is, that some of them claimed that right to choose the bishop, which had formerly belonged to their body, but was now transferred to the canons regular of Aberdeen. The second is exhibited against them all. They "were not afraid to erect themselves into a canonry," as Goodall expresses it; or, as it should be rendered, according to the chartulary of Aberdeen, " to erect a certain regular canonry, notwithstanding the resistance of the bishop, contrary to justice, and to the prejudice and grievance of his church. Those of the second class are distinguished by their place of residence. They are said to be " certain others, of the diocese of Aberdeen, below the village of Monimusk belonging to him." Both those who acted as canons, putting themselves forward in the election of the bishop, as perhaps residing at Aberdeen, or in its vicinity, and others who did not, concurred in this erection.

There is, however, a variation, as to phraseology, between the copy of this deed as given in the Chartulary of Aberdeen, and that which we have in the Register of St Andrews. In the former the phrase is, *quandam canoniam regularem ;* in the latter, *quandam canonicum parochiam.* It can scarcely be supposed, that this difference has been owing to the careless-ness of a copyist. Or, if there has been an error in transcrib-ing, it would be more natural to suppose that this was in the Chartulary of Aberdeen, because the Bishop of St Andrews, having managed this cause would of course have the original agreement. It may indeed be supposed, that the phrase, *canoniam regularem,* had been used in the original deed: but that, when it came to be examined by the bishop, he found the assertion contrary to truth, and therefore made the necessary alteration. For, to whatever cause the variation be owing, it is obvious that the expression, "a certain regular canonry," was not applicable to the foundation at Monimusk. It is in fact at war with all the rest of the deed.   For, as the bishop was eager to convert the Culdean monasteries into regular canonries, he could have no scruple to comply with those of this place, if they were willing to adopt the new rule, on the ground of the restrictions which the deed of agreement actually contains.   Can it be conceived that, if they wished to be canons regular, he would have constrained them to retain the designations of *Kelidei* and *Con-Kelidei*, and their ancient rule and mode of discipline, as far as was consistent with his modifications?   Or would he have added these words? *Et in electione Prioris vel Magistri Kelideorum ita fiet in perpetuum.*   It is not said, that they were not to become canons regular without the consent of their bishop; but that they were not to become Culdees, or canonical brethren; that is, none, though pretending to be Culdees by succession, were to be received into their monastery without his consent; nor were they ever to exceed the prescribed number.   Had they been any wise inclined to become canons regular, the Bishop of St Andrews, if he acted in the usual manner, instead of depriving them of the donations made by the Earl of Mar, would most probably have added to them.   But, that they never testified any such inclination is evident, not only from the tenor of this agreement, but from a posterior deed formerly referred to, enjoining the return of the fugitive Culdees.

It must at the same time be evident that the phrase, *canonicam parochiam*, is most consonant to the whole strain of the agreement; and may be viewed as the language that Malvoisin had used in the complaint against the Culdees, which he made to the Pope.   There seems no good reason to doubt that it refers to what had been done by Gilchrist, Earl of Mar, who had built for them a new priory at Monimusk; to which, *donarit coenobio suo quod construrit*, he gave the church of Lorthel, properly Lochel, with its lands and pertinents; and the church of Innerochtin, now Strathdon, with the same.

It is this which seems to be designed "a certain canonical parish;" and properly enough, because of the intention of the donor, Earl Gilchrist, to support the Culdees by this means. The bishop might have continued to connive at their establishment, had they still been confined to their old priory. But now, when they had got a new one built, with such ample endowments, he thought it necessary to humble their pride. He seems, indeed, to have been afraid that they might become too powerful for him. He therefore takes the shortest course, by complaining to the Holy Father at Rome that the lands, which the Earl of Mar had given to them, were his property.

CHAPTER XIII.

Suppression of the Culdees at St Andrews.—Preparatory Mea-sures adopted with this view.—Their Controversy with the Canons Regular as to St Mary's Church.—Remarks on Good-all's Account of this.—State of the Culdees at Iona.—Their Subjection to the authority of Rome; and Expulsion of those who were refractory.—Of the Translation of the Reliques of Adamnan, and of Columba.

LET us now attend to the means used for the suppression of the Culdees at St Andrews. Before the introduction of canons regular there, the bishops, it is admitted, were elected by the Culdees. But we need not be surprised to find, that when these canons were brought in by David I., the authority of the Culdees was much diminished; as this was one thing specially designed in their introduction. Henceforth the chapter consisted chiefly of canons; while the Culdees were merely permitted to form a part of it on certain conditions. Their temporal emoluments were also greatly abridged. When Robert de Burgo had seized upon that part of the lands of Kirkness in Fife, which had long been their property, the king indeed enjoined restoration; and it was undoubtedly with his approbation that Constantine, Earl of Fife, and Macbeth, Thane of Falkland, raised an army for the purpose of resisting this oppressor. But although he so far preserved appearances, as to repress measures of gross violence, it is evident that he was determined to cast the religious societies in Scotland into a new mould.

Even in the metropolitan see, it cost the labour of nearly two centuries to accomplish the extinction of this society. Here, as in other places, the great plan adopted was the advancement of the canons regular. But, in subserviency to this, a variety of steps were gradually taken, some of which seem not to have been noticed by former writers on this subject.

In the Register of St Andrews, we have the deed of foundation of the priory of this place, by Bishop Robert, A. 1144. Besides all his other donations of lands, tithes, &c., he gives all his books to this priory. Of the seven portions, which belonged to the altar of St Andrews, he devotes two to the canons regular, and one for an hospital.

This register also contains a deed of David I., authorising the prior and canons of this new foundation to receive the Culdees of Kilrymont among them as canons, with all their possessions and revenues, if they be found willing to adopt this character. If they refuse to comply, it is enjoined, that the Culdees then living shall be permitted to retain their possessions during their natural lives; and that, on their demise, canons shall be appointed to succeed them individually; and that all their possessions shall thus successively be converted to the perpetual use of this canonical priory. This deed was enacted about the year 1150.

Bishop Robert, mentioned above, by another deed extends his donations to the new priory. For he grants all the portions of the offerings at the altar, without any restriction, except the seventh, which belonged to the bishop. A similar grant was made by Ernald, who filled the see a few years after him, and renewed this grant. He assigns a reason for the gift, which affords the fullest confirmation of what has formerly been mentioned as one great cause of offence at the conduct of the Culdees. "Every offering at the altar used formerly to be divided into seven parts, which were held by seven persons; not living in common." He affirms that this offering "ought not to be divided into parts, because community of living gives, in a certain sense, community to all that is possessed." This Ernald was admitted to the see A. 1158.

From the extracts from the Larger Register, it appears, however, that the bishop does not here give a very accurate statement of the appropriation of these portions, or one favourable to the Culdees. The bishop had always one, and the hospital another; the other five belonged to the Culdees. Sibbald thinks that they had always the care of the hospital, and of attending on strangers. But all that certainly appears from the passage, as he has himself translated it, is, that "when there happened more than six to come, they were wont to cast lots, who, whom, and how many, they should receive and accommodate with themselves." He adds: "They counted obedience, in the performance of these charitable works, as good as sacrifice." These grants of the offerings to the canons were confirmed by a charter of Malcolm IV. The register contains another, by the same prince, confirming the agreement made between the canonical priory of St Andrews, and the Culdees of the same church, concerning the lands of Stradkines and Lethin.

Richard, who succeeded to the episcopate in the year 1163, gave to the canons regular the church of the Trinity at St Andrews, with the lands of Kindargog.

By a rescript of Pope Adrian, A. 1156, it is enjoined, that in case of a vacancy in the see of St Andrews, there shall be no exercise "of craft or violence, but that the election shall be made with their common consent, and according to the determination of the sounder part of the brethren of the priory." This is evidently pointed against the Culdees, concerning whom it is ordained, in the sentence immediately following, that, "upon their demise, their places shall be supplied by canons regular."

We have an ordinance of Pope Lucius, dated A. 1183, similar to that with respect to the Culdees of Monimusk; prohibiting them to leave their monasteries without permission from their prior, and discharging other religious houses from granting them protection.

The canonical priory of St Andrews, while striving to suppress the Culdees, was careful to strengthen its own dependencies. Accordingly, we find Prior John, and his convent, "because of the slender means belonging to their priory of Lochlevin, formerly the property of the Culdees," granting and confirming, with consent of the bishop and chapter, to this priory, the whole barony of Kirkness, the lands of Admore and Rialie, Bolgin, Balcristin, Markinche, Auchmotie, and the tithes of the church of Portmoak with certain limitations. Some of the lands formerly mentioned, as belonging to the priory of Lochlevin, are here omitted, and others are mentioned. This deed is dated A. 1240.

A few years after this, the adverse parties mutually tried their strength. This severe struggle seems to have hastened the overthrow of the Culdees. I shall give an account of it in the words of a writer who is not at all partial to them. He has extracted it from an instrument taken in the church of Inverkeithing, A. 1250, preserved in the Advocates' Library. This is transcribed by Sir Robert Siblald.

"The prior and convent of St Andrews claimed the precedency and superiority in the direction and management of affairs in St Mary's church of St Andrews, which the Culdees would not allow: for they maintained, and with a good deal of reason too, that Mr Adam Malkirwistun, their prior, was provost of St Mary's church, and that they themselves were the canons. The matter was appealed to the Pope of Rome, and he delegated the priors of St Oswald and Kyrkham in England, (who, being of another kingdom, it was to be supposed, would deal the more impartially,) to enquire into the matter, and to determine according to justice. The delegates found the Culdees in the wrong, and in the mean time suspended them from their office; but delayed to pronounce their final sentence, which they had appointed to be done by Robert, Abbot of Dunfermline, one of the Pope's chaplains, and chancellor of Scotland, and [R.] the treasurer of Dunkeld, upon the 7th November, 1250, whom they ordained to enquire also, whether these Culdees, and their vicars, had in the mean time celebrated divine ordinances, while they were thus under ecclesiastical censure: Et ad inquirendum utrum divina celebraverint sic ligati.   The Culdees did not make their appearance at the day appointed: yet, notwithstanding their contumacy, the delegates mildly enough delayed the publication of the sentence till another time."

It may not be improper to make a few remarks on this account.   Goodall admits, at the outset, that the Culdees had right on their side, at least in so far, as it would appear that their prior was the provost, and that they were themselves the canons of St Mary's church.   But, towards the close, he exhibits the charge of contumacy against them, almost in the same terms with their enemies.   His mode of expression would also seem to bear, that their contumacy lay in not appearing.   But there is no evidence, in the original instrument, whether the Culdees were present or not; or that their absence was viewed as the proof of that contumacy with which they are charged.   There is reason to believe, that the resistance of that claim of precedency which they exhibited, on the ground of their prior being provost of St Mary's, was a plan laid by their enemies for their complete overthrow. Although, as their last resource, they appealed to the Pope, it is more than probable, that their enemies had so much interest at the court of Rome as to procure the appointment of judges, who had their minds completely prejudged before they heard the cause.   There is great reason for this suspicion from the description of the persons.   Goodall wishes it to appear, that they had been brought from "another kingdom," under the impression that "they would deal the more impartially."   The very reverse is the natural supposition. They, being strangers, could not at any rate be sufficiently acquainted with the religious customs of the Scots.   But they had been brought from another kingdom, which was by this

time almost entirely cast into the Roman mould, the clergy
of which were therefore of course prejudiced against the Culdees. To appoint the prior of St Oswalds, indeed, as one of
the judges, was virtually to secure their condemnation. For
this priory had been long before noted for its zeal for the
Romish innovations. We have seen, that, so early as the
year 1114, the canonry belonging to it was proposed as the
pattern of that reformation which appeared necessary to
Alexander I. in regard to the service of God. When, therefore, he converted the ancient Culdean church at Scone into
an abbey, he applied to Adelwald, the prior of St Oswalds,
that he would send him canons from his monastery, and
obtained them.

This suspicion derives additional confirmation from the
severity of their determination. It might have been supposed
sufficient, in a question ostensibly about mere precedency,
especially where it is admitted that the Culdees had a good
deal of reason on their side, had the judges repelled their
claim of precedency as ill-founded. But let us observe their
decision. They not only gave the cause against the Culdees,
but they suspended them, all those at least who were
engaged in the controversy, from all exercise of their office;
that is, as appears from what follows, from all "celebration
of divine service." We are even left to suppose, that they
did so, till they should acknowledge the justice of a sentence
that deprived them of the rights which they had possessèd
for several centuries. Their enemies evidently wished to
exclude them from all public ministration. As if this had
not been enough, they meant, by their suspension, to lay a
trap for them. For they appoint enquiry to be made, whether
they resumed to perform divine service after this interdict.
The papal delegates not only determined the original controversy, apparently with the greatest injustice, against them;
but wished to subject them to the dreaded fulminations of
the Holy See.

In the instrument referred to, they are not merely pronounced contumacious, in consequence, as would seem, of its
being proved by witnesses, that they had celebrated divine
ordinances during their suspension ; but, in the very sentence
of the two judges appointed by the Pope, merely in relation
to the dispute between them and the canons, they are
described as "certain persons who were disobedient and
rebellious against the church of St Mary," or "belonging to"
it. Or perhaps this may respect the friends and adherents of
these Culdees.

When we attend to these circumstances, not to speak of
Goodall's glaring inconsistency, we see how little reason he
had for saying that "the delegates mildly enough delayed the
publication of the sentence till another time." From the
whole tenor of their conduct there is not the slightest ground
for ascribing any part of it to mildness. For both he and
Sir James Dalrymple have mistaken the sense of the language
used by these gentlemen. There were indeed two publications.
The first was that of the sentence given by the priors of St
Oswald and Kirkham, by which the Culdees were subjected to
suspension. This, it is said, the Abbot of Dunfermline, and
the treasurer of the church of Dunkeld, "solemnly published
on their proceeding to make inquiry, whether they had
celebrated divine ordinances, *sic ligati*." Having made this
publication, they then admitted witnesses, made out a record
of their evidence, and appointed a day to the parties, the
first Sabbath after the festival of St Andrew, for publishing
the evidence exhibited by these witnesses, in the church of
the preaching friars of Perth ; and for proceeding further
against the Culdees referred to, "according to the form of the
papal mandate." Here was a second publication appointed,
which, we have no reason to doubt, would be carried into
effect. Where, then, is the proof of the mildness of these
inquisitors ? All that they delay is a present infliction of
"that penalty, which they might have justly inflicted," to the

day of this last-mentioned publication. Whether they had any papal authority for proceeding as far as excommunication, I shall not pretend to say.

One thing is evident here. The adversaries of the Culdees, who well knew their spirit, laid a snare for them. The two priors appointed by the Pope suspended them for no other reason, as far as we can discern, but for pertinaciously adhering to their ancient rights; and at the same time appointed their persecutors to watch them, to see whether they would practically acknowledge the justice of this sentence by submitting to it; that, if they did not they might have a ground for further procedure against them. When they obtained a proof which they so earnestly desired against the Culdees, they made a show of forbearance; not from any good-will to them, but because they judged it necessary, after having taken one strong step, not too hastily to proceed to another. We have no accounts with respect to any subsequent procedure in this cause. Fear might at length so far operate on the Culdees as to produce their submission. We learn that, when William Wishart was postulated to the see of St Andrews, "at his election or postulation [A. 1272], the ancient Culdees were not allowed to vote."

They had, indeed, been excluded from the election of Gameline, as Keith also remarks, so early as the year 1255, in which year Gameline appears as elect. The Chronicle of Mailros says, that he was elected by "the prior and convent of St Andrews."

Notwithstanding this exclusion, the Culdees "neglected to make any appeal, till the year 1297, and then they sent their provost or prior, William Cuming, to plead their cause at Rome, before Pope Boniface VIII.; where they lost their plea *non utendo jure suo*, because they had suffered two former elections to proceed without them, and entered their appeal only against the third."

As it appears that these religious men were by no means

indifferent with respect to their rights, we can account for
their listlessness, in this instance, in no other way, than by
concluding, that, from the spirit which was manifested in the
management of their cause, as narrated above, they had for
a long time viewed it as hopeless. Either from the more
sanguine temper of Cuming their prior, or from his supposed
interest, as it was a powerful name in that age, or from some
other circumstance now buried in oblivion, they had been
induced, after a silence of twenty-five years, to try the effect
of an appeal to Rome. But their cause, it would appear,
had been finally determined there long before.

It has been generally supposed that, from their defeat at
Rome, we are to date their extinction. But, from certain
articles in the Index to the Extracts from the Register of St
Andrews, Sir James Dalrymple concludes, that they continued in that city for some time after this. One article is,
Decisio contraversiae inter Keledeos *et Episcopum de juris-
dictione agri per Thomam Ranulphum Guardionem citra mare
Scottorum*, An. 1309. "This," he says, "behoved to be with
William Lamberton." He mentions another, of which if the
contents were known, it would throw much light on the
whole matter. This is, *Petitio* Keldeorum *et subjectio eorum
Episcopo Sancti Andreae*. This last has evidently been their
dirge.

Here it may not be improper to take a cursory view of
the state of their brethren at Iona, for some centuries previous to the extinction of their monastery.

It is worthy of observation, that the decline of their prosperity, as well as of their respectability and influence, may
be dated from the æra of their submission to the encroachments of Rome. As God had punished the apostacy of professing Christians on the continent of Europe, by letting loose
on them the barbarians of the north, he permitted the same
unrelenting instruments of his displeasure to desolate the
remote islands of the west.

The ostensible grounds of controversy between the Culdees and the Church of Rome, were in themselves trivial. It did not signify on what day they began to celebrate a feast, which had no divine authority in the Christian Church; nor in what manner they practised a tonsure, which had no better origin than the blind superstition of the priests of heathenism. The proper question was, whether any church or bishop had a right to prescribe to all who bore the Christain name. And although the Church of Rome, conjoining policy with her power, attacked the Culdees more immediately on these points, it has appeared, that the object she had in view was far more extensive; and that she was resolved to accomplish either their total extinction, or their complete subjugation.

Adamnan, in consequence of a visit which he made to the monks of Girwy, when sent as ambassador from his nation to Aldfrid, King of Northumbria, had become a convert to the Romish rites; and attempted, on his return, to introduce them at Iona. But, great as was their veneration for their patriarch, they continued firm in their adherence to those customs, which, as they believed, had been transmitted to them from the apostles of Christ. Thirteen years after the death of Adamnan, the Annals of Ulster take notice of an event in the history of Iona, which merits our particular attention, as marking the commencement of the many vicissitudes to which the Culdees were henceforth subjected. "716. *Expulsio familiae Iae trans Dorsum Britanniae, a Nectano Rege.* The expulsion of the family of Hij beyond Drum-Albin, by King Nectan."

The notices which have reached our times concerning these dark ages are so slender, that it is not possible to ascertain the causes of those facts which are barely narrated. We can only form conjectures, from a comparison of what is stated in the Annals of Ulster, and of the Quatuor Magistri, in the Chronicon Pictorum, in the Martyrologies, and by

Colgan. There can be little doubt, however, as to the cause of this expulsion. Nectan, the third of the name, king of the Picts, being convinced, as is said, by reading ecclesiastical writers, of his own error, and that of his people, with respect to Easter, resolved to embrace the catholic mode. But, "that he might accomplish this with greater ease, and with more authority, he wished for aid from the nation of the Angles. He accordingly sent ambassadors to Ceolfrid, Abbot of Girwy, requesting that he might write a hortatory letter to him, by means of which he might be enabled to confute those who presumed to observe Easter out of the proper time, and also concerning the mode of tonsure by which the clergy ought to be distinguished: informing him, that he was himself pretty well instructed on these subjects." Nectan received such a letter as he requested. In this Ceolfrid says, that by him Adamnan had been convinced of his errors, but that he was "not able to reduce to a better way the monks who lived in the island of Hij, over whom he presided as ruler." When this letter was read and interpreted to Nectan, it is said that he greatly rejoiced at the exhortation, gave thanks to God, and protested before all present, that he, with all his nation, would for ever henceforth observe this time of Easter; and decreed that the Roman mode should be received by all the clergy in the kingdom. Here we have an early specimen of Roman *finesse*. Bede also informs us, that, not long after this, the monks of Hij, with the other monasteries which were subject to them, were, by the assistance of our Lord, reduced to the "canonical observation of Easter and the tonsure." For, in the year 716, the priest Ecgberht went from Northumbria to Hij, and prevailed with them to submit to this change· "These monks," he says, "by the instruction of Ecgberht, received the catholic rites of life, under the Abbot Dunchad, about eighty years after they had sent Aidan to preach to the nation of the Angles." Ecgberht remained thirteen years in the island, and died A. 729.

Yet it seems unquestionable, that "the family of Hij were expelled in the year 716." How shall we reconcile these apparent contradictions? May we not suppose, that the excellent Bede, zealous as he was for conformity to the church of Rome, was ashamed of the means employed at Iona, and therefore drew a vail over the expulsion itself, and the circumstances connected with it? By comparing his account of Ecgberht's visit to Iona, and long residence there, with what is said in the Annals of Ulster, it is evident that the language of the latter cannot be understood of a total expulsion. It appears that, by the authority of Nectan, all the refractory monks were expelled; while those who submitted to the innovations remained. But perhaps we may safely infer, from the use of the term *familia*, that a great part, if not the majority, were removed.

I am inclined to think that, on the part of Nectan, some degree of policy had been blended with this severity. He expelled the monks "across," or "beyond Drum-Albin," *i.e.* beyond the Grampian mountains, apparently into the low country, or that of the Southern Picts, of which Abernethy was the capital. It is evident, that, about this time he had formed the plan of adorning the religious foundation at Abernethy, and perhaps of extending it. With this view, when he wrote to Ceolfrid, for the purpose already explained, he at the same time requested that he would send him architects to build a church in his nation after the Roman manner. Now, as the refractory monks of Iona were sent beyond Drum-Albin, it is not improbable that he wished to increase the religious establishment at Abernethy, and thus gradually diminish the dependence of his people on Iona, which lay at such a distance from his capital, and at the very extremity of his kingdom. He might at the same time hope, by a change of situation, to wean them from their former prejudices; and especially by retaining them in or near his capital, and immediately under his eye.

It would appear, that Faolchuo, or Faolon, also called Felim, had been elected Abbot of Iona, after Dorbhen, A. 714. But it may be supposed that, in consequence of the schism with respect to the Romish rites, he had been obliged to resign his dignity to Duncha or Dunchad. For, in the chronicle compiled by Dr Smith, it is said, under the year 716, when Dunchad died: "Faolchuo, who had resigned his office to him, again resumes it." There is a slight difference of two years between Dr Smith's Chronology and that of the Ulster Annals as given by Usher, Pinkerton, and Johnstone; the former fixing the expulsion of the monks of Hij A. 714, the same year in which Faolchuo had been elected, and two years before his restoration. If we trust to the narrative given by Bede, we may suppose the expulsion to have taken place a year or two before the time mentioned in the Ulster Annals. For we learn from him that Nectan, on receiving the letter from Ceolfrid, "immediately performed, by his royal authority, what he had said. For forthwith, by public proclamation, the circles of nineteen years were sent throughout all the provinces of the Picts, to be transcribed, learned, and observed, the erroneous revolutions of eighty-four years being everywhere suppressed. All the ministers of the altar and the monks had their heads shaved in the form of a crown; and the corrected nation rejoiced, as anew subjected to the instruction of the most blessed Peter, the prince of the apostles, and put under his patronage for protection."

He adds: "Not long after, those monks also of the Scottish nation, who lived in the island of Hij, were reduced to the canonical observation of Easter and the tonsure. For in the year 716, Ecgberht was honourably received," &c.

From the Ulster Annals we learn that "the reliques of Adamnan were transferred into Ireland," A. 726. This was probably in consequence of the continuance of the schism, and by those who had adhered to the ancient rites. For it follows: "and the law renewed." This may signify that the

law, or established custom received from their fathers, which
had been broken by the tyranny of Nectan, was renewed
among all those who at this time retired into Ireland.   This
conjecture receives confirmation from what is said under the
year 729: "The return of the reliques of Adamnan from
Ireland."   This was the very year in which Ecgberht died:
and it appears probable that the adherents to the old system
flattered themselves that, in consequence of this event, they
might be restored to the peaceful enjoyment of their former
privileges in Iona; especially as their persecutor Nectan,
who had been put in chains by Drust, A. 725, had died in the
year 727, that is, two years before the return of the reliques;
unless we suppose that it was the same year, according to the
error ascribed to the chronology of Tighernac.

From this time the island of Hij seems to have enjoyed
tranquillity for more than sixty years.   A. 793, all the
western isles were desolated by the Gentiles.   Hij was burnt
by them, A. 801.   They returned in 805, and "reduced the
family of Hij to sixty-four."   Blathmac, the son of Flain, was
martyred in Hij by the Gentiles, A. 824.   In 828, "Diarmaid,
Abbot of Hij, went into Scotland with Columcille's reliques:"
The same person, it is added, in the year 830, went into
Ireland with the same reliques.   A. 848, Jurastach, Abbot of
Hij, "came into Ireland with Colum Cille's oathes, or sanctified
things."

It is evident that the reliques, venerated at Iona, were no
longer reckoned safe there, by reason of the perpetual inroads
of the northern nations.   But it is not easy to account for
their perpetual change of place.   A learned writer supposes
that, when under the year 848, Jurastach "is said to have
brought Columcille's oaths, or sanctified things, into Ireland,"
it is "mistakingly put for Scotland, into which they were
brought at this epoch."   He apprehends that, in the year
849, they were deposited in a church built at Dunkeld by
Kenneth Macalpin in honour of Columba.

The repetition in the Annals of Ulster gives great probability to the idea, that there is a mistake as to the designation of the country; as these reliques are previously said to have been carried into Ireland, A. 830.   To this it must be added, that, in the year 877, it is said: "The shrine of Colum Cille, his oathes and reliques, brought into Ireland, for refuge from the Gentiles," or "for fear of the Gâls."   If Jurastach actually deposited these at Dunkeld, we must either suppose that they were allowed to remain there only about twenty-eight years: or that the writer of the Annals speaks of some other reliques, which had been retained at Hij till this time, as a succession of abbots was still kept up there.   It seems certain, from Innes's Old Chronicle, No. 3, that A. 849, Kenneth translated the reliques of Columba to the church which he had erected. But as Constantine, the son of Vergust, King of the Picts, built the church of Dunkeld, A. 815, it is said, in Dr Smith's Chronicle, under the year 816, "St Dermit, Abbot of Hij, goes to Albin with Columba's coffin or box *(scrinium)*."   If this event happened so early, it is probable that Diarmaid had gone with them to Dunkeld; as knowing that Constantine had erected a church in honour of Columba.   This agrees with Myln's account of the building of a church by Constantine; although he dates the erection about the year 729.

At any rate, it is impossible to account for their being so early transported into Ireland as A. 830.   If we shall suppose a mistake in the date of the Ulster Annals, as to the time of their being brought into Scotland, and that they were really deposited at Dunkeld A. 816, they may have remained there for some time, and been afterwards removed; because Ungus, who succeeded Constantine, A. 819, founded Kilrymont, in honour of Regūlus, and was determined to give it the pre-eminence above Dunkeld.   For, at this time, there does not appear to have been any internal disturbance in Pictland, nor any invasion from the northern barbarians, that could render Dunkeld insecure.

If we may credit Colgan's Chronology, these reliques could not have been carried into Albin by Diarmaid later than the year 816; for he says that in this year he died. But at what time soever they were carried thither, it would appear that they were soon transported into Ireland. If we admit the idea, that they had been formerly deposited in Constantine's church, whether in the year 816, or 828, we must suppose that, in 848, or 849, they were only brought back by Jurastach to the place which they had occupied before. As it is said these reliques were carried to Ireland A. 877, or, according to Smith, A. 875, "for refuge from the Gentiles:" some light may be thrown on this by comparing it with what is said in the same Annals, under the year 865. "Anlaiv and his nobilitie went to Fortren," i.e. Pictland, "together with the foreigners of Ireland and Scotland; and spoiled all the Cruthens," or Picts, "and brought their hostages with them." This Anlaiv, or Olave, was leader of the Danes and Norwegians who had taken up their residence in Ireland. He invaded Pictland a second time, A. 870. In the year 874, the Picts were defeated, with great slaughter, by the black Gâls. He remained a whole year in Pictland. Thus in about a year, or at farthest three years, after this last defeat of the Picts, the reliques of Columba seem to have been removed to Ireland, as at that time in a state of greater tranquillity than Pictland. For this was a very disastrous reign to the Picts. It is evident, however, from what we have formerly seen, that the monks of Dunkeld still boasted the possession of at least one precious wonder-working bone of the saint.

Notwithstanding the great decline of power, there continued to be monks, if not abbots, of Hij at least till the year 1203, when, it is said, " Ceallach built a monastery, in opposition to the learned of the place; upon which the clergy of the north of Ireland held a meeting; after which they came to Hi, and demolished the monastery of Ceallach." It is probable that this was erected for the reception of one of the Romish orders of religious men; as it was opposed not only by the Irish clergy, but by " the learned of the place."

CHAPTER XIV.

Of the Library at Iona.—Account given of it by Pennant, from Boece.—Causes assigned for its Destruction;—Devastations by the Danes;—by Edward I.;—by the Reformers;—by Cromwell;—during the period of Persecution.—Books, formerly belonging to it, said to be still extant.—The Culdees preserved till about the Time that the Lollards appeared.—Of the Reformation in Scotland, whether by Bishops?—Of those called Superintendents.

NOT a little has been said with respect to the Library at Iona. But, besides having to regret the loss of this very ancient collection, we have not even the slender consolation of certainly knowing what was its fate. It is more than probable, however, that, like other monuments of antiquity which have fallen a sacrifice to the depredations of time, its value has been considerably overrated.

"The public," says Pennant, "was greatly interested in the preservation of this place, for it was the repository of most of the antient Scotch records. The library here must also have been invaluable, if we can depend upon Boethius, who asserts that Fergus the II., assisting Alaric the Goth in the sacking of Rome, brought away, as share of the plunder, a chest of books, which he presented to the monastery of Iona. Aneas Sylvius (afterwards Pope Pius II.) intended, when he was in Scotland, to have visited the library, in search of the lost books of Livy, but was prevented by the death of the king, James I. A small parcel of them were, in 1525, brought to Aberdeen, and great pains were taken to unfold them, but, through age and the tenderness of the parchment, little could be read; but from what the learned were able to make out, the work appeared by the style to have rather been a fragment of Sallust than of Livy."

But the account given by Boece is clogged with difficulties. 1. It is said that, besides the chest of books, there fell to the share of Fergus *sacra quedam rasa*, "certain sacred vessels," which he also brought with him.   Now, Boece himself has told us what we know from other sources, that the Goths respected the sacred edifices.   Alaric gave a peremptory order, that all the consecrated vessels belonging to St Peter should be transported, without damage or delay, to his church. But, although these only are mentioned, in consequence of their being found by the soldiers under the care of an aged virgin; it is most probable that this prince would show the same regard to all other vessels consecrated to the purposes of religion.

2. This account involves a gross anachronism.   Fergus must have made his donation to the monastery of Iona about a hundred and sixty years before the foundation-stone of it was laid.   For Boece says that Alaric sacked Rome A. 412. Now, Columba did not land in Iona till the year 563, or as some say, 565.   Here, we are told, Fergus employed approved scribes, for reducing the manuscripts to the form of books, several ages, as would seem, before the art of writing was known in the country.

3. The same writer elsewhere says that, although Fergus had appointed Iona to be a repository for the public records, yet Alexander I., on account of the great difficulty of the access to Iona, had caused our annals to be transferred to the priory of Restennet, in Angus.   Maitland has observed that hence it was evident, that in Boece's time there could be no records at Iona; and, therefore, that he could not get his *Veremundus* from this island.

As Boece mentions our annals only, it may be said, that he did not refer to the ancient classical works, which Alexander might not think of demanding from the monks of Iona.

It might even be supposed, that Maitland had not sufficient

ground for charging Boece with self-contradiction, as to our annals; as some of them, notwithstanding the requisition made by Alexander I., might have been retained at Iona, being concealed by the monks, or afterwards procured by them from other quarters: of which circumstance Boece might be informed, when he made more particular inquiry with the view of writing his history. But it cannot be denied, that, by referring to works unknown to all our historians, as to those of Cornelius Hibernicus, Veremund, and Campbell, of whose writings, nay, of whose existence, we can discover no other vestiges, he has greatly injured the credibility of his whole story with respect to the communications from Iona. The most favourable opinion which can possibly be formed of the conduct of Boece, and it is very little to his credit indeed, is, that he had destroyed the manuscripts which he had used, that his own history might be in greater request. This, as we learn from Gordon of Stralogh, was the tradition which, when a young man, he had heard at Aberdeen.

Nor can it at all be believed, that the classical MSS. were brought from Rome by Fergus. There is little probability indeed that Fergus ever was at Rome; and still less, that an Irish prince, in that early age, would encumber himself, during his military labours, with a chest of books, written in a language to which, we may reasonably suppose, he was an entire stranger.

It must be admitted, however, that from a writer, who has frequently substituted fable for history, credit is sometimes withheld, even when he may have a just claim to it. This may have been the fate of Boece, in the instance before us. It must be acknowledged, that he does not, as Pennant says, assert that these books were brought from Rome by Fergus. He only gives it as a tradition, or report; Ferunt, &c. Besides, there is a considerable appearance of integrity in his account of the transmission and examination of these works. He claims no merit in the discovery. All the honour that he claims, is the partial execution of a plan previously formed by a person warmly attached to the interests of literature, who had come to this country as papal legate, not a century before the time Boece wrote. If a foreigner, holding such a distinguished place, entertained the design of making a visit to Iona, for the express purpose of inspecting the library there, it must have been well known, and highly gratifying to our countrymen. Nor could the memory of this design have perished in so short a time among those who had any regard to learning: especially as it was frustrated by a calamitous event that so deeply interested every friend to his country. Even Boece, therefore, would not have ventured such an assertion, had he not been assured of the fact.

He also says, that it was in consequence of the great celebrity of these books, preserved in Iona, that he was so anxious to examine "what they were, and what they treated of." He assumes nothing to himself, in the account which he gives of their transmission. On the contrary, he owns that the religious men of Iona did not comply with his request, till after the third application; and this chiefly by the good offices of the noble and learned Campbell, his majesty's treasurer. Boece published his history while Campbell was alive; and can it be supposed, that he would have introduced a man of his respectability as a witness to a gross falsehood, liable also to contradiction from all the monks at Iona? His history was published, indeed, little more than a year after the time assigned as the date of the receipt of these books. He had even exposed himself to recrimination from these monks, if there was any ground for it: as he ascribes the deplorable state of the manuscripts rather to the carelessness of their guardians than to the waste of time. A reflection of this kind might well be supposed to excite *l'esprit du corps*.

Having mentioned the lost books of Livy as the great *desideratum*, had the story been entirely a fabrication, it would

15

have been as easy for him to have said, that the fragments
which he examined indicated the style of this author, as to
have ascribed them to Sallust; and more natural, as giving
greater importance to his pretended investigation.

It also deserves observation, that Boece speaks of these
manuscripts as inspected while in his custody by a variety
of learned men; and candidly confesses, that it could not be
determined whether they had been written in Scotland or
brought from abroad, being written after the Roman mode,
as they treated of Roman affairs. "This only," he says,
"appeared to the judgment of all who saw them, that they
savoured more of the style of Sallust than of Livy." Had he
never received these manuscripts, or had he shewed them to
none of his literary friends, would he ever have hazarded
such a declaration?

It may be added, that while the learned Usher scouts the
idea of their being brought from Rome by Fergus, he admits
the narrative of Boece, as far as it regards these fragments.
Gibbon also, a writer abundantly fastidious as to evidence,
has no hesitation in saying, that Iona was "distinguished
by a classic library, which afforded some hopes of an entire
Livy."

"There can be no doubt," it has been said of late, "but
the many learned men that flourished at I, had the classics
among them, and all the books on divinity and sciences these
ages could afford. It can be as little doubted, that, like
other societies of learned men, they committed their own
works to writing, as well as the transactions of their countrymen." With respect to classic works, however, it must be re-
gretted, that we have no better proof than conjecture besides
what may be supposed to arise from the testimony of Boece.
I am rather inclined to think, that their collection of theo-
logical works was never very extensive; because, in early ages
at least, the religious members of this seminary were chiefly
devoted to the reading and transcribing of the scriptures, and

of sacred hymns. Columba spent much of his time in writing. He employed his disciples in the same manner; and was at pains that they should transcribe with the greatest accuracy. Dr Smith, speaking of his successors, says: "How well they studied the languages, appears from the excellent Latin of Cumin, and of Adamnan, who discovers also his knowledge of Greek and Hebrew; and wrote a geography of the Holy Land." This work Bede not only ascribes to Adamnan, but highly commends. "The same person," he says, "wrote a book concerning the holy places, most useful to many readers. He received his information from Arcuulphus, a French bishop, who had gone to Jerusalem to visit the holy places; and who, having surveyed all the Land of Promise, travelled to Damascus, Constantinople, Alexandria, and many islands, and returning home by sea, was, by a violent storm, brought to the western coast of Britain. After many accidents, coming to Adamnan, the servant of Christ above mentioned, as he appeared to be learned in the scriptures, and well acquainted with the holy places, he was most readily received, and attentively listened to by him; so that what things soever he had seen in these places worthy of remembrance he forthwith committed to writing. Thus, he composed a work very useful, and especially to those who, being far removed from these places where the patriarchs and apostles dwelt, know nothing more of them than what they learn by reading." Bede then proceeds to give some extracts from this work, which occupy two chapters. The work itself is extant in Mabillion's Collections.

Many works, both in Latin and in Irish, are said to have been written by Columba, himself; and among these, the life of the patron saint of Ireland. The life of Columba, we are told, was written, in Irish metre, by his cousin, disciple, and successor, Baithan, who was also canonized. To Abbot Cumin several writings are ascribed, beside the life of Columba, published by Mr Pinkerton, and referred to above, which was undoubtedly his work. Of these, of the writings of Adamnan, and of other Abbots who succeeded him, there is every reason to believe that copies would be carefully preserved in the monastery. Men, who were so much devoted to writing, would strain every nerve to increase the number of their books.

"What then," may it be inquired, "has become of this library? How can it be accounted for that it should entirely disappear?" This has been primarily ascribed to the inroads of the Danes. These were frequent and fatal. The monastery of Iona was burnt by them, A. 797; a second time, 801; and it was destroyed by fire in the year 1069. A. 805, the family of Iona, to the number of sixty-eight, was destroyed by the pirates of that nation; and in 985 they rifled the monastery, and killed the abbot, with fifteen of his disciples. "If the barbarians," it has been said, "had the library in their power, no doubt they would destroy it." According to the information of Pennant, it would appear, that, perhaps, while the Norwegian princes were sovereigns of the isles, they judged it proper to carry some of the more valuable MSS. to a place of security in their own country. "I am informed," he says, "that numbers of the records of the Hebrides were preserved at Drontheim, till they were destroyed by the great fire that happened in that city, either in the last or present century." This, however, might take place after the cession of the Hebrides; for, by the treaty made on this occasion, "the patronage of the bishopric of Sodor was reserved to the Archbishop of Drontheim in Norway."

The learned Torffaeus does not seem to have been so well informed, with respect to the depredations made by his countrymen in the island of Iona, as might have been expected. He says, that in the year 1210, a squadron of piratical ships, to the number of twelve, under Birkibein and Bagli, taking advantage of the intestine divisions of the princes of the Hebudae, committed many depredations in this quarter, and plundered the Holy Island, or that of St Columba, which, till that time, had never been subjected to any injury from the Norwegians, as being protected by its sanctity.   He asserts this, as attested by all their annals. The facts formerly quoted, however, rest on the combined testimony of the Annals of Ulster, and of the Irish martyrologists.

Bishop Nicholson, speaking of the library at Icolmkill, says : " Our King Edward the First, having claimed the sovereignty of Scotland, made a most miserable havock of the histories and laws of that kingdom ; hoping that, in a very short time, nothing should be found in all that country, but what carry'd an English name and face."

" The second great loss of the Scotch records," according to his mode of enumeration, " happen'd upon the mighty turn of the Reformation ; when the monks, flying to Rome, carry'd with them the register-books, and other ancient treasure of their respective monasteries." " At the Reformation," says another writer, " the MSS. of I were in part carried to the Scotch colleges of Doway, or to Rome, at least the chartularies, and such as were esteemed most valuable by the monks.   The college of Ratisbon has also been mentioned as possessing part of this spoil.   But, from all that I have been able to learn from such of our countrymen as have resided, or been trained up, in the Scotch colleges on the Continent, it would appear, that there has been far less ground for this assertion than has been generally imagined. If an accurate search were made, by such travellers as really possessed a literary character, and took an interest in the ancient history of our country, more perhaps might be discovered among the treasures of the Vatican than any where else.

The indiscreet zeal of the Reformers has also with too much, reason, been viewed as a principal cause of the destruction of this library. "The register and records of the island," according to Pennant, "all written on parchment, and probably other more antique and valuable remains, were all destroyed by that worse than Gothic synod, which at the Reformation declared war against all science." He might perhaps allude to the act of the convention of estates, A. 1561, "passed at desire of the church, for demolishing all the abbeys of monks and friars, and for suppressing whatsomever monuments of idolatrie were remaining in the realm, the execution whereof in the west parts was committed to the Earls Arran, Argile, and Glencarne." In consequence of this appointment, "ensued a pitiful vastation of churches and church-buildings throughout all the parts of the realm; for every man made bold to put out his hand, (the meaner sort imitating the greater, and those who were in authority). They rifled all churches indifferently, making spoil of everything they found.—The very sepulchres of the dead were not spared, but digged, ript up, and sacrilegiously violated. Bibliothecks destroyed, the volumes of the fathers, councells, and other books of humane learning, with the registers of the church, cast into the streets, afterwards gathered in heaps, and consumed with fire." Could we give full credit to this account, who could read it without regretting, that men, whose intentions were good, should act with as little discrimination, as if they had reckoned learning inimical to religion, or proposed, as their pattern, the sentence of the Saracen caliph with respect to the inestimable library of Alexandria! But it can scarcely be supposed, that any of the nobility or ministry would give their sanction to the destruction of libraries. What happened in this way must be attributed to the unbridled licentiousness of the ignorant rabble, when once let loose. Spotswood himself views it in this light. For he subjoins: "But popular fury, once armed, maketh no difference; nor doth it any thing with advice and judgment."

With respect to the library of Iona, "it is said that some of the MSS. were carried to Inveraray, and that a Duke of Montague found some of them in the shops there, used as snuff paper." This traditionary account most probably respects the time referred to in the sentence immediately subjoined: "If any of them were in the library of the family of Argyll, the persecution that family underwent, in the time of Charles II., accounts for none being there now." What is here said receives considerable support from a circumstance mentioned by Sacheverell, in relation to a book which had certainly been brought from Iona. "The dean of the isles, Mr John Frazer, an honest episcopal minister, told me his father, who had been dean of the Isles, left him a book with above 300 inscriptions," taken from the monuments of Iona, "which he had lent to the late Earl of Argile, a man of incomparable sense, and great curiosity; and doubts they are all lost by that great man's afflictions."

With respect to our ancient registers in general, Bishop Nicolson says: "The third, and killing blow was given them by Oliver Cromwel; who brought most of the poor remains that were left into England; and they likewise were mostly lost in their return by sea." It is probable that he alludes to those of the monastery of Iona, in common with others. Whether Cromwell actually sent to Iona, with an intention to carry off any gleanings that might be found there in his time, we cannot determine. But it will afterwards appear, that his usurpation has been viewed as at least the accidental cause of the destruction of a considerable portion of its precious remains.

Whether it was owing to the depredations of the Danes or to the indifference of the Culdees of Iona to the works of the fathers, it is not easy to determine; but the fact seems well authenticated, that, in the ninth century, the only book of this description which they had, was one of the writings of Chrysostom. The anonymous author of the life of this father gives the following account. "Certain clergymen, who, from among those who inhabit the extremities of the world, coming, upon the account of some ecclesiastical traditions, but particularly the observation and exact calculation of Easter, to the royal city [of Constantinople] did wait upon the patriarch who at that time resided therein. This was Methodius, a man famous in the days of our ancestors; by whom being question'd from what place, and on what occasion, they had travelled thither? they answer'd, that they came from the Schools of the Ocean; and withall they clearly explain'd to him the occasion of coming from their own country.—He demanding, by what traditions of the fathers and doctors they govern'd themselves? they said that they had one onely book of the father Chrysostom, from whence they happen'd clearly to learn the faith, and the exact observation of the commands; affirming, that they daily reap'd great advantage by this piece, which was very agreeable and acceptable to all, being handed about from one to another, and diligently transcrib'd; insomuch that there was no city, as they said, nor any of their clans, or territories, that remained void of so great and important a benefit."

A few books have been mentioned, by different writers, within the last century, or a little farther back, some of which may have once formed part of the library at Iona.

In the account of the island of Mull, which is separated from Iona only by a narrow sound, it is said: "Since the Reformation, the parish has produced none eminent for learning, if we except the Beatons of Pennicross, who were doctors of physic. The family is now extinct: but they are still spoken of in the country with admiration for their skill in physic. It is said that one of them was sent for to attend one of the kings of Scotland. They had a large folio MS. in Gaelic, treating on physic, which was left with a woman, the heiress of the Beatons, and seen by some now living; but what became of it, the incumbent, after all his inquiries, could not find. It is perhaps lost, as the heirs of this woman are quite illiterate."

In this monastery particular attention seems to have been paid to the science of medicine. "The Olla Ileach, and Olla Muileach," says Dr Smith, "the ancient and famous line of physicians in Hay and in Mull must no doubt have derived their first knowledge from this seminary. I had from Major Maclachlan, in the neighbouring island of Luing, a MS. in the Irish character and language, on the subject of medicine and surgery, which appeared, from being compared with Astle's specimens, to have been of a most remote antiquity: and it is likely that it was written by some of the learned men in Iona."

"Of what has been written at Iona," says Mr M'Nicol, "I have heard, in particular, of a translation of St Augustine *De Civitate Dei*, and a Treatise in Physic, which is very old The former was in the possesion of the late Mr Archibald Lambie, minister of Kilmartine, in Argyleshire; and the latter was preserved in the Advocates' library at Edinburgh, where, no doubt, it is still to be seen."

Many copies of the Life of Columba seem to have been dispersed through the islands, in the vernacular tongue. "The Life of Columbus," Martin says, "written in the Irish character, is in the custody of John Mack-Niel, in the isle of Barry: another copy of it is kept by Mack-Donald of Benbeenla."

"We are informed by Mr. Lloyd," says Dr Macpherson, "that there is still in the Bodleian library at Oxford, an Irish manuscript, entituled *The Works of Columbcille*, in verse, containing some account of the author's life, together with his prophecies and exhortations to princes.

"The same industrious writer observes, that there is in the library of Trinity College at Dublin, some other most curious and wonderfully ancient manuscript, containing the four gospels, and a variety of other matters. The manuscript is called *The Book of Columb-cille*, and thought to have been written by Columba's own hand. *Flann*, King of Ireland, ordered a very costly cover to be given this book. On a silver cross, which makes a part of that cover, is still to be seen an Irish inscription, of which the literal meaning is, 'The prayer and blessing of Columb-cille to *Flann* the son of *Mailsheachnail*, King of Ireland, who made this cover: and, should the manuscript be of no greater antiquity than the reign of that prince, it must be about nine hundred years old.' This story, however," Dr Macpherson adds, "carries with it a great degree of improbability; and it is more than probable that this *Book of Columb-cille* arose from the pious fraud of a much later age."

I shall conclude this meagre account of a library once so famous, with the latest notices which I have met with on the subject. They occur in a posthumous work of the late learned Dr Walker of the University of Edinburgh. "All that I could learn of its fate," he says, "was, that the reformers came so suddenly upon Icolumbkill, that the inhabitants had time to carry little or nothing away. Some of the books and papers, however, were conveyed to the castle of Cairnburg, belonging to the chief of the Macleans, and then judged impregnable. Here they remained till a siege, in the time of Cromwell, when they were mostly destroyed by fire. Some of them, however, still escaped, of which I got notice of one manuscript, and saw an old gentleman in whose hands it had been for some time; but found, after hunting it through three or four islands, that the last leaves of it, as it was unhappily vellum, had fallen a sacrifice for measures to a taylor. It was a Latin translation of an Arabian work on physic."

From what we have formerly seen, "it is plain," as Sir James Dalrymple has observed, "that the Culdees continued till the beginning of the fourteenth century." In this century, he adds, "Renatus Lolardus appeared in France, and

Wicklif in England.—The Lolards appeared in this kingdom under the government of R. D. of Albany ; and shortly thereafter James Resby and Paul Craw were burnt for maintaining these doctrines. In the reigns of James the Third and Fourth, great numbers of them appeared in Kyle and Cunningham ; and the first beginning of the Reformation of religion was embraced in these districts."

Here we have a singular proof of the providence of God in preserving the truth in our native country, even during the time that the Man of Sin was reigning with absolute authority over the other nations of Europe; and in transmitting some of its most important articles at least, nearly to the time of its breaking forth with renewed lustre at the Reformation. It would be inconsistent with the design of this inquiry, to enter into any discussion with respect to the scriptural warrant for the presbyterian form of government. But it cannot reasonably be supposed that the memory of the Culdees had, even in the sixteenth century, completely perished in a country, in which, only two centuries before, they had been contending for their ancient rights, not merely in opposition to the whole power of the primacy, but to the additional support of papal authority ; and where they seem to have constituted the majority of the ordinary pastors, till within a short time of their overthrow. Although we have no written documents concerning them as a body, later than the beginning of the thirteenth century, it is by no means improbable, that individuals, trained up by them, or adhering to their principles, continued to discharge the pastoral duties, especially in those places which were more remote from the episcopal seats.

It is no inconsiderable confirmation of the accounts given of them by our later writers, before the Reformation, how much soever some affect to despise their testimony ; and no contemptible proof of the strong bias that was in the mind of the nation in opposition to prelacy ; that, as soon as they had the power in their hands, they preferred a form of government nearly allied to that ascribed to the Culdees.

It has been asserted, indeed, by the friends of the hierarchy, that the government adopted by our Scottish reformers was not presbyterian but episcopalian. The ground of this assertion is the appointment of those ministers who were denominated Superintendents. It cannot be denied, that a greater degree of power was given to those office-bearers than to ordinary pastors. But those by whom they were appointed had no idea of any distinction of office : and even the power, entrusted to them was so limited, that they appear in a very different light from those usually denominated Bishops. Such, indeed, were the limitations to which they were subjected, and the services required, that any one who chiefly sought his ease, or wished to sacrifice to ambition, might, with respect to this pre-eminence, have said, with a safe conscience, *Nolo episcopari*. They were elected by the people who were to be committed to their charge. For although one, in the first choice, was previously nominated by the lords of secret council, his edict was regularly served ; and not only were all the people at liberty to object to his instalment, but " question was moved to the haill multitude, if there was ony uther quhome they wuld put *in electioun* with the said" person. In case of a vacancy, it is ordained, that " the cheefe towne within the province, to wit, the ministers, elders, and deacons, with the magistrate and conncell of the same towne, shall nominate, and by publick edicts proclaime, as well to the Superintendents, as to two or three provinces, next adjacent, two or three of the most learned and godly ministers within the whole realme, that from amongst them one with publick consent may be elected and appointed to the office."

They were to be strictly tried by the ordinary pastors, as to their learning, prudence, piety, and character : to be set apart by them, and the Superintendents, where any had been appointed ; and severally subjected to the censure and correction of the ministry and elders of the whole province. They were equally subject to deposition with the ordinary pastors. Each of them had a particular congregation especially under his charge. He was required to preach thrice every week. He was not to remain more than three or four months in his principal residence; but to visit the province for eight or nine months in the year. He was prohibited to reside more than three weeks in any one place during this visitation.

Our reformers did not admit of any ordination of the Superintendents, as this would have implied investiture with an office different from that of the ordinary pastor. Therefore they say: "Other ceremonies then [than] sharp examination, approbation of the ministers and superintendents, with the publicke consent of the elders and people, we cannot allow."

Their office, at any rate, was meant to be merely temporary. To some, this idea may appear as the interpretation of a later age, when, it may be supposed, the notion of presbyterian parity had gained more ground. But let us attend to the declaration of those very men who first recommended, and who digested, the plan with respect to the choice of superintendents. "We consider," they say, "that, if the ministers whom God hath endowed with his singular graces amongst us, should be appointed to severall places, there to make their continuall residence, then the greatest part of the realme should be destitute of all doctrine; which should not onely be the occasion of great murmur, but also be dangerous to the salvation of many. And therefore we have thought it a thing most expedient at this time, that from the whole number of godly and learned men, now presently in this realm, be selected ten or twelve, (for in so many provinces we have divided the whole,) to whom charge and commandment should be given to plant and erect kirkes, to set, order, and appoint ministers as the former order prescribes, to the countries that shall be appointed to their care where none are now," &c.

Although this measure was adopted merely as a matter of temporary expediency, because of the great scarcity of reformed pastors, that no part of the church might be altogether neglected; they thought it better that several provinces should be vacant, than that any should be appointed who were unfit for so important a trust. Accordingly, although ten or twelve superintendents were, as we have seen, judged necessary, no more than five were ever appointed.

This plan, in another point of view, was very different from that of prelacy. For, as Calderwood observes, " in this head of superintendents, we have no degrees of superior or inferior, provincial or general superintendents, but all of one rank, without subordination of some to others; which is otherwayes in the hierarchie of the prelats, where we have bishops, archbishops, primats, and patriarches."

Such is the resemblance between these superintendents and the first bishops of Scotland, and also as to the mode of appointment, that one might almost suppose that our reformers had taken the college of Iona for their model. Both were chosen out of the common body. Both were subject to the authority of the presbyters or seniors. We have not the slightest proof of ordination by any claiming superiority of office. They were equally teaching bishops. The principal design of the appointment of both, was the planting of churches, or, as it is expressed in the First Book of Discipline, " the establishment of the kirke ;" neither being suffered to live, as our reformers say, " as your idle bishops have done." They were not distinguished from others, under any pretence of divine authority, but by man, merely for expediency. Thus the superintendents are described only as one class of preachers. Hence the compilers of the Book of Discipline say: "We have thought good to signifye to your honours such reasons as moved us to make difference betwixt preachers at this time." Although, during several successive reigns, the crown still endeavoured to restore the hierarchy which had existed before the Reformation, it was still keenly opposed; and on every opportunity which the body of the nation had of expressing their inclinations, a national, (may I not say?) an hereditary, antipathy to this form of government was unequivocally manifested.

CHAPTER XV

Objections considered.—The supposed Inconsistency of the Monks of Iona sending Bishops, or Improbability of their being applied to for such a Mission, if unfriendly to the Order ;— The Culdees said to have been merely the Episcopal Chapter of the Diocese in which they resided.—Assserted, that there were never any Culdees at Iona, or within the Territories of the ancient Scots ; and that they made their first Appearance at St Andrews.

In the progress of this investigation, I have considered the principal exceptions to the arguments brought to prove, that the ecclesiastical power, established at Iona, bore a striking analogy to the presbyterian form. Before leaving the subject, it may be necessary to advert to some of the objections that have been made to this hypothesis.

1. It may seem a powerful objection to this scheme, that, when application was made, on different occasions, by the Saxon princes to the monastery of Iona, for bishops, those who resided there had no scruple to ordain and give a mission to pastors of this description. On the other hand, it may appear inconceivable, that "the English would, once and again, have concurred so heartily with those who wanted to abolish the episcopal order in Scotland, while they still kept it up among themselves."

So little weight is there in the last part of this objection, that it scarcely merits a reply. Those who made application to the seniors at Iona were principally concerned about the preaching of the word of faith ; and it may naturally be supposed, that, in the first instance at least, they scarcely passed a thought about the form of ecclesiastical government. With the same propriety might it be argued, that they would not have applied to those who were schismatical as to the mode of observing Easter; because the Angles, when they submitted to the authority of Rome, viewed the Scottish clergy in this light. By the use of the appellation English, an ignorant reader might be led to suppose that the correspondence had been maintained even after this became the general designation of the inhabitants of South-Britain. But the intercourse with Iona was long previous to this time; and was maintained only for about thirty years. The influence of Rome at length so far prevailed, that none were received from this island who refused submission to papal authority.

Of this we have a striking proof from the conduct of Wilfrid, a Saxon monk, who carried on the debate with Colman, Bishop of Lindisfarne, about the time of observing Easter. Bede merely says, that King Alchfrid sent the presbyter Wilfrid to the King of France, who caused him to be consecrated a bishop. But the good man was, perhaps, ashamed of the real cause of this mission. Wilfrid was so violent, that he would not submit to Scottish ordination. William of Malmesbury speaks it fairly out: "But he persisted in refusing to be ordained by Scottish bishops, or by those whom the Scots had ordained, because the apostolical see scorned to have any fellowship with them."

The other branch of the objection deserves more attention. No pastor can have any reasonable prejudice merely against the name of Bishop. For it is of scriptural authority; and was originally given, in common with that of Presbyter, or Elder, to all who were overseers of the flock. Our excellent translators were well assured that there was a number of Elders in the church of Ephesus; and that not only the Apostle Paul gave them all, without exception, the designation of Bishops, but that "the Holy Ghost had made" them all "bishops." But here carnal policy prevailed over conviction. They could not but know, that if they translated the term επισκοπας, as they did everywhere else, in its proper sense, as being the very origin of our word bishop, they would give a fatal stab to the divine right of episcopacy; and therefore, according to the dictates of worldly prudence, they substituted overseers.

The objection is solely to the abuse of the name. In early ages, such was the piety of the ministers of religion, such their humility, that no idea of pomp was attached to this designation. This was eminently the character of "the family of Hij": and they could scarcely form the apprehension that one of their own number, merely because he received the name of Bishop, would lord it over his fellows who had conferred on him this character. For, after the most impartial investigation of this subject of which I am capable, I have not found a shadow of proof that any of those sent forth as bishops from that island were ordained by such as claimed a dignity superior to that of presbyter.

1. I am much disposed, indeed, to think that all the difference which they, in a more early age at least, admitted between presbyter and bishop, was, that they conferred the latter title on those only who were delegated to a particular charge, as to that of planting a church among the Angles, or who were to have a pastoral relation to a certain people; whereas the presbyters, although they by themselves dispensed ordinances in the vicinity of their monastery, or assisted the bishop on his mission in preaching and baptising, were viewed merely as preachers at large, without having any such pastoral relation.

Bede uses the terms Bishop and Priest, with respect to what was transacted at Iona, as if they admitted of no difference of signification as to office. When speaking of that bishop who had been sent to King Oswald, but, meeting with no success, returned home, he with the same breath gives him both designations: using both the term *Antistes*, and *Sacerdos*: and the import of both, nay, the great dignity of his office, is made to lie in this, that he was a preacher. It was in his room that Aidan was sent. It is indeed said, that he deserved to be made a bishop, and that he was ordained. But, besides the circumstance of his being ordained by the *conventus seniorum*, it may be difficult to prove, as we have formerly observed, that he was a preacher before. As it is admitted, that in these monasteries there were laymen, can it be shewn that Aidan was any thing more before his ordination as a bishop?

2. There is undoubted evidence, that, in these early times, the term bishop was used in a sense very different from that attached to it afterwards. Of this the most ample proof might be brought from the general history of Christendom. But I shall confine myself to that of our own islands. Ninian is called a bishop by Bede: and he probably received the title during his life. He says that the Southern Picts were converted "by the preaching of Nynias," as he gives his name, "the most renowned bishop, who had been instructed at Rome in the faith and mysteries of truth, whose episcopal see, of the invocation of St Martin the bishop, and stately church, the nation of the Angles is now possessed of." This place was not within the Pictish territories, as Mr Pinkerton shows in his Enquiry, but among the Cumraig Britons. Ninian receives the same designation from Alcuin, Boece, Leslie, and a variety of writers. Yet he seems to have been no more a bishop than was Columba. Nor could Bede use the term in that canonical sense which was become common in his own time. For he afterwards says: "Pecthelm is Bishop of Candida Casa, or Whithern, which, in consequence of the increase of the number of the faithful, has been lately added to the list of episcopal sees, and had him for its first prelate." In the MS. History of Durham, under the year 664, and long after the age of Ninian, it is expressly said: "Candida Casa as yet had no bishop." William of Malmesbury also, in his account of the bishops of this see, although, after Alcuin, he calls Ninian a bishop, using the term in its

loose and general sense, says that, "towards the end of Bede's life, Pethelm was made the first bishop;" that is, as Selden explains it, "according to the canonical ideas of the episcopacy then generally received throughout Christendom."

The character of the Irish bishops, in early times, may assist us in judging of the rank of those who were ordained at Iona; especially as Columba, who was not a bishop, but an abbot and presbyter, is designed not only "primate of the Scots and Piets," but "primate of all the Irish bishops." Till the year 1152, they seem to have been properly *Chor-episcopi*, or Rural Bishops. In Meath alone there were fourteen bishoprics; in Dublin thirteen. Their number, it is supposed, might amount to above three hundred. They, in the same manner with the Scottish and Pictish bishops, exercised their functions at large, as they had opportunity. "That Bishop in Ireland," says Toland, "did, in the fifth or sixth centuries (for example) signify a distinct order of men, by whom alone presbyters cou'd be ordained, and without which kind of ordination their ministry was invalid; this I absolutely deny; as I do that those bishops were Diocesan Bishops, when nothing is plainer, than that most of 'em had no bishopricks at all in our modern sense; not to speak of those numerous bishops frequently going out of Ireland, not call'd to bishop-ricks abroad, and many of 'em never preferr'd there."

We have a similar account of the Irish bishops in that rare and curious work, the *Monasticon Hibernicum*. "It is to be observ'd," says the author, "that Colman having been a bishop in England, was no sooner settled at Inisbofinde, but that place became a bishoprick; so that St Colman, who had before been called Bishop of Lindisfarn, was afterwards stil'd Bishop of Inisbofinde; and the same saint going afterwards to Mayo, that place was likewise a bishoprick, which was united to that of Inisbofinde: so certain it is that formerly, in the British islands, bishopricks were not regulated and settled, but the bishops were movable, without being confined to any certain diocese. This is the reason that, in the first ages, we find so many bishops in Ireland; for in St Patrick's days there were three hundred and fifty at one and the same time, though, as Colgan owns, there were never near so many bishopricks in Ireland. It is very likely, that, when the ancient historians speak of so great a number of bishopricks in Ireland, they only meant those abbies in which these moving or titular bishops were abbots; and those houses, that were so numerous, ceas'd to be bishopricks the very moment the titular bishops and abbots happen'd to die or to shift their monasteries."

3. We have formerly seen that the Abbots of Hij, because of their great authority and extensive influence, were sometimes called Bishops. Besides the proofs already mentioned, it may be observed that, for this very reason, in relation to that monastery, the terms *Abbas* and *Episcopus* seem to have been used as synonymous. Hence Sigibert speaks of "Adamannus, the presbyter and abbot of the Scots." As the prelacy gained ground, the rage for multiplying bishops, in preceding times, also increased. On this principle, as would seem, Spotswood includes both Columba and Adamnan in his list of the early bishops of Scotland, appended to his history. According to Fordun, Regulus was only an abbot. The Register of St Andrews, however, makes him a bishop.

4. During several centuries, none of those who were called bishops in Scotland had dioceses. Hence, in ancient deeds, they are simply designed *Episcopi*, or *Episcopi Scotorum*. The latter title was that taken by the Bishop of St Andrews so late as the year 1188; as appears by the seals of Robert, Ernald, and Richard. No satisfactory reason can be assigned for this loose mode of designation, but that none of these bishops had a fixed charge. It is admitted that "it was altogether consistent with the universal practice of the church in the earliest ages to consecrate bishops who did not enjoy distinct jurisdiction." There seem to have been no regular

dioceses in Scotland before the beginning of the twelfth century. The foundation of diocesan episcopacy was indeed laid in the erection of the bishopric of St Andrews. In this erection we may perceive the traces of a plan for changing the whole form of ecclesiastical government, as it had hitherto been exercised within the Pictish dominion. This seems to be the true meaning of two passages in ancient writings to which the attention of the public has formerly been called on this subject. Mr Pinkerton has justly denominated one of them "a very singular passage." It occurs in the register of the priory of St Andrews, in relation to Grig, the Gregory of our historians. "He first gave freedom to the Scottish church, which till that time was in servitude, by the constitution and custom of the Picts." "This surely refers," says Mr Pinkerton, "to the subjection of the Pikish churches to Hyona: from which they were delivered by erecting St Andrews into a bishopric. Our clergy, in gratitude, gave much fabulous praise to Grig, as was their custom in such cases; and say that he conquered Ireland, and most of England."

Now, the foundation of this honourable ascription to Grig was his erection of St Andrews into a bishopric. For, according to Fordun and Wyntoun, Kellach, who seems to have been the first bishop of this see, lived in the time of Grig, who began to reign about the year 883. The same honour is given to this prince in the Elegiac Chronicle.

Qui dedit Ecclesiae libertates Scoticanae,
Quae sub Pictorum lege redacta fuit.

The erection of this bishopric might be viewed, by those in the interest of Rome, as the emancipation of the Scottish church; especially as St Andrews seems to have been directly opposed to the monastery of Dunkeld, which had been erected in imitation of that at Iona, and as its substitute in respect of power. One thing, as we have formerly seen, which renders this highly probable is, that Tuathal is called both "Archbishop

of Fortren," and " Abbot of Dunkeld." It must be admitted,
however, that, so far as the transactions of Grig are explained
by Fordun, this could not be the only thing implied. For he
says, that he "gave liberty to the persons of ecclesiastics,"
apparently meaning that he delivered them from the cognisance
of civil judicatures. But his language may include both. For
he clearly distinguishes between the church and the persons
of her ministers. " He gave," says the historian, " with the
consent of the nobility, perpetual liberty both to the Church
of God and to ecclesiastical persons; which was confirmed by
Pope John VIII."

There is another passage, which deserves more particular
attention. It occurs in the more modern History of Durham,
in the account given of Turgot, prior of that see, who was
made Bishop of St Andrews. " In these days," it is said, "all
the right of the Culdees throughout the whole kingdom of
Scotland, passed into the bishopric of St Andrews." He was
consecrated by Thomas, Archbishop of York, in the year
1109. Sir James Dalrymple makes no further use of this
passage, than to oppose the idea of the Culdees having ceased
to exist from this time. But there is no evidence that this
was the idea of the original writer. Nothing is here asserted
which might lead us to conclude that they were even immediately deprived of their revenues, that is, of the temporal
rights which they enjoyed. This could not be meant; for
their privation in this respect was gradual. The learned
Selden seems justly to view the term *Ius* as denoting the
right, which they had long claimed and exercised, of electing
and ordaining bishops, without the interference of any others
in order to their consecration. Had the writer meant to speak
of their temporal rights, or even of the privileges attached to
particular priories, he would most probably have used a
different term. At any rate, had these been in his eye, he
would have spoken of rights in the plural, as referring to the
whole extent of their property. But when he speaks of "the

right of the Culdees throughout the whole kingdom of Scotland," it is evident that he must refer to one distinguishing privilege, belonging to them as a body, by virtue of which their jurisdiction had no limit, save that of the kingdom itself. And what could this be but the right of choosing, without any *conge d'elire* from the sovereign, and of ordaining, without any consecration from a superior order of clergy, those who were called bishops in a general sense, or bishops of Scotland, as exercising their authority somewhat in the same unlimited way in which the Culdees exercised theirs?

This right is said *transire*, to pass, which, "with lawyers," as Selden observes, "denotes the legal transference of a right or dominion, so that it entirely belongs to the person to whom it is thus transferred. The Bishop of St Asaph conjectures that "it might be the right of confirming the elections of all the bishops in Scotland. This had been done by them" [the Culdees], he says, "as being the primat's dean and chapter; but was now taken from them, and performed by the primat himself. For this interpretation I think there is ground enough in the account that a Culdee of St Andrews hath given of the foundation of his church; where he says that the archbishoprick of all Scotland belongs to that city, and that no bishop in Scotland ought to be ordained without the consent of the Seniors of that place."

Here the learned prelate finds himself under the necessity of conceding to the Culdees a very extraordinary power. But this power must originally have centered in the monastery of Iona. This monastery, then, must have been to all intents the primacy of Scotland, of the country, at least, which has now received this name. This power must have belonged to the college, as the chapter, if it must be so. But who was the primate? No bishop, from all that we have seen; but the abbot himself. Thus the Bishop of St Asaph finds it necessary to admit, however reluctantly, what he elsewhere tries to set aside, the testimony of Bede with respect to the subjection of "all the province, and even of the bishops themselves, in an unusual manner," to this abbot. Even after he has made an ineffectual attempt to shew that the province referred to by the ancient writer could signify only a single diocese; he inadvertently gives up the point in controversy, making all the bishops in Scotland to be at least so far subject to the Culdees, that they had the "right of confirming their elections."

It should also be observed that he supposes not only a transition as to the power, but a very important change with respect to the exercise of it. This right formerly belonged to the *Keledei*, to them as a body, or at least to their college. But at this time it "was taken from them, and the act of confirmation performed,"—by whom? by the dean and chapter, in correspondence to their supposed rank before? nay, but "by the primat himself." Here we have the admission of a change, from something which strikingly resembles presbytery, to the very *acme* of prelacy. All the right of the Culdees, "throughout the whole kingdom of Scotland," although at this time they were very numerous, is transferred to a single person.

But the bishop's attachment to prelacy has, in this instance, carried him farther than he was warranted to go, according to the authority to which he refers. For his "Culdee of St Andrews" does not attribute this right to "the primat himself;" but says that "no bishop in Scotland ought to be ordained without the council of the seniors of that place." Now, to whom does the Culdee give the name of seniors? Undoubtedly to his own brethren. For, as we have seen from Bede, this is the very designation that had all along been given to the members of the College of Iona. This seems indeed to be admitted by Bishop Lloyd. Sir James Dalrymple carries it farther with respect to the bishopric of Glasgow. For in Pope Alexander the Third's bull to the dean and chapter of that see it is said that, "in the electing of the bishop, they must have *consensus religiosorum virorum civitatis*, which must be meant of the laicks; and it's like also the laicks had the same share in the settling the Culdees, who were their pastors." I question, however, if in that age, the term *religiosus* was extended to any laics, save those who adhered to some monastic rule.

When the Bishop of St Asaph quoted the narrative of the Culdee on this subject, had he subjoined the words immediately following those which we have already considered, he would have given a just exhibition of the design and tendency of this transference of power from the Culdees to the bishopric of St Andrews. "This is Rome the second, formed after the model of the first; this is the chief city of refuge: this is the metropolitan city of Scotland."

As Turgot was the first bishop who was introduced at St Andrews from another country, he was the first who was consecrated by a foreigner. Thus a very important branch of the right which belonged to the Culdees was lost by this extraneous consecration. Notwithstanding all the pains, however, which were taken by the king and the bishop to unhinge the more ancient form of ecclesiastical government, we are under a necessity of concluding that Turgot found his situation very uncomfortable. It is justly said by Keith that there was a "misunderstanding betwixt the king and him." After he had continued about six years at St Andrews, "as, from certain causes which sprung up, he could not worthily discharge his office, he made preparations for going to Rome, that he might spend his life according to the counsel of the Pope. But that this plan might not be carried into execution, the breach was widened between him and the king; and, from vexation of spirit, he fell into melancholy. He received permission, on account of his infirmity, to reside for some time at Durham;" where, in less than three months, he died.

Thus, Alexander, notwithstanding his great zeal for changing the form of religion, soon learned that it was

scarcely possible to retain his own authority, in connexion
with those who were so much devoted to a foreign jurisdiction.
But, although disappointed with respect to Turgot, and,
according to the general account, also as to Eadmer, who was
chosen to succeed him, but would not submit to be consecrated
by any other than the Archbishop of Canterbury; he was
determined virtually to take even the right of election into
his own hand. Accordingly, as we learn from the Chronicle
of Mailros, he caused Robert, Prior of Scone, to be chosen to
the vacant bishopric.

On the whole it plainly appears from our history, that it
was during the age of Turgot, that the Scottish bishops began
to have distinct dioceses. "The bishops of the Scots," says
the learned Camden, "exercised their episcopal functions
everywhere without distinction to the time of Malcolm III.,
about the year 1070, when their dioceses were confined to
certain limits. Afterwards, in the lapse of time, this
hierarchy was established in Scotland." This seems to have
taken place somewhat later, although within the age of
Turgot. "At the accession of Alexander I., 1st Jan. 1106-7,
he found prelates performing their undefined functions
within the Scottish territory."

II. It has been objected, that "the convent of Culdees
constituted the chapter, and had the election of the bishop;"
and that, in some instances, they "would needs be canons
regular, and would erect themselves into a canonry, not only
without the consent, but even against the declared will of
the bishop their patron and founder."

That they submitted to act as dean and chapter, in some
sees, is undeniable. That they might occasionally manifest an
eagerness to do so, as has been asserted with respect to those
of Monimusk, might easily be accounted for. The introduction of canons regular, we have seen, was particularly
intended for accomplishing the exclusion of the Culdees
from the exercise of their ancient privileges. As they could

not be blind to this design, it is very natural to suppose, that they would contend for the liberty which they still retained by charter, however much it had been abridged. Many of them would rather submit to be canons regular, although they hated the institution, than be brought down to the level of mere laymen. But neither their submission to act as the chapter, nor any anxiety to have a place in it, can be sustained as a proof that they never enjoyed any higher authority. Their being retained as the chapter in some bishoprics, and admitted into it in others, affords a presumption, nearly amounting to proof, that their power had, in former times, been much greater. For is it at all conceivable, that men so much disliked by the Roman clergy, and, in their mode of life, so different from the canons, would be preferred to them, or even associated with them, without some urgent necessity? And what was this necessity? The strong plea arising from almost immemorial possession, and the strong prejudices of the people in their favour. The new bishops, and their adherents, well knew that they were persecuting those, who had formerly been superior to themselves in authority; those to whom, in fact, the bishops owed all the authority which they possessed, however "unusual the manner" in other countries. We know that, during the reign of James the Sixth, there were many presbyterians in Scotland, who submitted to a more moderate kind of epis-copacy, received episcopal ordination, and sat in the synods in which bishops acted as perpetual moderators. Would any sound reasoner hence conclude, that they were friends to episcopacy? It cannot be doubted that they acted this part, because they did not think of any more eligible plan of conduct. Far less would any one dream of inferring from this fact, that presbyterial church-government had not been previously established in Scotland.

In several places, afterwards erected into episcopal sees, as we have already seen, the Culdees had monasteries erected long before; as at Brechin, Dunkeld, Dunblane, &c. But they had establishments in many other places that were never converted into episcopates. Were they the chapter at Dunfermline, at Lochlevin, or at Scone? Had they bishops in all these places? For, to the friends of the hierarchy, a Culdee establishment seems to resemble a hive of bees, that cannot exist without a queen. If they all had bishops, for performing what is exclusively viewed as episcopal duties, they could only be of an inferior class; for there must have been a considerable number of bishops in the districts of Fife alone. It they did exist, how are all their names buried in oblivion; whence is there not even a vestige of the office in these places? If there were foundations of Culdees without bishops, their acting in an episcopal see as the chapter can be sustained as no proof that they depended on the see, or were the creatures of the bishop.

The extent of their possessions, in an early period of the episcopate of St Andrews, is a strong proof that their establishment preceded that of the see. They received several important donations from Bishops Malduin, Tuthald, and Modach, who had most probably been Culdees, and elected by them. But they seem to have had considerable endowments, before the see itself was erected. Ungus II., King of the Picts, who died A. 833, gave the Boar's Raik to St Regulus. Yet this appears to have been the property of the Culdees; as it is designed *Baronia Caledaiorum infra Cursum Apri*. This gift must have been made about sixty years before the election of Kellach, the first bishop of St Andrews. Brudi, the last King of the Picts, who died A. 843, gave them the isle of Lochlevin. This proves their celebrity, at least in the neighbourhood of St Andrews, long before the erection of the bishopric.

III. It has also been objected, that "we read of no Culdees that ever were at Hy, or in any other place where the Scots anciently dwelt. But, as oft as they are mentioned, we find them still at St Andrews, which was in the country of the South Picts; and they are not said to have been there till it had been many years the see of a diocesan bishop."

How little foundation there is for the last assertion, we have already proved. It has also been seen, that, as Ungus gave the Boar's Raik to St Rule, and as it appears that it was in fact the property of the Culdees; if any faith can be given to this story, we may reasonably infer that they were accounted the legitimate successors of the Abbot Regulus and his thirty companions. The account which Fordun gives of him and his followers perfectly corresponds with that given of the monks of Iona. "Having laid the foundation of a monastical cell, these blessed men went through the country, not on horseback, but, like the apostles of old, in pairs, everywhere preaching the word of God." But, should we view the story with respect to Regulus as a mere legend, it must at least leave a strong impression on the mind, that there were men of this description, who held lands at St Andrews, in consequence of a royal endowment, a considerable time before the eversion of the Pictish monarchy.

The account which the learned Stillingfleet has given of the Culdees is truly ludicrous. "St Andrews," he says, "was called Kilremont;—Kil, as appears by the Scottish historians, was a place of devotion; Kilruil was the church of Regulus; —and Kilremont, as being the royal seat, and the principal church, for Remont is *Mons Regis;* and from hence the clergy of this church were called Killedees, from which title the fiction of the ancient Culdees came."

These worthy prelates seem actuated with such zeal against the Culdees, that they will not allow them common historical justice. Under this obnoxious name, the ghost of presbytery so haunts them, that they shrink back from those proofs of existence that are far stronger than any which they have ever been able to produce in support of diocesan episcopacy. Bishop Nicholson discovers the same temper, and cannot conceal the reason of it, when he calls Dr Lloyd's work "an undertaking becoming a bishop of our English church;" adding, "The story of the Culdees" is "an argument put into the mouths of our schismaticks by Blondel and Selden, out of the abundant kindness they had for our establishment."

But "we read of no Culdees that ever were at Hy." I shall not urge as a proof what Dr Smith has said respecting the disciples of Columba, that "they themselves seem to have assumed no other name than that of *Famuli Dei*, or servants of God; or, in their own language, *Gille-De*, which was Latinized into *Keledeus*." For I do not know that there is any evidence from ancient writers of their having assumed this name. Did it appear that they had thus denominated themselves, even in the Latin language, it would not only settle every dispute with respect to the origin of the name, but would be a sufficient reply to the objection.

If, however, we may credit an intelligent and well-informed writer, the name Culdee is, even at this day, not unknown at Iona. He views them indeed as prior to Columba. "The first Christians," he says, "that possessed themselves of I were, in all probability, the Culdees.—As they affected retired places, as their name imports, they could not in any country find a place more happily suited to their purpose. One place in I is still called the Culdee's Cell [Gael. *Cathan*, or *Cathan Cuildich*, N.] It is the foundation of a small circular house upon a reclining plain. From the door of the house a walk ascends to a small hillock, with the remains of a wall upon each side of the walk, which grows wider to the hillock. There are evident traces of the walls of the walk taking a circuit round, and enclosing the hillock."

But although it were certain that the name had never been used in Iona, this would by no means prove that the same class of religious persons did not exist there. Names arise often from accident, or from some very trivial circumstance which totally escapes the most accurate investigation of succeeding ages.   Names, which seem to have been quite unknown in a preceding age, appear at once in the history of nations, as if they had been long familiar, and universally known.   We have but very few instances of the use of the name Jew before the Babylonian captivity: and all these occur only a little time before this event.   Would any one hence conclude that the Jews were not the same people with those formerly known by the name of Israel?   Yet, as we know that the name Jews originated from the circumstance of the great majority of those who adhered to the family of David when the ten tribes apostatised being descended from the patriarch Judah; we are assured that the same reason for this distinctive name existed nearly three hundred and forty years before the captivity, more than four hundred before it came to be generally used.

That the Culdees of St Andrews, in almost every respect, resembled those of Iona cannot be doubted by any unprejudiced mind.   Their mode of life, their doctrine, their opposition to the Roman corruptions, all point out the same society.   Can it be supposed that they would receive the sovereignty of several islands from the Pictish monarch; and that neither he, nor any of his successors, although making a profession of Christianity, would ever invite any of them to the seat of government, or retain them there?   Was this at Abernethy? and whence the strength of its religious foundation, but from those men who had been so early patronised by the crown? Do we not know that Columba sent his disciples throughout Pictland; and have we not seen that a certain right, with respect to the election of bishops, is attributed to the Culdees at St Andrews, apparently the same which Bede ascribes to the monastery at Hij?

From the Annals of Ulster we learn that "the family of I," or Hij, was "expelled by King Nectan beyond Drum-Albin," A. 716.   But they were only sent from an island into what was to it the mainland, indeed, as would appear, into the territory of the Southern Piets; and thus must have spread themselves, although they had never done it before, through modern Perthshire, Angus, and Fife. Although a considerable number of them were driven from Hij, there is no evidence that they were subjected to personal suffering. The learned author of a very interesting work on the antiquities of our country, while he denies that the Culdean establishments afford any proof in favour of presbytery, discovers more candour on this subject than the Bishop of St Asaph has done. "In the united kingdom beyond the firths," he says, "there remained, at the epoch of the union, in 843, A.D., various cells, which had been settled, in early times, by *Columbans;* and still continued the abundant fountains, whence flowed religious instruction to a confiding people. One of the first acts of the reign of Kenneth, was to shew his respect for the memory of that apostle of the Scots and Piets, by building a church, wherein the reliques of the saint were deposited, in A.D. 849. [Chron. in Innes's App. No. 3.] The site of this sacred depository has not yet been fixed by antiquaries. Yet, was it at Dunkeld, where Kenneth built the church, which he dedicated to Columba. Thus Dunkeld and its church became sacred to Columba, who equally became the patron saint of both. A religious house was here built, upon the same system as the original establishment at Iona."

Bishop Lloyd has said that the name Culdee "is not found in any other place where the Scots dwelt," save in St Andrews. But he has certainly forgot that the name was well known in Ireland, where "the Scots dwelt" before their settlement in this country, and whence Columba and his companions came. The Irish antiquaries confess that they do not know when it was introduced. Yet it was commonly used there, as early as at St Andrews; which clearly shews, that it was not transferred from the latter to the former. "*Ceile-De*, both name and thing, cannot be deny'd by any

17

man, who's tolerably versed in the language of the Irish, or in their books; one of which, a chronicle mostly in verse, entitul'd *Psalter Na'rran*, was written by a Keldee, Aonghus *Ceile-De*, Latiniz'd Aeneas Colideus, about the year 800."

Whatever be the origin of *Ceile-de*, of which *Culdee* seems to be merely a corruption, there is no good reason to doubt that the first part of the word is incorporated with the name of the founder, in the designation of Columkill, given to the island of Hij. While Dr Shaw explains *Keledee* as "a word compounded of *Ceile* or *Keile*, i.e. a servant, or one devoted, and *Dia*, in the genitive *De*, i.e. God, q. d. the servant of God, or one devoted to him," he subjoins; "A church or place of worship was called *Kil*, because it was set apart for divine service."

After all, how little Bishop Lloyd felt the force of his own objection, and how much he must have been at a loss for argument when he introduced one of so trivial a nature, appears from what he had previously said concerning the origin of the name: "Thus as Columba was called by the Irish *Columbeylle*; that is, 'Columb of the cell,' so all those that lived in such houses might be, and I doubt not were, called by their names, with the addition of *Kyldee*, that is such a one of the cell-house."

After the concession made by the author of Caledonia, that "there remained—in 843,—various *cells*, which had been settled in early times by Columbans," &c., it is rather surprising that he should say: "There does not appear to be any appellation, in the maps of Scotland, which bears the least analogy to the Culdean monks." He seems to adopt this idea, because he views the term *Kil* as primarily signifying a retreat. But the testimony of Bede, with respect to the origin of the name of Icolumkill certainly deserves some notice; as the venerable writer was so well acquainted with the history of the island. He says, that "Hij is now by some called *Columbeill*, the name being compounded from *Columb* and *cella*." Although he substitutes the Latin word, it is evidently used as synonymous with the Gaelic *ecile* or *cill*.

The Celtic term does not in fact differ in signification from the Latin, and may be radically the same. For as *cella* properly denotes a private chamber, it is deduced, by etymologists, from *cel-are* to conceal: and what is this but a *retreat* or place of retirement? The sense of the term, as embodied in the designation given from Columba, and explained by Bede, is confirmed by Jocelin, a monk of Furness, who flourished about the year 1140. In his life of St Patrick, he says that Columba was called *Coluimcille*, and was the founder of a hundred monasteries. The purport of his language evidently appears from that of Notker Balbulus, who wrote in the tenth century. "In Scotland, in the island of Ireland, deceased St Columba, surnamed by his own people *Columkilli*, because he was the institutor, founder, and governor of many *cells*, that is, monasteries or churches, whence the abbot of the monastery over which he last presided [Iona,] and where he rests, in opposition to the custom of the church, is accounted the primate of all the Hibernian bishops." By the way, we may observe, that the claim of superiority, on the part of the monastery of Hii, was acknowledged, even in Ireland, so late as the tenth century. This translation of the term is still admitted. "For, in the language of the country," says Dr Smith, "he is called *Colum-cille*, (or Colum of the Cells), from his having founded so many churches and monasteries. Thus it appears that *killi* or *cille* is viewed as the plural.

When we find the same form of combination, not only in the neighbourhood of the Culdees, but in what is supposed to have been their original seat;—not only the names *Kilmenie*, *Kilconquhar*, *Kilrenny*, *Kilbirnie*, &c., but *Kelremont* and *Kilreul*;—it affords a strong presumption of analogy between the name of the *Keledei* as a body, and the names of the places that have been denominated from individuals, many of whom, in all probability, belonged to this very society.

With respect to the Irish Culdees, it may be added, that Colgan mentions Comganus *Kele-De*, or *Keledeus*, and also Aengusianus *Keledeus*. The latter seems to be the same person to whom Toland refers. Have we any reason to suppose that the Culdees of St Andrews emigrated to Ireland, after they were ejected from their offices and possessions here? "In the greater churches of Ulster," Archbishop Usher says, "as at Cluaninnis and Daminnis, and principally at Armagh, in our own memory, there were priests called Culdees, who celebrated divine service in the choir. Their president was stiled Prior of the Culdees, and acted as praecentor."

Their influence in Ireland was similar to that which they had so long enjoyed in Scotland. "Corruption," says a learned writer of that country, "was powerfully retarded by the firmness of the hierarchy and the Culdees. The latter were looked up to as the depositaries of the original national faith, and were most highly respected by the people for their sanctity and learning." It was not, indeed, till the eleventh century, that Ireland was completely subdued to the Roman authority. Here also we perceive the same opposition to this society. Wherever the influence of Rome prevailed, the Culdees were removed, and Columba himself was not supplicated as a patron and saint before the year 1741; although, in ancient times, acknowledged as "the primate of all the Irish churches," and "of all the Irish bishops."

Giraldus Cambrensis, who went to Ireland with King John in the year 1185, thus describes the island Monaincha: "In North Munster is a lake containing two isles; in the greater is a church of the ancient religion, and in the lesser, a chapel, wherein a few monks, called Culdees, devoutly serve God." On this passage Dr Ledwich observes: "We may easily understand what Cambrensis meant by the church here being of the old religion.   The Culdees, its possessors, had not even at this period, when the council of Cashel had decreed uniformity of faith and practice, conformed to the reigning superstition; they devoutly served God in this wild and dreary retreat, sacrificing all the flattering prospects of the world for their ancient doctrine and discipline."

The same Cambrensis gives an account of Culdees in Wales.   "The isle of Bardsey," he says, "is inhabited by religious monks, quos Coelicolas vel *Colideos* vocant."   Goodall seems to admit that the Culdees had been introduced into the north of England, in consequence of the conversion of the inhabitants of that region by missionaries from Iij.   For he says: "As to the Culdees, it is very certain, that there was a sort of monks, and secular priests too, who went under that appellation, not only among the Scots, but also among the Britons and Irish, and even among the northern English, who were first converted by the Scots, particularly in the cathedral of York, [Monast. Anglican. tom. 2. p. 367, 368."]

I have given a more full answer to this objection than it deserves, partly to shew its extreme futility; but especially, because the warm friends of diocesan episcopacy have been so eager to avail themselves of even a shadow of argument, in their attempts to disprove, not only the authority, but the early existence of a society, to which the cause of religion, in this country, has been so deeply indebted.

THE END.

PRINTED BY W. JOLLY AND SONS, 23 BRIDGE STREET, ABERDEEN.

www.ingramcontent.com/pod-product-compliance
Lightning Source LLC
Chambersburg PA
CBHW031426020726
47499CB00005B/1612